HITLER'S RENEGADES

Other Books by Christopher Ailsby

A Collector's Guide to World War 2 Medals and Political Awards

SS: Hell on the Eastern Front: The Waffen-SS War in Russia 1941–1945

Waffen-SS: The Illustrated History 1923–1945

Images of Barbarossa: The German Invasion of Russia 1941

Hitler's Sky Warriors: German Paratroopers in Action 1939–1945

The Third Reich Day by Day

SS: Roll of Infamy

Combat Medals of the Third Reich

A Collector's Guide to German World War 2 Medals & Political Awards: The Satellite States

Waffen-SS: Hitler's Black Guard At War

HITLER'S RENEGADES

Foreign Nationals in the Service of the Third Reich

Christopher Ailsby

BRASSEY'S, INC.

THIS BOOK IS DEDICATED TO DR WERNER NOWAK
AND THE MEMORY OF LEO BECK

First published in the United States of America by
Brassey's, Inc.
22841 Quicksilver Drive
Dulles, Virginia 20166

ISBN 1-57488-838-2

Brassey's books are available at special discounts for bulk purchases for
sales promotions, fund raising or educational use.

First Edition
10 9 8 7 6 5 4 3 2 1

Editorial and design:
The Brown Reference Group plc
8 Chapel Place
Rivington Street
London
EC2A 3DQ
UK
www.brownreference.com

Editor: Peter Darman
Picture Researcher: Andrew Webb
Designer: Reg Cox
Production Director: Alastair Gourlay
Map artworks: Darren Awuah

Printed in China

COVER PHOTOGRAPHS
Front cover photographs (left to right): Cossacks in German service
(AKG); Flemish SS recruits (AKG); Turkmenistani members of the
Wehrmacht (Robert Hunt Library).
Back cover photograph: Members of the *Légion des Volontaires Français*
(Robert Hunt Library).

CONTENTS

European Frontiers 1919–37

Legend:
- Lost by Germany 1919
- Saar: League of Nations control 1919–35
- Former territory of Imperial Russia
- Austria-Hungary until 1918
- Demilitarized Rhineland
- Plebiscite areas

Legend:
- Occupied by Germany
- Greater Germany
- Occupied by Italy
- Axis satellites
- Neutral
- Allied territory

THE GREATER GERMAN REICH, OCTOBER 1942

OUR FLAG
IS GOING FORWARD TO

INTRODUCTION

In European warfare, the hiring of mercenaries was common practice even before the establishment of the nation state. In the eighteenth and nineteenth centuries, foreigners fought to further political ends. But by the beginning of the twentieth century, foreign mercenaries had disappeared from European armies. In World War II, ideological mercenaries would fight for Nazi Germany.

This book is about foreign volunteers in the service of the German armed forces in World War II. To understand more fully the reasons why hundreds of thousands of foreign nationals should fight for Nazi Germany, it is necessary to provide a brief background to the rise of Germany prior to the twentieth century, and the employment of foreign nationals in European armies.

The Modern readers, especially those from the United States and Britain (countries whose borders have remained fixed for 200 and 300 years respectively), might view the foreign nationals who fought for the Nazis with particular disdain for two reasons. First, because they fought to preserve one of the most murderous regimes in modern history. Second, because they were mercenaries, a type of soldier often associated with lawlessness and atrocities. However, though the first reason has some merit, foreign mercenaries have been a

Left: A Waffen-SS recruiting poster in World War II aimed at British prisoners of war. The SS programme to create a British foreign legion was a dismal failure.

part of warfare throughout history and have not all been marauding bands of outlaws. In ancient times, for example, Greek mercenaries served the Persian Empire. And it was not unusual for a ruling power to hire mercenaries during the Middle Ages. Barbarossa (died 1546), for instance, was a Barbary pirate and later admiral of the Ottoman fleet whose efforts resulted in Algeria and Tunisia becoming part of the Ottoman Empire. For his own protection he created a bodyguard of renegade Europeans that formed the nucleus of a professional army, owing its loyalty and support to him alone. Between the tenth and the thirteenth centuries, the Varangian Guard of Viking mercenaries served the Byzantine emperors.

In the fourteenth century, Genoese crossbowmen fought in many European armies, while Flemish "hand-gonne" men in the fifteenth century were highly sought after. In Germany during the same period, Landsknecht mercenaries imitated the tactics of the mercenary Swiss pikemen, the latter being the most highly prized professional soldiers in Europe (though apt to mutiny or to changing sides if their pay was not forthcoming). Some

Above: *Fascist brothers-in-arms. Soldiers of the 29th SS Division on parade in northern Italy in 1944. Many of these men had seen service on the Eastern Front, where Mussolini's troops suffered heavy losses due to poor equipment and inadequate motor transport.*

200 years later, Oliver Cromwell's New Model Army in England relied on the expertise of German artillerymen. The hiring of mercenaries was thus a common, if rather expensive, practice of European warfare. And in the eighteenth century the military use of foreign nationals developed further.

Many European states employed foreign professionals in permanent regiments. They found their manpower from such countries as diverse as Scotland, Ireland, Germany and Switzerland. The "Wild Geese", the young men of Ireland who left their native land to serve in the armies of Europe, fought for France (in the Irish Brigade), Spain, Austria and Russia.

The early nineteenth century saw the term "legion" applied to many detachments of émigré patriots, notable among them being Napoleon's Polish Vistula Legion and the King's German Legion (in 1803 the French occupied

Hanover and disbanded the Hanoverian Army; thereafter, many Hanoverian soldiers made their way to England and were formed into the King's German Legion, the king being George III). Some members of these units were seeking to free their homelands from foreign occupation; others fought purely for profit. Today, the surviving legions are the French Foreign Legion, with its romantic overtones, and the Spanish Legion, which actually stopped recruiting foreigners in 1987. In addition, there is the Swiss Guard of the Vatican, which has the honour of guarding the Pope. In the British Army, the Gurkhas on occasion stand guard at Buckingham Palace, the seat of the British monarchy. Thus, it can be seen that the use of foreign nationals is part of the European military tradition. In this, the Third Reich was no different from other regimes throughout history. But what about individual motives for fighting for Nazism?

The title of this book, *Hitler's Renegades*, may give cause for debate. The word renegade conjures up the idea of a rebel or outlaw; a person who fights outside the law. On one level it can well explain or describe the position of non-German men and women who fought for Germany in World War II. But, to use a well-known phrase, one

man's terrorist is another man's freedom fighter. In reality, many of the foreign volunteers who fought for Adolf Hitler and the Third Reich did not see themselves as outlaws or renegades. Their attitudes and loyalties were to be influenced by the political and economic conditions experienced in the aftermath of World War I.

By 1914 foreign legions had largely disappeared from the armies of the main European powers. They may have deployed colonial units, but the concepts of patriotism and nationalism had made them out-moded (it could be argued, though, that the armed forces of the polyglot Hapsburg Empire were nothing more than a collection of foreigners). The four years of bloodshed that took place in Europe between 1914 and 1918 brought about the defeat of Germany, the destruction of the Austro-Hungarian Empire and the end of Romanov rule in Russia.

Nineteenth century imperial-style nationalism had been discredited. However, in its place would emerge an ideology that would transcend national boundaries to appeal to racial brethren to unite in a common cause. That ideology was National Socialism, and the appeal was to unite the Aryan race in a fight to the death against ideological foes and "race polluters" who threatened Western civilization. It would be a call that would be answered by hundreds of thousands of non-Germans.

Below: *During World War II, despite Nazi ideology, the Germans recruited hundreds of thousands of Russians to serve their military machine, such as the group of motley individuals shown below. Their duties ranged from digging latrines and cooking to frontline combat.*

Chapter 1

THE NEW ORDER IN EUROPE

National Socialism was a dynamic, expansionist ideology whose main aim was the reintegration of German lands and peoples "stolen" under the terms of the Treaty of Versailles into the Third Reich. Once this had been achieved, Germany would need "living space" in Eastern Europe to sustain the Reich.

When at last the fearful bloodletting of the conflict, with its 10 million dead and 20 million wounded, was over, there seemed good reason to believe that World War I would indeed be the "war to end all wars". Unfortunately, it culminated in an uneasy peace. The Allies, who had finally succeeded in destroying Germany's formidable war machine, had, in the peace treaty agreed at Versailles, imposed conditions designed expressly to make it impossible for the world again to be disturbed by German militarism. Germany's army was to be reduced to

Left: Adolf Hitler in Nuremberg for the 1937 party rally, at which he proclaimed that the Third Reich would last a thousand years.

100,000 men, and her navy to 15,000. She was forbidden to possess armour or an air force, and there were safeguards to ensure that she was not able to build up a hidden military reserve.

The Treaty of Versailles was draconian and sowed the seeds of many future grievances. The population and territory of Germany were reduced by about 10 percent. In the west, Alsace and Lorraine were returned to France, and the Saarland was placed under the supervision of the League of Nations until 1935. In the north, three small areas were given to Belgium, while northern Schleswig was returned to Denmark. In the east, Poland was resurrected and given large chunks of German territory: most of former German West Prussia and Poznán (Posen), a "corridor" to the Baltic Sea (which separated East Prussia

Above: *Freikorps members of the Ehrhardt Brigade in Berlin in 1920. Note the swastika symbol on their vehicle and helmets, which later became the official Nazi emblem. The anti-communist Freikorps was made up of ex-soldiers who had fought in World War I.*

from the rest of Germany), and part of Upper Silesia after a plebiscite. Danzig (Gdansk) was declared a free city. All Germany's overseas colonies in China, in the Pacific and in Africa were taken over by Britain, France, Japan and other Allied nations. The Versailles Treaty thus left many ethnic Germans outside post-war Germany. Called Volksdeutsche, around 10 million of them lived outside Germany in Central and Eastern Europe (this figure also includes ethnic Germans who had lived in the Hapsburg Empire). This caused resentment in Germany, and later the idea of uniting all Germans became a central plank of Nazi racial policy, not by bringing them back to Germany but by absorbing them into an expanded Reich.

A point often overlooked alongside the emasculation of Germany was the destruction of the Austrian Empire and the collapse of the Ottoman Empire. Austria, the former military superpower, was reduced to a rump state. From the splintered empire the new countries of Yugoslavia and Czechoslovakia were formed, with other countries, notably Italy, absorbing lesser or greater slices of Austrian territory. The Treaty of St Germain limited the Austrian Army to 30,000 men and prohibited the building of an air force (no air force existed between 1919 and 1934, but then Austria secretly created one). Europe now descended into a period of turmoil and civil unrest.

The "war guilt clause" of the Treaty of Versailles deemed Germany the aggressor in the war and consequently made her responsible for making reparations to the Allied nations in payment for the losses and damage they had sustained in the conflict. It was impossible to compute the exact sum to be paid as reparations for the damage caused by the Germans, especially in France and Belgium, at the time the treaty was being drafted. However, a commission that assessed the losses incurred by the civilian population set an amount of $33 billion in 1921. Although economists at the time declared that such a huge sum could never be collected without upsetting international finances, the Allies insisted that Germany be made to pay, and the

Right: *SS-Reichsführer Heinrich Himmler, who believed implicitly in the racial theories of National Socialism. His vision of creating a pure Aryan German Reich was responsible for the SS creating foreign legions from "racially suitable" non-Germans.*

treaty permitted them to take punitive action if Germany fell behind in its payments. Events would verify this prediction: in January 1923, French and Belgian troops occupied the Ruhr in response to Germany falling behind in reparation payments.

The social and political turmoil of inter-war Germany does not concern this study, but two elements that emerged from the 1920s and 1930s would have a dramatic influence on the way foreign units were subsequently raised and employed by the German armed forces in World War II. The first was Adolf Hitler; the second was National Socialism.

A drop-out and failed artist before World War I, Hitler fought for the German Army and afterwards became leader of the National Socialist German Workers' Party (Nationalsozialistische Deutsche Arbeiterpartei – NSDAP).

Hitler and National Socialism

Without the individual magnetism of Hitler there would have been no National Socialist mass movement, and no Third Reich. To his followers, Hitler had the historical personal greatness of Caesar or Napoleon. A man of monstrous egotism, his total self-confidence made him believe himself to be a man of destiny, chosen by an act of providence to lead the Nordic world. Whatever we may believe about Hitler with the benefit of hindsight, in the 1930s the great majority of Germans believed both in him as a leader and in his vision of a greater Germany. And this is all the more astounding given that the Germans were among the best-educated people in the twentieth century. As this chapter will show, by 1938 Hitler had made Germany the most feared and powerful state in Europe (a feat achieved without firing a shot in anger). In Germany, this made him an almost Messianic figure, but beyond the Reich's borders such leadership also had an effect on impressionable non-Germans, especially young men. This theme will be explored in later chapters, but suffice to say that in the 1930s Hitler's admirers could be found throughout Europe.

The second element that was to have a profound effect on the recruitment of foreign nationals in particular was National Socialism. Though an ideology with peculiarly German roots, its main themes – violent nationalism, contempt for the Slavs and anti-Semitism – had widespread appeal throughout much of Europe in the 1920s and 1930s. Essentially a radically conservative ideology, National Socialism contained concepts that were

Below: *Richard Walther Darré, Nazi racial theorist who became head of the SS Central Office for Race and Resettlement. His theory that the Germans were a race of farmer-warriors appealed greatly to Himmler.*

Above: *The triumph of bluff over military reality. The German Army reoccupies the Rhineland on 7 March 1936. The French Army, capable of easily defeating the fledgling Wehrmacht, did nothing.*

very attractive to young males in particular. These included the subordination of the individual to the state, the inequality of men and races, unswerving obedience to a leader, and the right of the strong to rule the weak.

For Hitler and the Nazis, National Socialist ideology came down to space and race. His main aim was to achieve German unification with Austria and all those Germans wrenched from the Reich as a result of Versailles; thus, all German-speaking peoples would be as one. Further, the concept of Lebensraum (living space) was crucial to Germany's survival. This required the conquest of Slav lands to the east, which would allow Germany to acquire sufficient land to become economically self-sufficient and militarily invincible. Having acquired the space, the Third Reich would be ruled by a German master race (Herrenvolk). The chosen race of Aryans (a term used from the nineteenth century to denote a race responsible for the progress of mankind; the Nordic or Germanic peoples came to be regarded as the "purest" Aryans), possessing blue eyes, blonde hair and striking Nordic features, would rule over the "lesser peoples", who would ultimately be reduced to a class of slaves.

Race lay at the core of Nazism. Nazi publications talked of the fragmentation (Zerreissung) of the German people, of the loss of tracts of land to "alien" states and peoples. The following is from the NSDAP monthly publication *Nationalsozialische Monatsschriften*: "Adolf Hitler and his National movement became the vehicle through which the work of bringing into existence a new Germany and a new Europe could begin. Its basis was the creation of the German national community which was no longer the sum of Germans living within the state borders, but its German people rooted in race, soil and history." Thus, the ideas of Nordism and Aryanism were not necessarily constrained by political boundaries. This would later make it possible for Nordic recruits to enter the SS, the Nazis' racial élite. Therefore, foreign nationals, as long as they were racially "pure" — not mixed with the blood of "inferior" peoples, especially Jews — could become part of the German blood community.

Hitler also portrayed National Socialism as being a bulwark against Bolshevik communism, and later the fight against Bolshevism was to be a popular reason why many non-Germans volunteered for military service in the Third Reich. However, anti-Bolshevism was not unique to the Nazis. In the aftermath of World War I in Germany, a great number of ex-soldiers had formed or joined ad hoc volunteer units collectively known as Freikorps. Freikorps units could consist of small groups of fewer than 100 men loosely thrown together along quasi-military lines to defend local areas; others were divisional-sized formations consisting of infantry, artillery, machine-gun and motorized units, logistical support, engineers and even air power. Estimates put the number of Freikorps units formed during the period 1918–23 at about 200–300. Freikorps units served as the basis for combating communist revolution across Germany, seeing service in the Baltic region where they fought the Poles along the eastern frontier during various Polish territorial incursions. The Freikorps saw themselves as being the saviour of Germany, and had taken to the streets to counter the communist thrusts that sprang up immediately following Germany's fall in 1918. In much the same way, foreign nationals would take up arms with Germany in World War II to defend Europe from the perceived Bolshevik threat.

After Hitler became chancellor in January 1933, he set about reclaiming German lands "stolen" under the terms of the Treaty of Versailles. Notwithstanding the subsequent brinkmanship of the Führer and the appeasement of Britain and France, the string of diplomatic victories Hitler won reinforced his image as a man of destiny and of National Socialism as an all-conquering ideology.

On 1 March 1935, the German Army, accompanied by armed SS units, marched into Saarbrücken. No resistance was encountered. Thus buoyed up, on 16 March Hitler made his famous proclamation repudiating the Treaty of Versailles and its disarmament clauses. He reintroduced military conscription, announcing this to the German Reichstag as a political statement (parts of his speech were, word for word, those written seven years earlier by Defence Minister Groner, but Hitler was the only German politician prepared to stand up and present it). He certainly expected some repercussions from the Allies (Britain and France), but they were too engrossed in their own internal affairs and took no notice.

At this time, Hitler also officially established the SS-Verfügungstruppe, the armed wing of the SS. The SS (Schutz Staffel) — Protection Squad — was founded in 1925 as a small personal bodyguard to protect Hitler at public meetings. From 1929, it was headed by Reichsführer-SS Heinrich Himmler, and entry into its ranks was governed by strict racial criteria. The SS was the racial and ideological élite of the Nazi Party and thus of the Third Reich. The intention was that the SS-Verfügungstruppe, which later became the Waffen-SS (Armed-SS), would benefit from the highest possible standards of training available. To facilitate this, two highly regarded former army officers, Paul Hausser (appointed Inspector-General of the SS-Verfügungstruppe in 1936) and Felix Steiner, were recruited. Both were ultimately to become among the finest field commanders in the Waffen-SS. The SS will be dealt with in later chapters, but suffice to say here that its armed units were never intended to rival those of the army in terms of manpower. Rather, they were to have experience of combat to enhance their reputation in the post-war Third Reich.

Hitler now turned his attention to the Rhineland. Under the terms of the Treaty of Versailles it had been demilitarized, producing between France and Germany an unoccupied buffer zone. It comprised all German territory west of the River Rhine and a 48km (30-mile)

Below: *Soldiers of the Austrian Army, preceded by a swastika flag, march through the streets of Vienna on 15 March 1938 following the* Anschluss (Union) *with Germany. Most German-speaking Austrians supported the idea of union with Nazi Germany.*

östr. Legion Lechfeld 1933

Above: The Austrian Legion, formed from Austrian Nazis who had agitated for unification with Germany. Himmler had stated: "We must attract all the Nordic blood in the world to us, and so deprive our enemies of it, so that never again will Nordic blood fight against us."

strip east of the river, which included Köln, Düsseldorf and Bonn. Hitler yearned to send troops into the Rhineland, both in order to assert that it was an indivisible part of his new Germany and to demonstrate his contempt for the treaty. The opportunity presented itself in early 1936.

In May 1935, a Franco-Soviet five-year treaty of mutual assistance had been signed (part of Stalin's policy of providing a counterweight to Hitler's Germany). While the French Senate was still debating whether to ratify the treaty, Hitler on 7 March 1936 repudiated the Rhineland clauses of the Treaty of Versailles and the Locarno Pact and announced that German troops had entered the demilitarized zone. The Locarno Pact had been signed on 1 December 1925 by Germany, France, Belgium, Britain and Italy. It guaranteed the borders as laid down in the Versailles Treaty and provided for mutual support and peace in Western Europe. Implicit in the pact was that Germany would renounce the use of force to change her western frontiers.

Against the advice of his more cautious commanders, Hitler ordered his army to march into the Rhineland, in an operation codenamed Winter Exercise, on the morning of 7 March. The new Luftwaffe fighter aircraft made their first public display, while the *SS–Leibstandarte* (Hitler's

bodyguard regiment) provided the advance guard. The Wehrmacht was ordered to retreat immediately should French forces move to oppose the occupation. The French General Staff refused to act unless partial mobilization was ordered, a request the French Cabinet refused. Thus, the French Army, one of the largest in the world at that time, stood by and did nothing. That evening the Führer made a gloating speech to a packed Reichstag. The occupation had been an enormous risk, which only a man as driven as Hitler would have taken. The German Army had mustered only one division, a mere three battalions of which had actually crossed the Rhine. If the worst had occurred, only a few brigades could have reinforced these minute forces. The French, on the other hand, with their Polish and Czech allies, could have immediately fielded 90 divisions and brought up reserves of 100 more.

Hitler had become the undisputed demigod of European fascism. He now became even more confident and began to look at the absorption of the other Germanic territories, which led to what has been euphemistically called the "flower wars".

The new Austrian republic, like Germany but on a much smaller scale, had embarked on its own rearmament programme. Her small army for defence had been secretly swollen. No air force existed between 1919 and 1934, but from the latter date Austria secretly created one. On 25 July 1934, Austrian Nazis, who together with German Nazis attempted a coup but were unsuccessful, assassinated Austrian chancellor Engelbert Dolfuss. An authoritarian right-wing government headed by Chancellor Kurt von Schuschnigg then took power in the country. During the next 44 months, Austria was overrun by Nazi agents who, with the support of Austrian sympathizers, were able to subject the citizens to a constant barrage of propaganda. This authoritarian right-wing government perhaps kept half the population from voicing legitimate dissent. In February 1938, Hitler invited von Schuschnigg to Germany and forced him to agree to give the Austrian Nazis a virtually free hand. Schuschnigg later repudiated the agreement and announced a plebiscite on the *Anschluss* (union with Germany) question. He was bullied into cancelling the plebiscite, and then obediently resigned, ordering the Austrian Army not to resist the Germans. President Wilhelm Miklas of Austria refused to appoint the Austrian Nazi leader Arthur Seyss-Inquart as chancellor. Hermann Göring ordered Seyss-Inquart to send a telegram requesting German military aid, but he refused, and the telegram was sent by a German agent in Vienna instead. On 12 March 1938, Germany invaded, and the enthusiasm that followed persuaded Hitler to annex Austria outright on 13 March. A controlled plebiscite of 10 April gave him 99.7 percent approval for his actions.

After his success in absorbing Austria into Germany, Hitler looked covetously at Czechoslovakia, where about three million people who lived in the Sudeten area were German in origin. It became known in Prague in May 1938 that Hitler and his generals were drawing up a plan for the occupation of Czechoslovakia. The Czechs were relying on military assistance from France, with which they had an alliance. As Hitler continued to make inflammatory speeches demanding that Germans in Czechoslovakia be reunited with their homeland, a general European war seemed imminent. Neither France nor Britain felt prepared to defend Czechoslovakia, however. In mid-September, Hitler agreed to take no military action without further discussion, and Neville Chamberlain, the British prime minister, agreed to try and persuade his cabinet and the French to accept the results of a plebiscite in the Sudetenland. The French premier, Edouard Daladier, and his foreign minister, Georges Bonnet, then went to London where a joint proposal was prepared stipulating that all areas with a population that was more than 50 percent Sudeten German should be returned to Germany. The Czechs were not consulted. The Czech Government initially rejected the proposal, but reluctantly accepted it on 21 September. On 22 September, Chamberlain again flew to Germany and met Hitler, where he learned that the Führer now wanted the Sudetenland occupied by the German Army and the Czechs evacuated from the area by 28 September. The Czechs rejected this, as did the British Cabinet and the French. On the 24th, the French ordered partial mobilization; the Czechs had

Below: *Another bloodless victory for Hitler. German troops enter the Sudetenland in October 1938 as a result of the Munich Agreement. The Sudeten area of Czechoslovakia was home to some three million German-speaking people. It was also rich in minerals.*

Left: *Looking the worse for wear following a street brawl on "Death Sunday" (see p53), these Nazis from Danzig pose for the camera. Danzig Nazis worked closely with their comrades in the Third Reich for the "free city" to be returned to German control.*

ordered a general mobilization one day earlier. In a last-minute effort to avoid war, Chamberlain then proposed that a four-power conference be convened immediately to settle the dispute. Hitler agreed and, on 29 September, Hitler, Chamberlain, Daladier and Mussolini met in Munich, where Mussolini introduced a written plan that was accepted by all as the Munich Agreement. The agreement stated that the German Army was to complete the occupation of the Sudetenland by 10 October, and an international commission would decide the future of

Below: *Adolf Hitler (bareheaded, standing in car giving a right-arm salute) dreamed of creating a Greater German Reich comprising all ethnic Germans and being fed from "living space" in the East. His grandiose scheme would plunge Europe into a second world war in 1939.*

other disputed areas (though Germany was given de facto control over the rest of Czechoslovakia as long as Hitler promised to go no further). Britain and France informed Czechoslovakia that it could either resist Germany alone or submit to the prescribed annexation. The Czechs capitulated. Following a little over five months of internal discontent between Czechs and Slovaks, the latter proclaimed their independence on 14 March 1939. Germany received Slovakia into its web of power as a satellite state the day after Germany had occupied Bohemia and Moravia as "protectorates". The annexation of Czechoslovakia was undoubtedly Hitler's greatest "bloodless conquest", and was the second of his "flower wars". This was the first time Germany was able to annex a state with a largely Slav population, and Czechoslovakia disappeared from the map of Europe.

In the aftermath of World War I, an area of East Prussia known as the Memel District with a population of 160,000 people was turned over to Lithuania following the Memel Convention of 1924. Its significance in the history of Nazi Germany came on 20 March 1939, when Hitler demanded the return of the area and its ethnic German population to the Reich. Surprisingly, Lithuania accepted and the bloodless turnover was effected on 23 March. In truth, the German

Left: *German troops are welcomed as liberators by Russians following their invasion of the Soviet Union in June 1941. Such views would not last, as the reality of Nazi racial policies became clear to the indigenous Slavs who were viewed by Berlin as "sub-humans".*

community had remained unreconciled throughout the decade and a half of Lithuanian rule. Martial law had been imposed on them in 1926 and again in 1938. National Socialism had gained favour among the German community, and anti-Semitism grew steadily during the 1930s. The Nazis won 26 of 29 seats on the local council in the December 1938 elections, for example, and Memel's Jews began a mass exodus. The acquisition of the Memel District marked the end of Hitler's bloodless conquests and thus the "flower wars".

Hitler also coveted the Free City of Danzig and the "Polish Corridor", a strip of land 32–112km (20–70 miles) wide that gave Poland access to the Baltic Sea. Despite their policy of appeasement, both London and Paris finally realized that Hitler was determined to absorb Poland just as he had the Austrians and Czechs. They therefore signed treaties with the Poles guaranteeing to declare war on Germany should Hitler invade. But the Russo-German Non-Aggression Treaty (23 August 1939), which sealed the fate of Poland, stunned the world. The details were as follows: the two countries agreed not to attack each other, either independently or in conjunction with other powers; not to support any third power that might attack the other party to the pact; to remain in consultation with each other on questions touching their common interests; not to join any group of powers directly or indirectly threatening one of the two parties; and to solve all differences between the two by negotiation or arbitration. The pact was to last for 10 years, with automatic extension for another 5 years unless either party gave notice to terminate it 1 year before its expiration. More importantly, perhaps, a secret protocol divided the whole of Eastern Europe into German and Soviet spheres of influence. Poland east of the line,

formed by the Narew, Vistula and San rivers, would fall under the Soviet sphere of influence.

On 1 September 1939, German forces attacked Poland – World War II had begun. The Blitzkrieg completely destroyed Poland, whose total armed forces exceeded three million men, in a campaign that lasted 36 days. Shortly after Warsaw had fallen, Hitler informed his military chiefs of his monumental decision to attack in the West that autumn. Great consternation was engendered among the German Army leaders, who felt that a decisive conflict with the Western Allies was not at this point within Germany's grasp. In fact, Hitler then ordered various postponements to the attack, which put back the offensive in the West to the following spring. Ironically, this was the date proposed by the OKH (Oberkommando des Heeres – Army High Command) in opposition to Hitler's original demand for an immediate offensive. A winter of inactivity on the British and French side, and preparations on the German side, followed.

The invasion of Denmark and Norway, codename Fall Weserübung or Operation Weser Exercise, began in the early dawn of 9 April 1940. The operation was characterized by lightning speed, meticulous planning and total secrecy. In Denmark it met with virtually no resistance. Two German aircraft were shot down, a few armoured cars were damaged, 13 Danish soldiers were killed and another 23 wounded. It was nothing more than a skirmish. Before the Danes had had breakfast, it was all over. The Volksdeutsche and pro-German Danes were as surprised as any by their fate, which literally fell from the sky upon them. It was the first example in any war of a successful airborne operation. However, once they had recovered from their shock, the North Schleswig Germans welcomed the arrival of "their" army. They offered hospitality, directed traffic and in some cases even took it upon themselves to round up and guard Danish prisoners of war. But nowhere did any Danish citizen indulge in any acts of premeditated sabotage. Before the invasion, the Germans had dispatched a small commando unit to Pagborg to ensure that the Danes did not try to impede their advance by blowing up the important bridge there – the Danes had not even mined it. Norway was a tougher nut to crack, but by 1 May only some northern parts of the country remained in Allied hands.

On 9 May 1940, Hitler decided to unleash the Blitzkrieg in the West the following day. At nine o'clock that evening, the codeword "Danzig" was given, signalling

Above: *A member of Vlassov's Russkaia Osvoboditelnaia Armiia (ROA – the Russian Army of Liberation), POA in Cyrillic. It was highly ironic that the Germans should recruit units from the Slavs, people that Hitler regarded as "vermin", fit only to serve the Aryan "master race".*

Below: *More Russian recruits in German service. The Wehrmacht, faced with the enormous strains on manpower in the East, found former Red Army members very useful for rear-area duties, including fighting the partisans who were an ever-present threat.*

the launching of Fall Gelbe or Case Yellow, the invasion of France and the Low Countries. The campaign concluded on 25 June, after which the French were forced into a humiliating capitulation. Hitler had enjoyed six years of continuous diplomatic and military successes, which was not lost upon the populations of Germany or Western Europe.

Despite the fiasco of Italian arms in the Balkans, which forced Hitler to divert divisions south to conquer Greece, Yugoslavia and Crete between April and May 1941, by June the Third Reich stood poised at the borders of the Soviet Union.

The invasion of Russia

There had been extended common frontiers between Germany and Russia before, and rarely had they proved anything but sources of constant friction and animosity. In October 1939, a sense of history had prompted many to wonder how long such bellicose neighbours could live in harmony. The war between Nazi Germany and communist USSR was inevitable. Ever since his days as an extremist in the political wilderness, Hitler had been obsessed with what he called the "Jewish-Bolshevik conspiracy", the bastion of which he saw as the Soviet Union. From the earliest days of Nazism, Hitler had looked eastwards to find Lebensraum for the German people. "If we speak of new land in Europe today, we can primarily have in mind only Russia and her vassal border states," he wrote in *Mein Kampf*. "Here fate itself seems desirous of giving us a sign." Now the time had come. France had been demolished by one quick thrust, the Balkan sideshow had been concluded, and Germany could now look to the East. Hitler and his party had unconcealed contempt for the Slavs. He lumped them with the Jews as an inferior race, and equated Bolshevism with Zionism.

During the spring of 1941, German units were massed on the Soviet border. Eventually, more than three million men were deployed on Russia's western frontier. Operation Barbarossa, the codename for the attack on the Soviet Union, began on the morning of 22 June 1941.

In many areas, the Germans were initially welcomed with enthusiasm. In the Ukraine, for example, there was little resistance. In fact, some of the villages and towns welcomed the German Army with flowers or the traditional Ukrainian bread and salt of hospitality and friendship. German soldiers were pleasantly surprised that they were welcomed and regarded as liberators from the communist yoke. In 1933, the Ukraine had suffered a man-made famine organized by Lazar Kaganovich, a henchman who followed Stalin's orders to the letter. An estimated seven million Ukrainians died of starvation.

Later in the 1930s, thousands of Ukrainians were arrested and started disappearing, including intelligentsia, writers, artists and even musicians whose patriotism was suspected by the NKVD, the Soviet secret police. The Soviet terror of the 1930s erroneously convinced many Ukrainians that there was nothing worse than communist Russian slavery; they were wrong.

Mid-1941 was to witness a surge in the number of foreign nationals volunteering for service in the German armed forces. In Central Europe, volunteers came from Albania, Bohemia, Bulgaria and Croatia. In Western Europe, recruits came from Denmark, Finland, France, Holland, Norway and Spain. As German armies rolled east towards Moscow, Leningrad and Rostov, a diverse range of nationalities came under German control – Estonians, Latvians, Lithuanians, Belorussians, Cossacks and Tartars – many of which would provide soldiers of varying quality to serve the Third Reich.

The many different nationalities that had fallen within the control of the Third Reich as a result of military conquests presented a vast array of opportunities and problems for the Nazi leadership. The addition of millions of people to the Reich's population meant an increase in the manpower pool of potential recruits that could serve the German war machine. In theory, hundreds of thousands of additional recruits meant more manpower for yet further military offensives, which meant more conquests and yet more peoples falling under the yoke of the swastika. The prospects were dazzling. And yet, conquests also threw up a number of problems. Integration of foreign volunteers into the armed forces of Germany was not simply a matter of bureaucratic procedure. Laying aside differences in language and culture, National Socialism was an ideology that had definite views on certain races both within and outside Europe. The peoples of the more "Germanic" nations, such as Denmark and Holland, could be viewed as Aryan brothers and willingly accepted into the fold of Nazism. But what about Slavs and Moslems? What future could Ukrainian and Tartar recruits have serving a military machine whose political masters viewed them as "sub-human", fit only for ultimate slave labour, or even extermination? The circle could not be easily squared. This would be a problem that would never be solved; though it was ultimately to be irrelevant when the Third Reich accepted anyone who would fight on its behalf in an effort to stave off military defeat.

If ideology complicated the subject of foreign volunteers, then practicalities added another layer of difficulty. For, having conquered vast tracts of Europe, the German military bureaucracy was not geared up for the processing of thousands of foreign recruits. Trainers and administrators had to be found, plus barracks, training facilities, uniforms and weapons. For volunteer and officials alike, the recruiting process would be fraught with difficulty.

Below: Two soldiers of the Cossack 623rd Battalion pose for the camera. This unit was in the service of Germany's Army Group Centre on the Eastern Front in August 1942. The Germans valued the Cossacks for their scouting and raiding abilities. Note the Russian submachine guns.

La ⚡⚡ t'appelle !

Chapter 2

WHY THE THIRD REICH?

This chapter examines some of the psychological reasons why foreign nationals fought on the German side in World War II. For many Western Europeans, anti-Bolshevism was the main motive, rather than an attachment to Nazism. In the East, nationalism drove many to wear the German field-grey uniform.

It would be wrong to suggest that there was one overriding reason why hundreds of thousands of foreign nationals joined the Wehrmacht and Waffen-SS. It would certainly be false to claim that the majority did so because of an ideological allegiance to fascism, or rather to German National Socialism. Their reasons, like their nationalities, were many and varied. That said, there were certain influences that acted as psychological motivators to young men who volunteered for service with Germany's armed forces in World War II.

Left: *"The Waffen-SS is calling you". The front cover of a recruiting pamphlet aimed at Frenchmen, 1943. The call was answered by hundreds of thousands of foreigners.*

When we talk of foreign volunteers, of course, we mean young men aged between 17 and 25. Though recruits were sometimes older, the majority of recruits were males in their early 20s. This is important, because Nazism contained many traits that were attractive to impressionable young males. These included its brutality, its stigmatization of certain races and populations, its culture of warfare, its demands for vengeance and national revival. All these appealed to the more basic instincts within young men. However, there were other more positive attributes that were equally appealing: its sense of comradeship, its criticism of the alienating aspects of capitalism, and its struggle against political and cultural decadence.

Of course, Nazism also made overtures to the more romantic side of human nature. Though totalitarian reality

Above: *This photograph appeared in the same French recruiting pamphlet, the caption reading: "Today, the Waffen-SS has become the Army of Europe and includes in its ranks volunteers from 17 nations." The pan-European idea was a myth propagated by the Germans.*

in the 1930s was often brutal, especially for those individuals and groups who were viewed as enemies, Nazi ideology contained many ideas that harked back to an age of heroes and myths. These included a belief in leaders of vision who commanded with a strong hand, and in return received the adulation and respect of those they commanded; a belief in the value of a strong and unified nation; and in the willing and eager sacrifice of individual goals and lives to strengthen the national purpose, with war and expansion being seen as tests of strength and arenas for heroic sacrifice. Nazism and fascism were also careful to reinforce a belief in at least some traditional hierarchies, such as the army, the family and sometimes the church (less so in Nazi Germany, where Hitler and most of the party hierarchy viewed priests with suspicion and derisively referred to them as parasitic "black crows").

Nazi Germany could also tap into the base instincts of young males in the conquered lands. Those who were members of indigenous fascist parties were already

converted, of course, but others could be wooed by the Nazis' poisonous views on enemy creeds and groups. Thus, National Socialist ideology espoused a hatred of socialists and liberals; socialists because they were opponents of national self-determination (they were also portrayed as potential betrayers of the people to slavery under a foreign Russian élite), and liberals because they were unwilling to take the steps necessary to fight socialists. Nazism despised both groups for being self-absorbed individualists who weakened the nation by not recognizing that the nation, rather than the individual, held rights. Above all, there was a hatred of Jews, who were seen as rootless cosmopolitans uninterested in national destiny; thieves and deceivers; people who made their money through financial manipulation rather than through heroic feats of engineering and construction.

The new ideology

Perhaps what most attracted young males to fascism was the thing it shared with them: youth. The old system of liberal capitalism had failed. It had had its chance but had been found wanting. Above all, it had failed economically: it had not guaranteed high employment and rapid economic growth. The Great Depression destroyed the credibility of liberal democracy among many groups, and the young Western Europeans who joined the German war machine in the 1940s would have experienced at first hand the economic hardships visited upon their families during the 1930s. Fascism and Nazism were youthful ideologies that offered a brave new world. They had worked in Germany and Italy, so why not in their countries?

The conquest of Western Europe in the spring and summer of 1940 would also have made an impression on the young males within the conquered states. They had witnessed at first hand the might of the German armed forces, their awesome firepower and modern military machines. Overhead had been the fearsome howl of the Stuka, while on the ground hundreds of panzers had made a lasting impression. The seemingly unstoppable progress of the Wehrmacht had led to glorious victories which were calculated in days, not years. Fortress Holland had been smashed, the mighty Maginot Line had been bypassed and the French and British armies had been defeated. At first, potential recruits were hostile to the Germans, especially after their indigenous armies had been humiliated. However, then came a turnaround. Instead of blaming the Germans, they blamed their own governments for the debacle. Young men were taken in by the notion that they, too, could be a part of Hitler's New Order in Europe.

Of course, there were other reasons why Western Europeans joined the Germans, pragmatic self-preservation being chief among them. In an occupied country one had to do what one could to survive, and serving in the Wehrmacht appeared a better option than being a Nazi slave at home or in Germany. For no matter how hard the Nazis tried to portray themselves as benevolent rulers, eventually the true face of fascism would show itself. Following Holland's capitulation, for example, and in the weeks that followed, the Dutch were in a state of bewilderment and numbness. Initially, it seemed that the German occupation might not be too unbearable. Seyss-Inquart, Reich Commissioner for the Netherlands, said that Germany would not impose its ideology on Holland and that he would respect existing Dutch law.

The occupation myth

In May 1940, German troops in Holland were on their best behaviour. There was no looting and no burning down of synagogues. The occupation soldiers were polite and even proved to be good customers at Dutch stores and cafes. In a conciliatory mood, German authorities had declared that Dutch soldiers would be not held as prisoners of war (something permissible under the rules of law), but would be allowed to return to their homes and families instead. It was German thinking, at least initially in the occupation, that the Dutch should be treated with kid gloves. The Germans were convinced that with some care it would be only a matter of time before the Dutch would accept the New Order and embrace Nazism as the Germans themselves had. Of course, the Nazis had no intention of respecting Dutch law or of sparing them Nazi ideology. Step by step, decree by decree, the Germans set out to transform Holland into a totalitarian state. The Dutch Parliament was abolished, as were virtually all elected bodies. In the courts, the existing Dutch system was quickly replaced by German justice, i.e. the law of a police state.

Young men could be conscripted for labour service by the Germans, which could mean being shipped off to any part of the Reich where they would dig ditches and haul materials for defences, an altogether unattractive proposition. Jutt Olafsen was a teacher in Norway, and his experience was typical of that of many European volunteers: "Then, when the war began in Russia, things became more difficult and the Germans began rounding up men for forced labour. But they offered me an alternative, and this was to join the Legion *Norwegen* and assist in the anti-Bolshevik crusade, as they called it. I hated communism, so decided I would rather join this legion than go to work in Germany."

Generally speaking, conditions in the Wehrmacht appeared attractive to those who were nationalist without being National Socialist, and anti-communist without being anti-British or even pro-German. In many cases, young men

Above: *In its recruiting efforts, the Waffen-SS was keen to promote the idea of a European Army locked in battle with the Bolsheviks defending the history and culture of Europe. In reality, foreign nationals always served the narrow interests of the Nazi hierarchy in Berlin.*

left businesses and careers behind them. Pay was less than they could earn in their homeland, but most volunteers probably anticipated a brief and victorious campaign, after which they would return home in triumph to privileged positions and other advantages, having thrown in their lot with the Germans.

A prime motivator among Western Europeans, and something that was exploited to the full by the Germans after the invasion of the Soviet Union in 1941, was anti-communism. In the 1920s and 1930s, both fascism and Nazism had gained popularity as defenders against an imposing communist menace. With the coming to power of the communists in Russia, and with Moscow's assertion that the revolution would be exported and abolition of private property would sweep away class differences, much of the middle class in Europe had a very real fear of the "Bolshevik menace" and the possibility of the forceful overthrow or subversion of the existing social and political order.

Both Mussolini and Hitler made opposition to communism a major element of their ideologies. For Hitler, communism and Nazism were competing world systems, locked in mortal combat. As he stated in his closing speech to the Nazi party rally at Nuremberg in September 1936: "Bolshevism has attacked the foundations of our whole human order, alike in State and society; the foundations of our concept of civilization, of our faith and of our morals – all alike are at stake."

Germans efforts to recruit foreign nationals in Western Europe continually played upon the communist threat and the importance of taking part in the anti-Bolshevik crusade. Thus, a Waffen-SS recruiting brochure of early 1943 aimed at Frenchmen stated: "It is evident that the constitution of a unit of French volunteers at the heart of the Waffen-SS represents a new step that is very significant in the union of European youth against Bolshevist nihilism." The text went on: "Volunteers from almost all countries in Europe, side by side with their German comrades, have distinguished themselves by their valour at the Eastern front, [and because of this] the SS, the essential basis of the National Socialist Party that originally was merely of German internal political value, has now transformed itself into an indissoluble community of European youth

Above: *Bronislav Kaminski, self-styled Warlord of the Bryansk Forest and commander of the "Russian People's Liberation Army". A fanatical Nazi and brilliant organizer, he was shot by the Germans in 1944 for looting.*

Below: *Cossacks in German service on the Eastern Front. Like many Russian nationals, the Cossacks fought for the Germans in order to establish an independent Cossack nation, which the Germans had no intention of granting.*

struggling for the maintenance of its cultural values and its civilization." Lieutenant-Colonel Kryssing, commander of the Danish Freikorps, urged his countrymen: "Along the Eastern Front the fight against the world enemy is in full swing. Join the fight against our common enemy for the safety of our Fatherland which shall give our children security and peace." It is interesting to note that Kryssing was a rabid anti-communist rather than a pro-Nazi.

The oath that was sworn by those who served in the foreign legions raised in Western Europe by the SS reinforced the myth that they were defending Europe, not just Germany, against the evils of Bolshevik Russia: "I swear by God, this sacred oath, that in the struggle against Bolshevism, I will unconditionally obey the Commander-in-Chief of the Armed Forces, Adolf Hitler, and as a faithful soldier am ready, at any time he may desire, to lay down my life for this oath."

However, one must be careful when saying that ideology was the sole reason why men joined the foreign legions. It must be remembered that of the 125,000 West Europeans in the Waffen-SS, for example, only a third belonged to pro-Nazi nationalist parties. What reasons did the other two-thirds have for serving? A study by a Dutch psychologist in the late 1940s, Dr A van Hoesti, of young Dutchmen who had fought for the Germans revealed some interesting reasons why they had joined up. They included boredom, a desire for adventure, better food, a desire to avoid labour

*Above: **Fighting for fascism. These are Italians serving with the 29th SS Waffen-Grenadier Division, a unit formed following the fall of Mussolini in 1943. Their motivation for fighting was purely ideological.***

service, the prestige of wearing an SS uniform, and a wish to avoid prosecution for minor offences. Political idealism hardly figured at all. As Gottlob Berger himself stated: "We will never be able to prevent men from joining the legions and the Waffen-SS who are neither National Socialists nor idealists, and instead take this step for more materialistic reasons. That is the way it is everywhere in the world and it is no different in Germany during the Kampfzeit [time of struggle]."

When it came to East Europeans, the Baltic peoples and Russian recruits, the reasons for fighting for the Germans were much more straightforward. Felix Steiner, the commander of the *Wiking* Division, summed it up succinctly: "The eastern volunteers fought primarily for the freedom and independence of their countries." Of course, many served the Germans simply in order to survive, such as the many Russian prisoners of war who preferred working for the Wehrmacht in preference to starving to death. And of course, many police and security units raised by the Germans from indigenous peoples for service in Russia and the Balkans contained individuals who were attracted by the prospect of loot, rape and killing Jews.

Prüfungsbuch

für die

Germanische
Leistungsrune

Herausgeber:

DER REICHSFÜHRER-SS

SS-Hauptamt – Amt für Leibeserziehung

Chapter 3

RECRUITMENT AND TRAINING

Nazi ideology was based on the premise that the Aryan race was an élite among nationalities. Similarly, the Waffen-SS was the ideological and racial élite of Nazi Germany. Recruitment and training reflected this, and only those foreigners deemed "racially acceptable" were accepted into its ranks.

Although the Waffen-SS was primarily an armed force at Hitler's disposal for the maintenance of order inside Germany, Hitler also decreed that in time of war it was to serve at the front under army command. He believed that frontline experience for the Waffen-SS was essential if such a force was to command the respect of the German people. He also insisted that its human material was to be of the highest calibre, and so restricted the size of the Waffen-SS to between five and ten percent of the peacetime strength of the German Army.

Left: An SS booklet on how to win the Germanic Proficiency Runes Badge, an award that encompassed the ideals of National Socialism and Nordism.

Unlike many armies, the German Army's recruits were immediately placed in their branch of service at the beginning of their basic training, which lasted three weeks. The recruits were also exposed to an above-average amount of multi-disciplinary training. Thus, those in the artillery arm would learn how to use radios; signals troops would learn how to fire heavy machine guns and so on. Nazi Germany used a system of Wehrkreis (military districts) to recruit and train troops, with a total of 21 districts at the height of the Nazi conquests. The Ersatzheer (Replacement Army), which was formed in 1938 and revised in 1942, administered these 21 districts.

The Waffen-SS was under the Replacement Army system, but maintained a degree of independence with its own supply and weapons depots, training camps and

The Waffen-SS offered advancement to promising candidates regardless of their education or social standing, but those charged with grooming the new SS élite set their sights high. They called their academies Junkerschulen (schools for young nobles) and devised a curriculum to transform the sons of farmers and artisans into officers and gentlemen. For some, this required basic training in matters that were not exclusively military. For example, incoming cadets were issued an etiquette manual that defined table manners. Correct form was further encouraged through cultural activities and lectures on Nazi ideology. When off-duty, officers and men addressed each other as "kamerad". Locks were forbidden on wardrobes (much emphasis was placed on trust), and obedience was unconditional at all times.

On selection to the SS school, the individual was designated an SS-Führeranwärter, or SS officer candidate. After completing the initial phase, he became an SS-Standartenjunker. Towards the end of the training period, the commandant of the SS-Junkerschule bestowed the designation of SS-Junker on qualified personnel, and when achieving this position the SS-Junker put on the rank insignia of an SS-Scharführer. Upon successful completion of training, but before being commissioned to the rank of SS-Untersturmführer, the officer candidate was elevated to the position of SS-Oberjunker, and was thus authorized to wear the rank insignia of an SS-Hauptscharführer.

Above: *SS-Oberstgruppenführer und Generaloberst der Waffen-SS Paul Hausser (right), the pre-war Inspector of the SS-Verfügungstruppe. He is seen here with SS-Obersturmbannführer Fritz Klingenberg.*

military schools. From the beginning, it was intended that the Waffen-SS would benefit from the highest standards of training available. Two highly regarded former army officers, Paul Hausser and Felix Steiner, were recruited for this purpose. The SS-Hauptamt (Main Office), established on 30 July 1935, organized all branches of the SS, and a special Inspectorate of the SS-Verfügungstruppe was also created on 1 October 1936 to supervise military training. The new inspectorate had the objective of moulding the mainly ill-trained and far-flung units of the Waffen-SS into an efficient fighting force. SS-Oberstgruppenführer und Generaloberst der Waffen-SS Paul Hausser, who was to become known affectionately as "Papa" Hausser to his men, was chosen as the Inspector of the SS-Verfügungstruppe, although he had only just been appointed inspector of the SS-Junkerschulen (Officer Schools) at Bad Tölz and Braunschweig (both came into existence in 1934). Once established, Hausser began attracting increasing numbers of former police officials and German Army noncommissioned officers (NCOs) into the fledgling SS-Verfügungstruppe.

Hausser readily accepted the responsibility for the organization and training of the SS-Verfügungstruppe, which enabled him to formulate the directives and codes of practice it was to use. Hausser remained in his post until the outbreak of World War II, when he took command of the *Das Reich* Division. During the war, the SS established two additional Junker schools at Klagenfurt in Austria and Prague in Czechoslovakia.

Waffen-SS training

At the heart of training was a mixture of athletics and field exercises designed to turn the Junkers into commanders. Thus, the facilities at Bad Tölz included a stadium for soccer, track and field events, separate halls for boxing, gymnastics and indoor ball games, and a heated swimming pool and sauna. The complex attracted outstanding talent. At one time, for example, eight of twelve coaches at Bad Tölz were national champions in their events.

Felix Steiner was the luminary when it came to the actual training programme of the Waffen-SS. He was 16 years Hausser's junior, and his motto was "sweat saves blood". Steiner believed strongly in the creation of élite, highly mobile groups whose training put the emphasis on individual responsibility and military teamwork rather than on rigid obedience to the rule book. His ideas had been formulated and refined during World War I, when he served as the commander of a machine-gun company, witnessing the formation of "battle groups", which had greatly impressed him. They were made up from selected men, withdrawn from the trenches and formed into ad hoc assault groups. Specially trained for close-quarter fighting, usually carried out at night, they wreaked havoc in their trench raids, employing individualized weapons such as

Right: *SS-Obergruppenführer Felix Steiner, the man responsible for moulding Waffen-SS training following his experiences at the front during World War I. During World War II he commanded the Wiking Division and then III SS Panzer Corps. He died in 1966.*

knuckle-dusters, cluster grenades and entrenching tools sharpened like razors. The enemy's customary notification of an impending attack, a long artillery barrage, was often dispensed with, thus reinforcing the element of surprise.

As their value became recognized, Steiner's reforms gradually filtered throughout the SS hierarchy. In concert with the "battle group" ideology, his training stressed three main points: physical fitness, "character" and weapons training. He structured a recruit's day with a rigorous hour-long physical training session beginning at 06:00 hours, with a pause afterwards for breakfast of porridge and mineral water. Intensive weapons training followed, then target practice and unarmed combat sessions. The day was broken by a hearty lunch, then resumed with a comparatively short but intensive drill session. The afternoon was then punctuated by a stint of scrubbing, cleaning, scouring and polishing and rounded off with a run or a couple of hours on the sports field. As a result of his men spending more time on the athletics fields and in cross-country running than on the parade ground, they developed standards of fitness and endurance enabling them to perform such feats as covering 3km (1.8 miles) in full kit in 20 minutes, feats that could not be matched by either army recruits or members of the *Leibstandarte* (who spent a lot of time on the parade square, hence their nickname "asphalt soldiers").

The training programme stressed aggressiveness and included live-firing exercises. It was interrupted three times a week by ideological lectures, which included understanding the Führerprinzip (leadership principle) and unravelling the meanings of Hitler's *Mein Kampf* (ideology formed an important element in examinations, and was responsible for failing one candidate in three during the five-month course).

For the successful candidates, there was a passing-out parade where they took the SS oath, at 22:00 hours on the occasion of the 9 November anniversary celebrations of the Munich Putsch. This took place in Hitler's presence before the Feldherrnhalle and the 16 smoking obelisks, each of which bore the name of a fallen party member. The oath was a major ingredient in the SS mystique, binding each successful candidate in unswerving loyalty to Adolf Hitler.

Bad Tölz and Braunschweig were the premier Waffen-SS training centres for officers from their inception in 1934 until the end of the war. By 1937, the SS schools were graduating more than 400 officers a year, in two sets of classes. These officers were very well-trained and in due course often later earned distinguished military reputations. The spirited aggressiveness taught at the school was not without cost, though, for by 1942 nearly 700 Waffen-SS officers had been killed in action, including almost all of the 60 graduates of the 1934–35 Bad Tölz class. During the war, the Junker schools accepted recruits from occupied countries. Most foreigners enlisted to fight the Soviet Union, so the SS lectures shifted from the sanctity of Nordic blood to the evils of Bolshevism.

Himmler established an SS Recruiting Office within the SS-Hauptamt on 1 December 1939. The running of this office was entrusted to the steady hands of Gottlob Berger. The armed forces were unwilling to relinquish the cream of German manhood to the SS as they were suspicious of all paramilitary forces outside their control. Their passive resistance made Berger's task of locating the recruits who were required all the more difficult. His pool comprised those who were too young and too old to be eligible for military service in the German armed forces, and by 1940 the SS was having difficulties in finding recruits. However, Berger was able to circumvent the armed forces' restrictions by recruiting from abroad. He availed himself of Himmler's contacts outside the Reich to encourage ethnic Germans living abroad, as well as non-Germans of Nordic blood, to enlist. Not only were these groups allowed to become members of the SS, they were also exempt from conscription in the German armed forces. By May 1940, more than 100 foreigners were serving with the Waffen-SS. Following the defeat of France in the summer of 1940, a vast recruiting ground had opened up, over which the Wehrmacht had no jurisdiction.

In preparation for the attack on Russia, the German Army was expanded, but the SS was allowed to recruit only three percent of the newly enlisted age groups, which meant that it had to fall back on foreign manpower. Hitler was insistent that the Waffen-SS should remain a small, exclusive police force, but he did agree to the formation of a new SS division on condition that mainly foreigners were recruited. In addition, his own personal bodyguard was to be expanded from a regiment to a brigade.

From the beginning of the war, German recruits had been apportioned on the basis of 66 percent to the army, 8 percent to the navy and 25 percent to the air force. Those for the Waffen-SS were subtracted from the army's percentage on a quota established by Hitler himself. During the Polish and French campaigns, German casualties had been moderate. From its share of the available German manpower, the SS had been able to replenish its losses, but it would be forced to cast its net further afield for its replacements when it began to look as if the war would last longer than expected. Hitler's decision to invade the USSR was announced in July 1940. One of the first to be informed was Himmler, who wasted no time in informing Berger. On 7 August 1940, he drew up his SS manpower forecast.

Below: A parade at the SS officers' school in Braunschweig. Following successful completion of officer training, candidates, including foreign officer candidates, would go on to attend a platoon commanders' course at the SS training school at Dachau.

In August 1940, there was still a strong possibility that England would be invaded, thus the navy and air force were demanding an increase of their percentages to 40 and 10 percent respectively. Berger estimated that 18,000 recruits per year would be required by the SS, but assumed that it would receive only 12,000 men, or two percent. Consequently, the Germanic areas of Western Europe, together with the ethnic German populations of southeastern Europe, were the areas where recruiting should begin in earnest. As long as the SS recruited personnel who were not available to the Wehrmacht, Berger did not anticipate any objections. He also requested permission to establish a recruiting office to deal with foreign countries.

In Western Europe, Berger's recruiting staff had sufficient response to form two new regiments, *Nordland* and *Westland*, and to make the new *Germania* Division, later named *Wiking*, a feasible proposition. Nevertheless, when the first enthusiastic rush of pro-German and National Socialist volunteers had been signed up, recruiting figures began to drop. Even when an existing SS regiment, *Germania*, was transferred to the new formation, and other Reich Germans provided cadres, there were still large gaps in its ranks. When the Soviet Union was invaded, for example, the *Wiking* Division contained Reich and ethnic Germans to such an extent that a mere 630 Dutchmen, 294 Norwegians, 216 Danes, 1 Swede and 1 Swiss were to be found in its ranks.

German diplomatic agencies received offers of help from individuals living in the occupied countries, as well as in the Independent State of Croatia and in neutral Spain and Portugal following the German attack on the Soviet Union. The German Government decided to accept these offers of assistance and to establish

Above: *SS officers' school at Bad Tölz. Foreign candidates were treated the same as German recruits. One Dane, Eric Brörup, who served in the* **Wiking** *Division, commented: "I wasn't personally subjected to any form of demeaning or degrading treatment because I was a Dane."*

contingents of foreign nationals. On 29 June 1941, Hitler gave his formal approval to the establishment of legions for foreigners who wished to take part in the crusade against the Soviet Union. Legions from the Germanic countries were to be the responsibility of the Waffen-SS, while the German Army was to organize those from non-Germanic countries. A Spanish formation was established on 25 June, and almost simultaneously Danish and Norwegian units were brought into being.

The German Foreign Office convened a meeting of interested parties on 30 June 1941. Represented at the meeting were the Foreign Office, the SS-Führungshauptamt, the Foreign Section of the Oberkommando der Wehrmacht (OKW), the German Plenipotentiary in Copenhagen and the Foreign Section of the Nazi Party. Its brief was to settle the details pertaining to the formation of the new units. Because of international law, it was agreed that non-German volunteers were to fight in German uniforms but would wear national badges. It was not envisaged that German citizenship would be conferred upon the volunteers, but they were to receive the same pay and allowances as German serviceman while those with previous military experience would hold ranks equivalent to their former

ones. The meeting also considered how the volunteers were to be organized. It was decided that they should be deployed only in closed units, some of which had already been formed. The Waffen-SS, being responsible for volunteers from the Germanic countries, had already set up a Freikorps in Denmark and a Freiwilligenverband in Norway, both independent of Regiment *Nordland*, a separate Freiwillingenkorps for the Netherlands and the Flemish parts of Belgium, in addition to and independent of Regiment *Westland*.

The Wehrmacht was responsible for the large volunteer formations that were being created by the Falangist Party and the Spanish armed forces. Spaniards were to serve in both the army and air force, but there was to be no separate Falangist formation. The High Command of the Wehrmacht wanted Croats to serve in all three branches of the military, to which end a Croatian volunteer formation was to be set up under its control. Those foreigners already serving in the Waffen-SS had signed on for two years, the duration of the war or for an agreed period, but the Wehrmacht had not yet decided on the length of engagement for its volunteers.

The delegates expected that other European countries would yield few volunteers. It was agreed not to approach the Swiss Government or to launch an appeal for Swiss recruits, but Swiss volunteers were to be accepted if they presented themselves (in fact, some Swiss were already serving in the Waffen-SS). The conference reached no decision about whether Walloons and Frenchmen were to

Above: *Political education/indoctrination was a core part of Waffen-SS training. Himmler and the SS hierarchy considered it essential that all members of the Waffen-SS had a National Socialist outlook.*

be accepted. Finns could hardly be expected to volunteer for the German Army when Finland was already fighting the Soviet Union, though some were already serving in Regiment *Nordland*. Swedes would probably prefer to volunteer for the Finnish armed forces, but if enough came forward a Swedish Volunteer Corps could be formed under the auspices of the SS. If equipping and training of Swedish volunteers was outside the capacity of the Finnish Army to cope with, they were to be directed to German reception centres. It was also considered probable that a number of Danes would prefer the Finnish forces. Portugal was expected to produce few volunteers, but if enough presented themselves there was the possibility of incorporating them in the Spanish formation. In fact, no Portuguese legion was formed, and it is doubtful if any Portuguese volunteered at all.

For the German Army, Hitler's newly authorized non-German legions did not represent an important increase in size, but for the Waffen-SS they provided a considerable accession of strength. Himmler was interested only in raising legions of Danes, Norwegians, Dutchmen and Flemings on racial grounds. The SS could have had a far larger share of Western European manpower but for this policy. Although in need of additional manpower, it relinquished to the army the Walloon Legion that it had sponsored because Himmler maintained that Walloons were not Germanic and that their presence in the SS might offend the Flemings.

In some cases, the Germans opposed enlistment. Russian émigrés had expressed a willingness to serve the Germans, but they were to be refused. However, some White Russians served as interpreters, and others served in both the French Volunteer Legion and in the Danish Freikorps. Czechs of the Protectorate of Bohemia and Moravia who offered their assistance were not to be accepted. The newly occupied Baltic areas were to be dealt with by the local German military commander while Balts in Germany who presented themselves were to be dealt with in a derogatory manner.

Himmler probably thought that it was just not worthwhile compromising the racial purity of the SS for the sake of short-lived units that might never see action (a long campaign against the Soviet Union was not anticipated in the summer of 1941). In any case, the SS would have had difficulty in providing facilities and cadres for a division of Spaniards, a regiment each of Frenchmen and Croats, and a battalion of Walloons, in addition to those already employed – even if it had wanted to.

Finland, Romania, Hungary, Slovakia and Italy were allied with Germany. Small as they were, their legions had considerable propaganda value. The presence of Western Europeans and Croats in the ranks of the German forces

Above: Recruits received intensive instruction in firing and maintaining weapons. These included not only German models, as shown above, but also the weapons of the enemy, particularly the Russians.

gave Germany's act of aggression the semblance of a European crusade against Bolshevism.

Apart from meeting the strict racial standards of the SS, volunteers for the Waffen-SS had to be perfect physical specimens. They signed on for an initial period of four years before the war. For the most part, volunteers came from the ranks of the Hitler Youth via the Allgemeine-SS. In 1938, Himmler authorized the enlistment of Germanics into the Waffen-SS. Now, SS men needed only to be of Germanic origin, provided that they were of Nordic blood. By the end of the year, 20 foreign volunteers had been accepted. In the Waffen-SS, one could enlist for as long as 12 years and become eligible for German citizenship. Like their German comrades, foreigners could on retirement take up a career in the German police or civil service or receive land in the Incorporated Territories.

Foreign nationals who volunteered for service in the Germanic legions found their conditions of acceptance

Right: Becoming a Waffen-SS soldier was not all work. This image is from an SS pamphlet aimed at French recruits, though one wonders how many foreign recruits actually had leave before being shipped off to Russia.

were less stringent than those for the Waffen-SS. Candidates still had to be able to prove Aryan decent for two generations, and to possess an "upright" character. They also had to be between 17 and 40 years of age, although for former officers and NCOs the upper age limit was raised. The minimum height was reduced to 1.65m (5.5ft) and later disregarded. They received the same pay and allowances as members of the Waffen-SS, and were subject to the same penal code. They wore the uniform of the Waffen-SS but with additional national insignia. Those accepted into the legions were not members of the Waffen-SS but of units attached to it. The material inducements for joining the legions were less than those of the Waffen-SS for the simple reason that the legions

formation sign of the *Wiking* Division, and later adopted by III Germanic SS Panzer Corps (made up largely of volunteers from Germanic countries). The badge was instituted in two grades, bronze and silver, with a higher standard required for the attainment of the silver. It was worn in the centre of the left breast pocket of the service uniform.

The Germanic Proficiency Runes

From his headquarters on 15 August 1943, Himmler officially introduced the Germanic Proficiency Runes. In the institution document, he stated that it, "should be an example in physical training and tests in the use of weapons in the National Socialist spirit, and confirmation of the voluntary attainment of the Germanic joint destiny". Physical requirements for award of the badge included the sprint, long jump, grenade throwing, swimming, shooting and camouflage skills (observation and description of objective), climbing and digging trenches.

The Germanic Proficiency Runes were open to members of the German General SS. Although all four branches of the Germanic SS were eligible, and the rules and requirements were published in the newspapers of each, record has only been found of awards in Holland, Denmark and Norway. It is possible that the runes were awarded to members of the Flemish SS, but as this formation was on the decline in 1944 it is believed that none of its members received them. Only one presentation ceremony is recorded for each of the three countries concerned, although there may have been others later in the war.

The awards of the Germanic Proficiency Runes in Denmark were made at Hovelte on 2 June 1944 by Berger. The presentation took place at a memorial ceremony for SS volunteers from Denmark killed in action, and in fact the test schedule had been timed so that the results would be ready for this ceremony. Berger spoke of the Danish SS volunteers killed in action, and how "their spirits could rest in peace knowing that new columns of Germanic fighters stood behind them". He stated that it was in the memory of the dead Danish SS volunteers and in their spirit that the first Germanic Proficiency Runes were being awarded on

were a temporary creation, in which a volunteer was not expected to make a career. In many cases, the legionnaires were not affected by the advantages that other nationals received when they joined the Waffen-SS proper.

Himmler wanted a badge that would be available to both the General SS in Germany and the Germanic SS abroad, and which would not only require a high standard in various sports but also ability in military activities and National Socialist ideology. But the badge had to reflect all of the Nordic principles, and be an emblem of commitment to the SS. On a much grander scale, he aimed at strengthening the pan-Germanic idea within the entire political SS organization.

The badge that Himmler introduced was called the Germanic Proficiency Runes, and its very design was geared to appeal particularly to the Germanic SS. The two runes of the SS were superimposed upon a mobile swastika, the

Above: *Himmler presents the Germanic Proficiency Runes at Avegoor, taking them from a board carried by an SS-Unterscharführer from the Germania Regiment of the Wiking Division. Several thousand had applied for the badge and undergone the tests, but only 95 had passed.*

Danish soil. No details are available of the number of badges awarded, or of the recipients. However, photographs suggest that the badges went to members of the *Schalburg* Corps, who were wearing black service uniforms.

The only recorded awards of the Germanic Proficiency Runes in Norway were made at the Norwegian SS school on 16 August 1944, when the Higher SS and Police Leader in Norway, SS-Obergruppenführer Rediess, acting on instructions from Himmler, awarded 10 in silver and 15 in bronze to members of the Norwegian SS.

Rediess spoke of the badge's meaning, and how the 25 recipients had, though their behaviour, been a good example to their comrades in the Germanic SS and to the youth of Norway. After the awards, Rediess made a short speech on the meaning of the SS victory runes and the sun-wheel swastika design of the badge.

Right: *At the awards ceremony, Himmler made a speech praising the achievements of the Dutch SS (and the Westland Regiment in particular). This member of the Wiking Division, who is wearing the Germanic Proficiency Runes Badge, was captured at Arnhem.*

Once the SS Main Office handed over Waffen-SS training to the SS-Führungshauptamt (SS-FHA), it was left with only ideological training, physical training and vocational training through its Branch C — offices CI, CII and CIII respectively. It was CII that was responsible for the testing. SS-Standartenführer der Reserve Herbert Edler von Daniels, Chef SS Hauptamt Amt C II, was the commanding officer and authorizing signatory for the test document. The office was in Prague, and it was here that the tests were now taken, with exams being held in the Beneshau / Prague area of Czechoslovakia. The first recorded test following on from those in Norway was held from 23 September 1944 until 26 September 1944, then from 26 October 1944 until 29 October 1944, and the last from 6 March 1945 until 9 March 1945.

Chapter 4

THE FIRST VOLUNTEER LEGIONS

The first foreign units recruited by Germany were raised from pro-Nazi fascists in Austria, the Sudetenland and Danzig. They were all eager for political union with Germany, and agitated for such in their respective countries. They were aided in their efforts by Berlin, and especially by Heinrich Himmler's SS.

The first "foreign" volunteers for the German armed forces came from Austria, the Sudetenland and Danzig. Initially, they were political fighters organized into legions by their respective fascist parties, which relied in varying degrees upon the Nazi Party in Germany for assistance. These volunteers were in the main modelled on the SA of the 1920s, though as the SS grew in importance and stature this organization became the more preferred model. The Sturmabteilung (SA – Storm Detachment, also called Brownshirts) was a Nazi paramilitary organization founded in Munich in 1921

Left: Members of the Sudeten Legion parade through their home territory in October 1938, following the handover of the Sudetenland to Germany.

from the Freikorps. It numbered 500,000 men in 1933. The volunteer units were home-grown, and though in some cases under the jurisdiction of the SS, they must be viewed as separate from Nazi Germany. However, with the annexation of Austria (March 1938), the absorption of Czechoslovakia (March 1939) and the "liberation" of Danzig with the invasion of Poland (September 1939), the majority were then incorporated into the SS.

These, then, were pre-war militia units, and the Wehrmacht had scant regard for them. The German Army viewed them as part-time rabble-rousers akin to the SA in Germany, which the officer corps detested. On the other hand, the SS saw the potential for exploiting these units, which in the future would enhance its standing. Himmler had grandiose ideas of a Pan-Germanic state,

Above: When Dollfuss' government in Austria banned the Austrian Nazi Party, thousands of Nazis fled across the border to Bavaria and into the arms of Himmler. The Reichsführer-SS formed them into the Austrian Legion under SS-Brigadeführer Alfred Rodenbucher, shown here.

superiority of the Aryan race, stressed the greatness and creativity of Europe, and the negative influence of Jewry (his book, *The Foundations of the Nineteenth Century*, became the main ideological text for German National Socialists).

The thoughts of all three found their way into *Mein Kampf*, and were taken further by the three Nazi Party doctrinal luminaries: the ethnologist Hans Günther, the "philosopher" Alfred Rosenberg and the agronomist Richard Walther Darré. Of the three, Darré's thoughts had more impact upon Himmler, as to the Reichsführer-SS they were the verification he sought for his own perspective on Nordic life and culture, which were to become the bedrock on which he would construct his "new church".

Darré was born in the German colony around Belgrano, Argentina. He attended the colonial school in Witzenhausen, went to school in Wimbledon, England, and afterwards to several universities, including Heidelberg. Darré served during World War I in the artillery, and afterwards led the young farmers in Insterburg. He decided to become an agriculturist, and became interested in stock-rearing problems. In 1929, he wrote his first book, which theorized his views of agriculture and society. In 1930, he joined the Nazi Party and met Himmler at a meeting of the Artaman League (a nationalist organization founded in the 1920s which was preoccupied with a general distaste of urban life, Jews and capitalists).

The SS order

Himmler, greatly influenced by the theories of Darré and Rosenberg, imposed his values on the SS: anti-Christian and an overriding belief in the nobility of the Nordic race. To these were added the general Teutonic values of racial solidarity, Prussian discipline and the glorification of conflict. In his view, his SS thus became an order to rival that of the Catholic priesthood. In 1930, he restored the ancient celebration of the winter solstice and instituted the feast of Yuletide in place of the Christian Christmas, and in the following year he issued the ordinances concerning the marriage of men belonging to the SS. RUSHA (Rasse und Siedlungshauptamt – Race and Resettlement Office) was now the SS marriage bureau. It also was concerned with research on racial Germans living abroad and safeguarding the racial "purity" of the SS.

Darré became the first head of RUSHA in 1932. He wrote another book on blood and soil (later published in 1935) in which he distilled all his previous thoughts; he became minister of agriculture in June 1933 with the resignation of Dr Hugenberg. Made an honourary SS general by Himmler, Darré's philosophy was that the Germans were both farmers and warriors. He recognized no clear division between nobility and peasantry. Darré came into conflict with Himmler in 1936 over ideology,

which would encompass all Nordic blood. Himmler became enthralled by a new vision: he would create a Nordic religion. He was to be the "Great Architect" of the new church, a holy order in which the Führer was to be the Messiah. Himmler looked to the Pan-Germanist theories of the nineteenth century, notably those propounded by Gobineau, Chamberlain and Treitschke. Joseph-Arthur comte de Gobineau (1816–82) was a French diplomat who advanced a number of racist theories, in particular the superiority of the white race (whom he labelled Aryans) over others. Heinrich von Treitschke (1834–96) was a German historian and political writer who advanced the theory that the state should be headed by authoritarian leaders, and that war and violence were spiritually liberating. Houston Stewart Chamberlain (1855–1927), a political philosopher, owed much to Gobineau. He advocated the racial and cultural

and in 1938 these differences forced him to resign the leadership of RUSHA. He was followed by a series of ruthless leaders: SS-Obergruppenführer Günther Pancke, SS-Obergruppenführer Otto Hoffmann and SS-Obergruppenführer Richard Hildebrant, who gave the researches of RUSHA a different orientation. For example, in the name of racial selection and the detection of Nordic blood, RUSHA kidnapped children to be brought up as Germans, decided who should be deported from desirable resettlement areas, who should be conscripted for slave labour in the Reich, and who should lose their property or be executed for miscegenation with Germans. In all of these matters, RUSHA was under the jurisdiction of the executive police of the SS.

On 22 September 1939, the Sicherheitsdienst (SD — Security Service) and Sicherheitspolizei (Sipo — Security Police) — the latter included the Gestapo and Kriminal-polizei (Kripo — Criminal Police) — were merged to form the Reich Security Main Office (Reichssicherheitshauptamt — RSHA), the central office through which the Nazis conducted their war against "enemies of the state". The RSHA was commissioned with the task of setting up the Einsatzgruppen (Special Action Groups) which were first employed in three areas during the invasion of Poland. Their

Above: *Alfred Rosenberg, leading Nazi ideologist (on podium at right), who was appointed Reich Minister for the Eastern Occupied Territories in July 1941. His work, The Myth of the Twentieth Century, became a sort of Nazi bible. He was hanged at Nuremberg in October 1946.*

back-up was provided by the local communities, but during the invasion of Poland they were greatly expanded to form Einsatzgruppe I, II, III, IV, V and VI, in which units of local militia, self-defence volunteers, police and disgruntled locals played an important role.

Returning to the raising of the first foreign legions, Austria provided a fertile potential recruiting ground. The early 1930s picturesque Austria of the holidaymaker's photographs disguised a period of extreme political violence that was taking place in the country. Nazis, communists and monarchists beat up each other's newspaper sellers, staged provocative marches and fought pitched battles in which "India rubbers", better known as coshes, and "match boxes" (pistols) were frequently used. It was in this supercharged atmosphere of violence that so many men, embittered by military defeat and economic depression, decided to join the Austrian SS. Indeed, an emphasis on physical toughness and swagger

came to characterize the SS. On 1 July 1932, all Austrian SA and SS units assembled in Linz in upper Austria for an inspection by Adolf Hitler, SA Chief Hermann Göring, General Franz Ritter von Epp and Graf du Moulin Eckardt (the Nazis in both Germany and Austria were pressing for political union at this time).

In the summer of 1933, the Austrian Chancellor, Engelbert Dollfuss, banned the Austrian National Socialist Party and its SS wing. His ban, however, inadvertently opened a door for Himmler and the SS. As thousands of Austrian Nazis fled across the border into Bavaria,

Himmler was waiting with open arms to receive them. Many chose to join the SS in preference to the less disciplined SA. With Hitler's approval, the SS armed the émigrés and organized them into the Austrian Legion under SS-Brigadeführer Alfred Rodenbucher. This "army in exile" trained at a camp near the border, ready to return home when an opportunity arose. At the same time, Himmler's henchmen secretly enrolled hundreds of SS members within Austria itself. Supplied with arms and explosives, the recruits energetically pursued a campaign of sabotage and terror, blowing up power stations and murdering supporters of Dollfuss's regime. By the beginning of 1934, the SS could count on 5000 clandestine members in Austria. But they were an unruly crew, eager but not always willing to follow the lead of

Below: *Austrian Nazi "martyrs" who were executed in the abortive coup in 1934. On the top row, third from left, can be seen Otto Planetta, who mortally wounded Chancellor Dollfuss when the insurgents seized the Federal Chancellery in Vienna.*

Above: *Members of the Austrian Legion in SS uniforms following the Anschluss with Germany in 1938. Note the blank right-hand collar patches, signifying that they had yet to be assigned to a regiment.*

their nominal German superiors. One such volunteer was an ambitious and headstrong ex-sergeant-major called Fridolin Glass. He was the leader of a group of men who had been drummed out of the Austrian Army for activities in the Nazi SA, which included the creation of his own little Brownshirt force of six companies. Glass gained the confidence of SS-Gruppenführer Kurt Wittje, who supported the Austrian's idea of forming a new SS standarte (regiment) under his personal command. Glass visited Himmler in Berlin and offered the services of his private force to the SS. Himmler approved, and the troop was incorporated into the SS as Standarte 89 in the spring of 1934 under the leadership of SS-Sturmbannführer Glass. The new leader of the SS-Standarte 89 had more than sabotage in mind, though, and was plotting with others to bring about Dollfuss's downfall and the overthrow of the Austrian regime itself.

Right: *The Death's Head regiment titled* Ostmark *was made up of Austrian recruits, and many members of this unit later fought in the* Totenkopf *Division. These Austrians of the division are about to embark for Russia in 1941. Note the three MP28 submachine guns.*

Himmler, carried along by the Austrian's enthusiasm, gave his approval for the coup attempt, which was to be codenamed Operation Summer Festival.

The plot was to capture Dollfuss, together with his ministerial council, then proclaim a Nazi government over the main Vienna radio station after they had seized it. Shortly before 13:00 hours on 25 July 1934, a number of Austrian Army lorries carrying 150 men of the SS-Standarte 89 arrived at the Federal Chancellery. Some were wearing army uniforms, and others were disguised as

Above: Members of the Sudeten Legion during a clandestine mission inside Czechoslovakia in September 1938. The legion conducted 300 commando actions in Czechoslovakia, though the Sudetenland was handed over to Germany before large-scale activities could begin.

police officers. Members of the assault party quickly overwhelmed the guards, took the building and then stormed upstairs to where Chancellor Dollfuss was supposed to be meeting with his ministers. A group of 10 SS men encountered Dollfuss, but his cabinet was not present (an hour earlier, a Nazi conspirator had betrayed the plotters to the government). Having learnt of the impending attack, Dollfuss had ordered all but two of his colleagues to their offices. Not realizing the precariousness of his situation, the Chancellor made an impatient gesture and was shot by an SS soldier named Otto Planetta at close range. The shot hit the Chancellor in the neck and mortally wounded him. Dollfuss was laid on a sofa, and with only moments to live he began to discuss the situation with his captors. Even as he was dying, Dollfuss attempted to dissuade them from their course of action. However, in response and while he was slowly bleeding to death, the putschists harangued him with insults and political bombast, denying his request for

a doctor and a priest. Elsewhere in the city, fellow Nazis who had seized the radio station were broadcasting news that Dollfuss had resigned. Unsupported by the SA, the putsch soon faltered as hundreds of armed men in Vienna reneged on their pledge to join the revolt. The Austrian SA members were evidently still resentful of the part played by the SS in the "Night of the Long Knives", in which Ernst Röhm and the SA leadership had been purged in Germany little more than a month earlier. More than 1000 SA leaders were executed in all, including Röhm. In addition, some old scores were settled. Thus Gregor Strasser, who was anti-Hitler and a former Nazi Party leader, was killed, as was Gustav Kahr, who was loathed by the Nazis for suppressing the 1923 Beer Hall Putsch. The SA looked on impassively as police and government troops surrounded the Chancellery. The coup had failed and the putschists were quickly arrested. Planetta and several others were executed, the remaining participants receiving long prison sentences (though they were released when Austria and Germany were united).

When Austria was annexed in 1938, it handed to the Reich an additional 6.5 million German-speaking people, encouraging the dreams of both Hitler and Himmler for a racially pure Europe. The Anschluss also provided a large pool of prospective manpower that would swell the ranks of the Wehrmacht. These recruits were not perceived as foreign volunteers, and they became eligible for call-up in the same manner as other German citizens. The quotas that were given to the three arms of the Wehrmacht (Heer, Luftwaffe, Kriegsmarine – Army, Air Force and Navy) meant that the SS could not increase in size as Himmler had hoped as a result of this expansion of German territory. However, this did not deter the Reichsführer-SS from his expansionist ideas, or indeed from quickly selecting a site for a new concentration camp in Austria. The site was a massive quarry close by the picturesque village of Mauthausen, near Linz. Franz Ziereis was appointed as its first commander. Himmler ordered the establishment of the SS-Totenkopfstandarte 4 *Ostmark* (SS Death's Head Regiment 4 *Ostmark*), which was formed on 1 April 1938 at Linz, to be garrisoned at the camp. Under the pro-German Nazi Minister of the Interior Arthur Seyss-Inquart, the Austrian police worked in conjunction with the SS security police and Gestapo (Geheime Staatspolizei – Secret State Police) agents, who immediately carried out actions against dissenters, subversives and prominent anti-German Austrians. Himmler now had the first opportunity to exercise his power in a foreign land.

The infamous Death's Head formations were an important part of the SS organization. The so-called SS-Totenkopfverbände (SS Death's Head Detachments) were armed SS personnel formed in late 1933 at Dachau (the first concentration camp in Nazi Germany). Their task was to guard inmates, and they were commanded by SS-Standartenführer Theodor Eicke. The latter became Inspector of Concentration Camps and Commander of the SS Death's Head Detachments after the "Night of the Long Knives".

Czechoslovakia, like Austria, also offered rich pickings to the German Army and SS with regard to recruits. In Vienna a pan-Austrian workers' party had been formed in 1910, which had been renamed the German National Socialist Workers' Party (Deutsche Nationalsozialistische Arbeiterpartei – DNSAP) by the end of World War I. November 1918 saw the creation of a Czech section of the party, which had some 200,000 supporters among German-specking Czech citizens by 1929. The German Gymnastic Association, or Deutsche Turnverband, was an innocent-sounding organization which had been founded in the early 1860s, but from its very inception it had been chauvinistic, aggressive, anti-Semitic, anti-Slav and was as much a political and nationalistic body as a physical training organization. It acted as a conduit for the promulgation of Hitlerite ideas among the German community. This influence was particularly effective along the border region known as the Sudetenland. However,

the overtly Nazi parties and political sports clubs were suppressed due to the increase in tension between the Czech Government and its German subjects. In October 1933, one day before the official decree ordering the DNSAP's closure, it went into voluntary disbandment. Following this, the Deutsche Turnverband in the Sudetenland, under the leadership of Konrad Henlein, formed a *Sudetendeutsche Heimatfront* (Sudeten German Home Front). The following year, to conform to ordinances pertaining to the organization of political bodies in Czechoslovakia, the front changed its name. It became the Sudeten German Party (*Sudeten deutsche Partei* – SdP). Throughout the mid-1930s, financed and encouraged by various Nazi agencies in the Third Reich, the SdP stepped up its activities.

Meanwhile, the Czechs found themselves in an even more precarious position after Hitler's occupation of Austria in March 1938, being surrounded on three sides by Greater Germany. The government was well aware of

Below: *Konrad Henlein (standing at right and saluting with right arm), leader of the SdP who became the Gauleiter of Czechoslovakia in 1939. He was captured by the US Seventh Army in May 1945, and committed suicide in an Allied internment camp on 10 May.*

the type of subversion that had preceded the invasion of Austria, activities that were now being practised by Hitler's henchmen within its own state.

For the German invasion of Czechoslovakia, specially formed Einsatzstäbe (Action Staffs) were organized to coordinate SD, Security Police and Order Police personnel and units in their special tasks. Two staffs were set up: "K" under SS-Oberführer Jost for Prague, and "L" under SS-Standartenführer Dr Stahlecker for Brno. Each staff consisted of an SD and Gestapo expert, Czech-speaking interpreters, specialists and technical personnel, and five Action Commandos (Einsatzkommandos – EK). Western Czechoslovakia was now enclosed on both flanks by the jaws of Nazi-controlled territory. The clandestine Austrian Legion's organizational structure in Germany had remained intact after the Anschluss. This unit now became the basis for a Sudeten German Legion, which was raised along similar lines. Like the Austrian Legion, the Sudeten Legion was not actually a single entity, but the generic term for a variety of units, some SA, some Allgemeine-SS (the main branch of the SS, which served as a political and administrative body) and a few SS-Verfügungstruppen. The SA units were grouped under the SS Hilfswerk *Nord–Ost* (SS Help Organization *North–East*) which had a nominal strength of around 8000. Some 1500 of its members who were of proven political dedication and who met high physical standards were accepted into the Allgemeine-SS. Subsequently, about 500 of these were considered fit enough to be admitted into the SS-Verfügungstruppen Standarte *Sudetenland*, which had recently been formed at Dachau. The regiment was incorporated into the SS-Standarte 2 *Deutschland*, which later was to become part of the famed *Das Reich* Division.

Ostensibly to furnish voluntary aid in the case of accidents or natural disasters and provide physical training, Henlein formed within the Sudetenland itself the Freiwilliger Schutzdienst (Volunteer Protection Unit) from physically fit members of the SdP. In reality, it was a strong-arm unit engaged in paramilitary training. From July 1938, the German Army held weekly five-day courses

at Neuhammer, near Breslau, for these men, who under the guise of holidaymakers or travelling businessmen secretly slipped in and out of Czechoslovakia. Each course comprised some 50 trainees who were furnished with makeshift uniforms and instructed in the arts of rifle shooting and the demolition of static defences – clearly in preparation for the sabotage of the Czech frontier installations. At the conclusion of each course, the volunteers took an oath of loyalty to Hitler. Unfortunately for Henlein, this thinly veiled secret was compromised when the local SdP leader at Eger referred to it as "a body of soldiers on duty at all times".

In September 1938, the Sudeten Legion had its name changed to Sudetendeutsches Freikorps, its headquarters being in Bayreuth in the castle at Donndorf. The SD organized the Sudetendeutsches Freikorps on the Czechoslovak border, and on 19 September 1938 it secretly penetrated Czechoslovakia in commando squads, each numbering 12 men. The Freikorps was to carry out more than 300 sorties and take more than 1500 prisoners during raids against Czech forces.

The Munich Conference opened on 29 September (see Chapter 1), which caused hostilities to cease before they had properly started. The following day it was decided that the Sudetenland would be officially handed over to Germany, eventually being incorporated into the Reich as Gau (a Nazi administrative region) Sudetenland with its headquarters at Reichenberg. The new Gauleiter (district leader) was Konrad Henlein, his reward from a grateful Führer for his part in

Above: *Achievement Badge for the Security Troops of the nominally independent state of Slovakia. The so-called Regierungstruppe was formed to assist the gendarmerie maintain internal order and security. The badge was awarded in gold (shown here), silver and bronze.*

the dismemberment of Czechoslovakia. After the absorption of the Sudetenland into Germany, the SdP no longer had a function to fulfil, and was thus dissolved. The Sudetendeutsches Freikorps officially passed to SS control and was allocated to police functions.

Bohemia and Moravia were declared to be a German protectorate in March 1939 (annexed in September of the same year) and assimilated into the greater Reich, whereupon the Czech Army was disbanded. The remnants of the Czech Republic now became the notionally independent state of Slovakia. In October 1939, President Emil Hacha of Bohemia and Moravia petitioned Nazi Germany for permission to raise an armed force to assist the gendarmerie in the maintenance of security and internal order. The Germans happily agreed to this proposition, with the caveat that the new Regierungstruppe (the name of the army raised in the protectorate; used mainly for ceremonial duties and guarding important installations) could not exceed 8000 personnel (in fact, it never exceeded 7000). The Regierungstruppe comprised three inspectorates – Prague, Brno and Hradec Krolové – each made up of four battalions, and each subdivided into four companies.

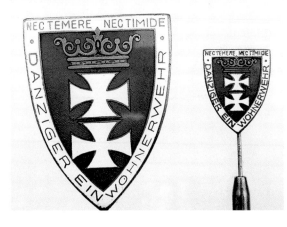

Above: *The Danzig Einwohnerwehr was the Danzig Home Defence Force. This shield, known as the "Danzig shield for true service to the State of Danzig", was awarded to its members. It was allegedly awarded only 15 times.*

Those who volunteered were usually former officers or noncommissioned officers (NCOs) of the Czech Army, with the additional support of some 350 uniformed civilian administrators. The officer corps comprised 280 men, of whom 40 were generals and 15 were civilian administrators who held a rank equivalent to army general. It was only in the latter stages of World War II that this unit saw anything approaching active service, when in May 1944 11 of the 12 battalions were deployed to northern Italy, leaving the first battalion for guard duty in Prague. The unreliability of the Regierungstruppe was illustrated by large-scale desertions, and so in the autumn of 1944 the force was returned to the protectorate. Few of the members wished to continue their service, as by this time their four-year engagement contracts had

lapsed, and it was becoming obvious that the Germans might not win the war. Before the end of the year, the formation had disintegrated.

World War II began on 1 September 1939 with the invasion of Poland. For this campaign, six Special Action Groups had been formed and attached to each of the five armies taking part in the conflict, plus one for the province of Posen. When the German troops entered western Poland, small groups of ethnic Germans (Volksdeutsche) immediately formed themselves into a militia. The advance was so rapid that newly occupied territories were often left devoid of German troops; the vacuum was filled by the militia. In fact, the army found the militia so useful that it undertook the arming and training of this irregular force. During meetings held between 8 and 10 September 1939 at Hitler's headquarters, the Führer suggested that the militia in Poland should be recognized and formed into self-protection units with the aim of defending German property and families in Poland.

Himmler undertook the task and instructed Gottlob Berger to place them under SS jurisdiction. Berger was a Swabian with numerous relatives in southeast Europe. He was probably the originator of the Waffen-SS as an international army, as well as bringing together the scattered Volksdeutsche of Europe. He would later become Himmler's chief of staff for the Waffen-SS. Subsequently, a self-protection force was organized in three regions. Each region was divided into a Kreise (district) under a Kreisführer des Selbstschutzes, and each district was divided into an Ort (locality) under an Ortichen Selbstschutzenführer. The southern and middle

Below: *The armband of the SS-Heimwehr Danzig, the local SS detachment in the free city. At full strength it numbered 1500 men and 42 officers. Two-thirds of the unit were German nationals, the rest were from Danzig.*

regions came under the overall command of the SS Main Office headed by SS-Obergruppenführer Heissmeyer, while the northern region of Poland came under Reinhard Heydrich's RSHA.

At the end of September, the so-called Selbstschutz (Self-Protection Force) was reorganized on stricter lines. It was under the overall operational jurisdiction of the Chief of the Order Police, technically making it a police organization, but SS leaders who were ultimately responsible to the HSSPF (Höhere SS und Polizeiführer – Higher SS and Police Leader) in their military region commanded the Selbstschutz. Service was voluntary in the Selbstschutz, being open to all racial Germans who were capable of carrying arms and were aged between 17 and 45. It was tasked with the guarding of important installations, stocks of war booty, the custody of prisoners of war and the escorting of refugees. The Selbstschutz earned itself a very unsavoury reputation among Germans with its indiscriminate treatment of Poles and close cooperation with the Special Action Squads, so much so that Gauleiter Albert Forster succeeded in getting Hitler to agree to its disbandment. Himmler ordered this on 8 November 1939 to take effect from 30 November 1939, with the exception that the

Above: *Troops and an armoured vehicle of the SS-Heimwehr Danzig in action in the port in early September 1939. Shortly afterwards, and following the swift German victory, the unit was disbanded and its personnel distributed as cadres for Death's Head units.*

Selbstschutz detachment in Lublin continued as the General Government Special Service (the General Government was the Nazi administrative title of the central and southern areas of Poland under German occupation; the northern and western border areas of Poland were annexed outright). In fact, it was not until April 1940 that the Selbstschutz was finally disbanded. Most of its personnel joined the SS, SA or NSKK (Nationalsozialisches Kraftfahrkorps – National Socialist Motor Corps), and it was estimated that between September 1939 and January 1940 45,000 men of all ages had served in the Selbstschutz.

The "Free City of Danzig" and its surrounding territory encompassed some 1166 square kilometres (729 square miles). The city contained just over 400,000 citizens, 96.7 percent of them being of German heritage, culture and language. The German nationals and Nazi movement inside the region gradually gained strength until by June 1933

Danzig had a Nazi-dominated government. From then until its reincorporation into Germany in September 1939, the "Free City" modelled itself on Nazi Germany. From the time it had been placed under the tutelage of the League of Nations as a "Free City", it had continued to cultivate close ties with Germany. Many of Danzig's officials, for example, came from the Reich, served a tour of duty in the city and then returned to their homeland. Danzig law followed German law in granting citizenship automatically with an official appointment. Special arrangements completed in 1921 allowed officials to transfer from the German or Prussian civil service to the Danzig civil service and back without any loss in seniority or other privileges. In this way, Danzig was able to maintain an administration similar in most respects to that found in any German town.

The first Danzig SA unit was formed on 28 March 1926 with 45 members. Even before the formation of the

Below: *Hitler's entry into Danzig on 19 September 1939. Ever since 1934, when the Nazis took control of the city's administration, Hitler had demanded that Danzig should be formally transferred to Germany, a demand that was welcomed by the city's German population.*

SA, the commander of the irregular citizens' militia, the Einwohnerwehr, which was the closest thing to an army in the demilitarized city, was disturbed by a distorted report that its Nazi members had been instructed not to extend their duty to defend law and order to protecting the existing government system. In reality, the local Nazis were no great threat at this time, as the party in Germany appeared to be stuck in the political wilderness. This produced despondency among the rank and file, a sentiment that affected the SA men in Danzig even more than those in the Reich itself. The Danzig SA was isolated, cooperation with the militia was poor, and the way to power appeared blocked.

The increase in political street violence in Germany during 1931 and 1932 had its parallel in Danzig. The SA clashed repeatedly with the communists and with the social democratic Arschufo, the Workers' Defence Formations. Gun battles were rare, but knives and improvised weapons were frequently used. Remarkably, there was only one fatality: 16-year-old Horst Hoffmann, who had been fighting alongside his SA and SS companions with the Arschufo in bloody riots in the village of Kahlbude on Sunday 12 November 1931. With

what was perceived as a hero's death, he was immediately elevated to the status of a martyr by the NSDAP, and the day passed into Danzig Nazi legend as "Totensonntag" or "Death Sunday". In the early summer of 1939, the Danzig Senate decided to form a home defence force, and with its closure on 3 June 1939 the responsibility for raising the unit was taken over by the Reichsführer-SS. In October 1938, the third battalion of the 4th SS Death's Head Regiment was formed in Berlin-Adlershof under the command of SS-Obersturmbannführer Hans Freidemann Götze. Himmler decided that this unit would be the cadre of the home defence force. It was joined by the Totenkopf Anti-Tank Training Company, also from Germany. In July 1939 the SS-Heimwehr *Danzig* (SS-Home Defence Force *Danzig*) was raised. Its full complement consisted of 42 officers and approximately 1500 men. Its demographic composition was two-thirds German nationals while the remainder were from Danzig. Gauleiter Forster presented the unit with its company standard at a special parade held on 18 August 1939, when SS-Obersturmbannführer Götze received it on behalf of the SS-Heimwehr *Danzig*.

The SS-Heimwehr *Danzig*

Earlier, in June 1939, the SS-Wachsturmbann Eimann (a reserve unit that saw minor action in the Danzig region between July and September 1939, carried out "police duties" after the invasion of Poland and which was dissolved in 1940) was formed on the orders of SS-Brigadeführer Schafer with the cooperation of SS District Northeast. It was a police reinforcement battalion that consisted of four companies and a motor transport echelon. Commanded by SS-Sturmbannführer Kurt Eimann, it also found time to shoot handicapped German civilians who were sent to Poland from the Reich. In addition, a number of Action Commandos were formed from members of the Political Police of the Danzig Criminal Police, Protection Police and General SS, all of which were exclusively at the disposal of the Danzig Police.

With the start of the war against Poland in September 1939, SS-Heimwehr *Danzig* saw action in and around Danzig, Gdingen and Westerplatte. Reichsführer-SS Himmler was particularly incensed at the treatment of one of its battalions which on 8 September had taken part in the storming of the spit of coastline known as the Oxhöfter Kämpe. But because this battalion had been attached to a Pomeranian local defence division under Colonel Graf Rittberg, it had been mentioned in orders as the Rittberg battalion. As insignificant as this may sound, Himmler was seeking as much glory and recognition for his SS units from the army as he could at the beginning of the war.

Above: *This is the Danzig Cross, created by Gauleiter Forster and awarded "For meritorious service in the building up of the Nazi Party within the free state of Danzig". The 1st Class, shown here, was awarded only 88 times, the 2nd Class 257 times.*

Shortly after the Polish surrender on 27 September, the unit was withdrawn to Germany and its personnel distributed as cadres for the new Totenkopf Infantry Regiment 3 of the *Totenkopf* Division. The regiment's formation was made official on 1 November 1939 in a ceremony that took place at the training depot at Dachau.

During Hitler's visit to Danzig, the SS-Wachsturmbann Eimann carried out security duties in Oliva and Danzig, while two companies guarded Hitler's headquarters in Zoppot. Following the fighting in Danzig, large numbers of civilians were taken prisoner and put in camps at Neufahrwasser, Stuthof and Grenzdorf, where two companies of the battalion acted as camp guards.

The first "foreign" volunteer units had, more or less, been a success. These Germanic units were relatively easy to raise and maintain since their main loyalty was to the government in Berlin. Nevertheless, they provided a useful blueprint for the raising of non-Volksdeutsche volunteer units for Germany's armed forces and the SS. The effectiveness of this blueprint would now be tested in those states conquered by Germany in Western Europe.

Constitution d'un régiment français
de
WAFFEN- ⚡⚡

Par la loi du 22 juillet 1943, le Président Laval avec l'assentiment du Chef de l'Etat, Monsieur le Maréchal Pétain, a reconnu à tous les Français le droit de s'engager dans les formations de la Waffen-⚡⚡ à l'Est, afin d'y prendre part aux combats pour l'existence et l'avenir de l'Europe.

En vertu de cette loi, les volontaires pour la Waffen-⚡⚡ jouissent du même statut légal que les membres de la L. V. F.

Le Gouvernement français a ainsi montré qu'il appréciait l'offre faite par le Führer et qu'il est prêt à prendre sa part des devoirs que commandent des heures décisives pour le sort de l'Europe.

Il est évident que la constitution d'une unité de volontaires français au sein de la Waffen-⚡⚡ représente un nouveau pas très important dans l'union de la jeunesse européenne contre le nihilisme bolcheviste.

Le fait est que par l'afflux des volontaires de presque tous les pays de l'Europe qui, côte à côte avec leurs camarades allemands, se sont distingués par leur vaillance au front de l'Est, la ⚡⚡ , fondement essentiel du Parti national-socialiste, qui n'avait, à l'origine, qu'une valeur politique interne allemande, s'est transformée aujourd'hui en une communauté indissoluble de la jeunesse européenne luttant pour le maintien de ses valeurs culturelles et de sa civilisation.

Que la jeunesse française ait d'instinct compris la portée de ce nouveau pas est démontré par le fait que, en quelques jours et sans la moindre propagande, plus de quinze cents volontaires se sont présentés. Les deux premiers bataillons existent, et bientôt le premier régiment ⚡⚡ français sera en mesure de faire la preuve de la permanence des hautes traditions militaires françaises et de l'esprit combattif de sa jeunesse.

La ⚡⚡ se fera un point d'honneur et considérera comme une tâche essentielle d'employer les qualités militaires et la volonté de combat de chaque Français disposé à engager sa vie dans la lutte pour l'existence et l'avenir de l'Europe, contre le bolchevisme, pour la justice sociale, pour la victoire !

(Communication faite à Paris, le 6 août 1943, à la Conférence de la Presse française et étrangère.)

Chapter 5

VICHY FRANCE

Vichy France occupied a unique position in Hitler's Europe. Neither a fascist ally nor an occupied state, Pétain's France was relatively autonomous. Soon after the German invasion of the Soviet Union in June 1941, a French legion was formed to fight on the Eastern Front. Thereafter, Vichy France supplied a steady number of volunteers to fight for Germany against the Red Army. Elements of the *Charlemagne* Division would also fight in Berlin in 1945.

After the defeat and occupation of France in May 1940, an armistice was declared in June between the French and German governments. France was split into two zones. The northern industrial region remained occupied and was placed under German administration. In the southern region, a collaborationist government had established itself in Vichy under the leadership of World War I hero Marshal Philippe Pétain, who was 84 years old.

When Germany invaded Russia in June 1941, it caused great excitement among French collaborationist political

Left: The constitution of the French Waffen-SS regiment formed in 1943. It stressed the fight to preserve European civilization rather than National Socialism.

parties and paramilitary home-based formations. In response, the first recruiting centre was opened at 12 Rue Auber, Paris, with additional recruiting centres placed all over France. On 7 July, all the leaders of these parties met at the Hotel Majestic in Paris to create an anti-Bolshevik formation; and on 18 July 1941, the grandly titled *Légion des Volontaires Français contre le Bolshevisme* (LVF) was formally established.

Initially, the Vichy Government had enacted a law that forbade Frenchmen from enlisting into "foreign armies" to prevent them from joining the Free French forces of exiled General Charles de Gaulle. Since the LVF was a private affair, Marshal Pétain amended the law so there would be no barrier to Frenchmen enlisting in the LVF. Hitler approved, but stated that membership be limited to

Above: *French volunteers for the LVF leave Paris to begin their training. At this point, French volunteers were under the control of the Germany Army. The Waffen-SS in 1941 could afford to be picky about the racial qualifications of recruits. The French were not considered to be Aryan.*

Below: *Members of the LVF in action on the Eastern Front in the winter of 1941–42. Attached to the 7th Infantry Division during the assault on Moscow, the LVF suffered heavy losses and was therefore withdrawn from frontline service in the spring of 1942.*

15,000. However, the LVF received a total of only 13,400 applications and, of these, 4600 had to be refused on medical grounds and a further 3000 on "moral" grounds. Many came from the militias of the collaborating political parties, prominent among them the men from Doriot's *Parti Populaire Français*, include Doriot himself. Eventually, 5800 Frenchmen were accepted into the LVF and trained at the Borgnis-Desbordes barracks at Versailles.

The recruits wore standard German Army uniforms and had the French national arm shield inscribed "FRANCE" placed on their right sleeve (the Germans made it clear that unless France actually declared war on the Soviet Union there could be no question of sending combatants to the front in French uniform). Colonel Roger Labonne, a 60-year-old military historian, assumed command of the legion.

On 4 September, the first draft of volunteers – 25 officers and 803 men – left Paris for Debica in Poland. On 20 September, a second contingent of 127 officers and 769 men, including Sergeant-Major Doriot, followed them to the same destination. By October 1941, the LVF comprised two battalions: 181 officers and 2271 other ranks, with a liaison staff of 35 Germans. The LVF was registered as the 638th Infantry Regiment of the German Army.

By the end of October, both battalions proceeded by rail to Smolensk and then by truck and on foot towards the frontline near Moscow, joining the German 7th Infantry Division near Golokovo. In early December, a third battalion of 1400 other recruits to the LVF was sent to the Debica troop training facilities. In February 1942, the 1st and 2nd Battalions were caught up in the Soviet winter counteroffensive. During the fighting, the 2nd Battalion was overrun by Soviet forces near Djunovo and virtually annihilated. The LVF lost half of its strength either due to enemy action or frostbite.

In March 1942, Colonel Labonne was recalled to Paris and relieved of his command. The LVF was pulled out of the frontline and for the next 18 months ceased to function as a unified formation but operated as two separate battalions — the 1st under Major Lacroix and the 3rd under Major Demessine — the 2nd having been virtually wiped out. The unit had no overall French commander and was employed on anti-partisan operations. During the summer of 1942, the 1st Battalion was subordinated to the German 186th Security Division and was deployed in anti-partisan activities, while the 3rd Battalion was southwest of Smolensk engaging partisans near Volost, where it suffered heavy casualties.

On 24 June 1942, the Controlling Committee of the LVF sent Prime Minister Laval a memorandum proposing that the unit be taken over as an official military force, be allowed to wear French uniforms, receive French decorations, be financed by the Ministry of War, and be made available for active duty "on any front where the national interest is at stake". It further suggested that a new name, the *Legion Tricolore*, be adopted "to underline the stoutly national ideal which inspired the legionary unit". These ideas were agreed four days later, the *Legion Tricolore* being financed by the Vichy Government and headed by Raymond Lachal, Pierre Laval's right-hand man.

The unit lasted only six months before being dissolved. Hitler did not approve. After all, if the LVF became a French-controlled unit what power would the Wehrmacht have to prevent it being withdrawn from Russia and brought back to France? Such a prospect could not be tolerated. The Führer decreed that the French volunteers must remain under German authority.

Former members of the *Legion Tricolore* were allowed to rejoin the LVF. By June 1943, after active recruiting and reorganizing, the LVF was refitted and prepared to serve under the German 186th Security Division at Smolensk.

Thus, at the end of December 1942, the *Legion Tricolore* was disbanded and its personnel transferred to the LVF. In June 1943, the 1st and 3rd Battalions were brought together under the 286th Security Division, and a reconstituted 2nd Battalion was added so that by the end of the year the LVF became a single regiment. It was commanded by Colonel Edgar Puaud, a regular soldier and former Foreign Legion officer who had spent most of his service career in North Africa.

In January 1944, the LVF was once again engaged in anti-partisan operations in Russia, in the forest of Somry. The operation was a success: out of the 6000 partisans estimated to be active in that region, 1118 were killed and a further 1345 captured. In April 1944, the 4th Battalion

Below: *French Waffen-SS recruits take their oath in February 1944. The oath stated: "Before God, I swear absolute obedience to Adolf Hitler, Commander-in-Chief of the German Army, and the superiors appointed by him."*

was added to the LVF from excess personnel from the disbanded LVF artillery detachment.

In June 1944, after the collapse of the German Ninth Army, the regiment found itself in the path of a major Red Army offensive (part of the massive Russian offensive codenamed Bagration). To stem the Soviet attack, a battalion of 400 Frenchmen under the command of Major Bridoux, plus various ad hoc German units, formed a battle group near Bobr, Ukraine. This unit fought so well that it enabled much of the Ninth Army to break out of a Soviet encirclement at Bobruysk. Withdrawn from the front, the regiment was regrouped at Greifenberg in East Prussia. In September 1944, the LVF ceased to exist. It found itself absorbed into the Waffen-SS (see below).

A small number (perhaps no more than 300) of Frenchmen succeeded in being accepted into the ranks of the Waffen-SS after 1940. They served mainly as private soldiers in the *Wiking* and *Totenkopf* Divisions rather than a national legion. It wasn't until July 1943 that full nationwide recruitment began in France, with a Committee of the Friends of the Waffen-SS being established under the sponsorship of Vichy Propaganda Minister Paul Marion. The committee's main recruitment office was located at 24 Avenue du Recteur Poincaré in Paris (where some 1500 applications were received), with regional offices distributed throughout the larger cities of France.

Left: *A happy Vichy Arab volunteer in German service. His sleeve shield is coloured red, white and green with the words "Free Arabia" in German and the Arabic translation over the top.*

Volunteers were required to be "free of Jewish blood", physically fit, and between the ages of 20 and 25. The initial recruits were drawn from members of Vichy youth movements, various collaborationist militias, right-wing politicals, plus a large number of university students.

Some 3000 applicants visited the assorted offices in the first few months. The first 800 volunteers were trained at Sennheim in Alsace, and following basic training another 30 were chosen as officer candidates and sent to the SS Junkerschule Bad Tölz. Another 100 were sent to specialized NCO training in Posen. In March 1944, 1538 French recruits, plus their officers and NCOs, were assembled at the Waffen-SS training ground at Beneschau near Prague. It was designated a sturmbrigade, and was commonly referred to as SS Sturmbrigade *Frankreich*.

In August 1944, the sturmbrigade was attached to the 18th SS Panzergrenadier Division *Horst Wessel*, and thrown into the fierce rearguard fighting against the advancing Soviets in Galicia. The new unit took heavy casualties, with 15 of 18 officers dead or wounded, and 130 dead and 660 wounded among the other ranks. Following its baptism of fire, the sturmbrigade returned to barracks for refitting and eventual amalgamation with the soldiers of the disbanded LVF.

The *Charlemagne* Division

By this date, much of France had been liberated by the Allies, giving Himmler the opportunity to combine the assault brigade, French Navy personnel and members of the LVF into a Waffen-SS grenadier brigade. By 1 September 1944, he had combined the remnants of Vichy military personnel into the SS Brigade *Charlemagne*. It consisted of 1200 former sturmbrigade soldiers, 2000 former LVF, 1200 former Kriegsmarine, 2300 former NSKK and Organization Todt members, and 2500 former Militia Police and new recruits.

In late 1944, these disparate elements were assembled for training at Lager Wildflecken, northwest of Frankfurt-am-Main. At Wildflecken, the volunteers were sorted out and assigned to their respective units. In February 1945, the brigade was formed into the 33rd SS Waffen Grenadier Division *Charlemagne*, but training was cut short when the "division" was sent to the Eastern Front.

On 25 February 1945, as the trainborne elements of *Charlemagne* Division pulled into the railhead at Hammerstein, Pomerania, armoured spearheads of the Soviet 1st Belorussian Front unexpectedly smashed into the division. The result was disaster, with the ill-trained French unit being split up into three battle groups. One group, commanded by General Krukenberg, made it north to the Baltic coast where it was evacuated to Denmark and sent back to refit at Neustrelitz in Mecklenberg. Another battle group, commanded by General Puaud, was cut to pieces by the Red Army soon afterwards. The third group, nearly wiped out at the railhead, conducted a fighting retreat west towards German lines, being destroyed in early March 1945.

At Carpin, Mecklenberg, the remnants of the *Charlemagne* Division – 1100 men – gathered to rest and refit. In early April, Krukenberg released the disillusioned and demoralized from their oaths of allegiance, which cost him a third of his men. On the night of 23/24 April, the remaining 700 were summoned to the defence of Berlin. Krukenberg organized a vehicle column, but because of enemy action and mechanical problems only 330 men were able to enter the northwestern suburbs of Berlin just hours before the Soviet encirclement of the city.

They were engaged immediately upon their arrival. They fought brief and bloody counterattacks at the Hasenheide and Tempelhof airfield, withdrawing back across the Landwehr Canal, and fighting through the district of Kreuzberg into the city centre. The Frenchmen continued to battle the Red Army until the general order of surrender announced by General Weidling on 2 May, when some 30 surviving *Charlemagne* members went into Soviet captivity near the Potsdamer station.

French naval volunteers

In February 1944, the German Navy began to appeal for French volunteers, the main recruiting office being at Caen in Normandy. But, as with other branches of the German armed forces, individual enlistment had certainly taken place before that late date, especially in the traditional coastal regions of Brittany and Normandy. Up to 2000 Frenchmen served in the German Kriegsmarine in World War II. In France, the German Navy also raised an indigenous naval police known as the Kriegsmarine Wehrmänner.

Another separate naval police unit of French volunteers was the Kriegswerftpolizei. This unit consisted of some 259–300 Frenchmen who assisted in guarding the important U-Boat base at La Pallice near La Rochelle in the Bay of Biscay. The Allied invasion of France in June 1944 does not appear to have deterred the German Navy from continuing its attempts to recruit Frenchmen. For example, the *Journal de Rouen* dated 29 June 1944, three weeks after the Allied landings, carried an advertisement urging young Frenchmen to join the Kriegsmarine. It stated: "To be a sailor is to have a trade, enlist today in the German Navy."

Above: *Some of the French volunteers who assembled in Germany for training in late 1944. The men in the front rank shoulder a mixture of German and Russian machine guns. No doubt, the French took what was available.*

In May and June 1941, an unsuccessful German-backed uprising took place in British-occupied Iraq led by Rashid Ali el-Kilani. The Germans and many of the coup leaders fled to Greece and found themselves in a training camp at Sunion near Athens under the command of Helmuth Felmy and Sonderstab F (Special Staff F). Berlin decided to form an Arab-speaking unit for clandestine operations in North Africa – Battalion 845 of the German Army was born.

By April 1942, the battalion contained volunteers from Algeria, Syria, Saudi Arabia, Egypt, Jordan, Palestine and Iraq (Tunisians did not volunteer for frontline duties but offered their services as labourers and security troops). Some 400 Arabs living in occupied areas were drafted into a local force called *Phalange Africaine*, who were all incorporated into a new unit called the Deutsch Arabische Lehrabteilung (DAL). The unit first saw action on the coast of the Gulf of Hammamet where a British commando team landed to blow up the headquarters of the German Brandenburg commando unit. The Arabs fought the British for 48 hours, taking 3 casualties and inflicting 8 on the enemy.

In total, 6300 Arab-speaking volunteers passed through the ranks of the German and Vichy forces. The frontline Arab volunteers were issued with the Bevo sleeve shield, and the auxiliary Arab volunteers with a printed sleeve shield. These shields were made in very limited numbers, and are now one of the rarest of all volunteer sleeve shields.

Chapter 6

WESTERN EUROPEAN VOLUNTEERS

Of all the foreign nationals who served the Third Reich, the Western Europeans were the best. They were the most enthusiastic, the most militarily effective and the most loyal. They formed the core of the *Wiking* Division, one of the best fighting units in the Waffen-SS, and indeed in the whole German Army.

Before the outbreak of war, only a handful of fanatical Western European Nordic volunteers had offered themselves for service with the Allgemeine-SS. In the main, these were devoutly anti-communist individuals who saw the "Red Menace" as a reality, i.e. as an ominous threat to their homelands and way of life. Few, if any, had made overtures to the other branches of the German military forces. By mid-1940, though, with Western Europe firmly in the grip of the Third Reich, the way was made clear for those with pro-Nazi beliefs to volunteer for service. In dribs and drabs,

volunteers from West European countries presented themselves for entry into the ranks of the Waffen-SS. The principles of such individuals fighting for Germany, whose countries had been devoured by the Reich's armed forces, were highly questionable. Service in the Waffen-SS appeared to compound their immorality. Two questions arise. First, why should these men desire military service within the German armed forces, let alone the SS with all its connotations of racial superiority? Second, why would the SS, or indeed any other branch of the German armed forces, recruit them? And, having done so, why would they trust them in battle? Surely these individuals could pose the threat of being a Trojan Horse? The simple answer to these questions is that the men were all volunteers, who for various reasons viewed service with

Left: *A Flemish SS volunteer. On his left breast he wears the Tollenaere Commemorative Badge, named after Reimond Tollenaere of the Flemish Legion.*

the Waffen-SS as being desirable – or at least tolerable. This being the case, they presented little threat of being unreliable in the field once they had been committed to battle. These men were desirable to the SS in turn because they were Aryan brothers, i.e. "racially pure" volunteers who would be a valuable part in the crusade against the "sub-humans" in the East.

From the SS standpoint, the administrative procedure to raise foreign volunteer legions had been perfected before the war, being a direct result of Himmler's goal of a pan-Germanic Europe. Himmler had decreed in 1938 that non-Germans of acceptable "Nordic" origins could join the Allgemeine-SS. It is important to highlight that, at this time, the distinction between the civilian "General" or Allgemeine-SS and the Special Purpose Troops or SS-Verfügungstruppe, which later became the Waffen-SS, did not exist.

Indigenous fascist parties

The occupied countries of Norway, Denmark, Holland and Belgium all had their own fascist parties, which in some cases modelled themselves on the German Nazi Party. Others took their inspiration from Rome (where Mussolini had ruled since 1922). Norway, the first to be overrun by the Nazis, also held the dubious distinction of spawning the most notorious of all collaborators, albeit

not the most accomplished, Vidkun Quisling. Norway had only one collaborative political party of any significance, which Quisling founded in May 1933 – the *Nasjonal Samling* (NS), which means National Unity. The organization of the NS paralleled that of the German Nazi Party. The NS was small, though after the German invasion it grew to around 50,000 members. It described itself as a "deeply rooted Norwegian, national, spiritual and Christian movement". Curiously, it contained a large number of Freemasons (whom the Nazis believed were helping Jews achieve world domination). Immediately after the German invasion in April 1940 (which, contrary to popular belief at the time, the NS did not assist), Quisling attempted to take power by declaring himself prime minister. Hitler, incensed at this arrogance, ordered him to step down one week later and then named Josef Terboven as Reich Commissioner for Norway. Terboven disliked Quisling intensely, a feeling that was reciprocated. However, eventually Quisling was appointed "Minister President" of Norway by Hitler on 1 February 1942, becoming the only foreign leader ever to achieve such high office in a German-occupied country.

Denmark was overrun and occupied with virtually no resistance on the part of the Danes. Denmark had several pro-Nazi political parties because no one individual had emerged who could weld them all together. For this reason, entrusting political power to the Danish Nazis never seems to have been considered by the Germans. The *Danmarks National Socialistiske Arbejder Parti* (DNSAP – Denmark's National Socialist Workers' Party), founded in November 1930, was the largest of the Danish Nazi parties. At first the leadership comprised a three-man committee, but in 1933 the alcoholic Frits Clausen took over (he had joined the party in 1931). It was an extremely well-disciplined organization. For example, it was administered by its own corps of political leaders, and for protection it could call on its own stormtroopers, the *Storm Afdelinger* (SA).

The Germans invaded Holland on 10 May 1940, which surrendered after only four days, giving rise to widespread panic and confusion among the population. The Dutch, who are related both linguistically and racially to the Germans, were taken aback by the confrontation. Prior to World War II, Holland had some 52,000 German residents who lived and worked in the Netherlands. It is not surprising, therefore, that a number of imitation Nazi movements emerged during the 1930s. The largest was

Right: *A member of the Danish Schalburg Corps, a unit set up in 1943. The corps was divided into two groups: the first made up of regular soldiers; and the second made up of civilians. It fought against the Danish resistance until mid-1944 when it became part of the SS.*

founded on 14 December 1931 by Anton Adriaan Mussert. It was called the *Nationaal Socialistische Beweging* (NSB – National Socialist Movement). It was a strictly nationalistic Dutch fascist movement, and proved ultimately to be the most successful.

On 18 May 1940, Arthur Seyss-Inquart became Reich Commissioner of the Netherlands, which was declared to be a Reich Commissariat. With complete control of the country's entire resources, which he exclusively directed towards the demands of the German war machine, Seyss-Inquart ruled authoritatively, answering only to Hitler. He generally followed the "carrot and stick" method of rule, though his rule was more stick than carrot. In March 1941, he had bestowed upon himself the power to administer summary justice, at least pertaining to dissension or suspected resistance. He levied swingeing fines, confiscating the property of all enemies of the Reich, including Jews, and instigated severe reprisals for acts of subversion and sabotage. He forced five million Dutch civilians to work for the Germans, and deported a total of 117,000 Jews to concentration camps.

Under these conditions, the main exponent of collaboration was the NSB, a party that was extremely well organized. The NSB was now to come to the fore, and on the tenth anniversary of its foundation was granted an exclusive political monopoly in the Netherlands by the Germans. All other parties were faced either with merger or disbandment. The NSB had its own stormtroopers, the *Weer Afdeelingen* (WA – Defence Section), but on 11 September 1940 it took a bold step by establishing its own SS within the party framework. J. Hendrik Feldmeyer, the former leader of the Mussert Garde, was the initiator of the plan; he had visions of it becoming the equivalent of the German Allgemeine-SS. It was at first simply known as the *Nederlandsche SS*, which was replaced by the more general term *Germaansche SS en Nederland* (or the Germanic SS in the Netherlands) on 1 November 1942. Until then it had been one of the paramilitary sub-formations of the NSB. Himmler gave orders that it was now to become part of a greater Germanic SS. Mussert's control was now marginalized, with an oath of loyalty to Adolf Hitler being taken by the Dutch SS men. Its membership, which stood nominally at 3727 (five regiments plus an SS police regiment), was constantly depleted by voluntary enlistment into the Waffen-SS. There were possibly up to a further 7000 Dutch volunteers in the Germanische

Sturmbann, an SS formation raised from the large pool of Dutch and other Nordic workers in Germany. Seven battalions were recruited from the industrial cities of Berlin, Brunswick, Dresden, Düsseldorf, Hamburg, Nuremberg and Stuttgart. In effect, the Germanische Sturmbann was never anything other than a recruiting agency for the Waffen-SS.

The Dutch NSKK

It would be wrong to state that all foreign volunteers were recruited into the more "glamourous" organizations within the SS. There were others formations that absorbed volunteers for the German war machine. These included the Nationalsozialisches Kraftfahrkorps (NSKK – National Socialist Motor Corps), Reichsarbeitsdienst (RAD – National Labour Service) and the Kriegsmarine. The NSKK, for example, was almost as voracious in the recruitment of Dutchmen as the SS. The invasion of Russia in 1941 led to additional loads being placed on the already overstretched German military transport system, and so the occupation authorities were always searching for foreign drivers. The WA, the Dutch equivalent of the German SA, had its own transport arm – the Motor WA – which provided the usual source of drivers for service on the Eastern Front. The Dutch drivers were passed through a unit called the Alarmdienst, which was created to provide the German forces in Holland with auxiliary transport. Its members were kitted out with Motor WA or other NSB uniforms.

Above: *Arthur Seyss-Inquart, the brutal Reich Commissioner for the Netherlands. He forced five million Dutch to work for the Germans, and deported 117,000 Jews to their deaths. He was executed in 1946.*

The service was rechristened the Transportactie on 12 January 1943, and thereafter its members sported German field-grey uniforms.

The German Army also raised a small unit of Dutch civilian drivers, which was known initially as the Kraftfahrt Transport Dienst. This was mainly to help with work on military construction projects, and after April 1942 it was renamed the Kraftfahrzeugüberführungs Kommando (KUK). When the need arose, some KUK drivers had to be coerced to serve in the Soviet Union in German rear areas. Due to the partisan threat they were permitted to carry arms for their defence, being kitted out in ex-French Army uniforms.

In November 1943, the Higher SS and Police Chief in the Netherlands, Hans Albin Rauter, upon being informed that the NSKK was proving very successful in drawing into its ranks young Dutchmen, was forced to issue an order forbidding the NSKK from accepting anyone below the age of 30. Volunteers under the age of 30 were to be directed into the Waffen-SS instead.

Most of the Dutch NSKK volunteers came under the jurisdiction of the Luftwaffe, with volunteers in the

Below: *Seyss-Inquart (centre) with the Dutch Nazi leader Anton Mussert (left) and SS-Gruppenführer Karl-Maria Demelhuber (right). Mussert was tried as a collaborator after the war and hanged on 7 May 1946.*

Frw Legion Niederlande

following formations: NSKK Gruppe Luftwaffe, NSKK Staffel WBN (Armed Forces Commander-in-Chief Netherlands) and NSKK Todt/Speer. The Organization Todt was the construction formation of the Nazi Party, auxiliary to the Wehrmacht. It was named after its founder, Dr Fritz Todt, who was replaced by Albert Speer following Todt's death in 1942. It should not be confused with the Organization Speer, which was a separate body concerned with engineering. Like many similar agencies in Hitler's Reich, they competed with each other for power and resources.

In January 1942, NSKK Gruppe Luftwaffe was created under Luftwaffe General Wilhelm Wimmer in Brussels, which brought together under one command all Dutch, Flemish and Walloon NSKK members. The Dutch NSKK saw active service in Russia as the NSKK Regiment *Niederland*. Luftwaffe General Kraus reported to Hermann Göring on 6 August 1942: "We have thousands of Dutchmen in transport regiments in the East. Last week one such regiment was attacked. The Dutch took more than 1000 prisoner and were awarded 25 Iron Crosses."

Above: The cuffband of the Dutch Legion Niederlande, which was formed in July 1941 under the command of the Chief of the Dutch General Staff General Seyffardt. It was committed to battle in January 1942, on the Eastern Front, earning itself a commendation for its actions.

Scores of Dutch NSKK men fought and died at Stalingrad as part of the German Sixth Army in 1942–43. In October 1942, the NSKK Todt and the NSKK Speer were merged to become NSKK Transportgruppe Todt; then NSKK Gruppe Speer; and, finally, in 1944, Transportkorps Speer. The Transportkorps Speer and KUK were made part of the NSKK Staffel WBN in the autumn of 1943. Volunteers wore field-grey uniforms with NSKK rank and other insignia, and signed on for one year or for the duration of the war, whichever was shorter. It is conceivable that 8–9000 Dutchmen served in the various branches of the NSKK in total during World War II.

The Dutch had a labour service of their own but also provided volunteers for the RAD. The number was small,

Below and right: Very rare service badges of the Dutch NSKK (two badges at right). The badge below is the dog tag of the badges's owner. These items were found in 2003 at a former Luftwaffe airbase just outside Berlin.

Above: *Dutch RAD personnel follow the advancing German armies east in Russia. Note the rifles slung on their backs. NSKK members were armed in Russia because of the constant threat of partisan attack.*

possibly around 300, but was enough for an all-Dutch unit to be formed known as Gruppe *Niederland*. Dutchmen also graduated as RAD officers, such as those of the Oostkorp (East Corps) of the Niederland Arbeits Dienst (NAD – Dutch Labour Service). Gruppe *Niederland* saw active service between May and October 1942 on the Eastern Front, behind the German frontline. Normally, RAD personnel were unarmed, but due to partisan activities guards were permitted to carry rifles or pistols.

For a nation with a distinguished maritime tradition, it is surprising that perhaps only about 1500 Dutchmen served in the Kriegsmarine. This may be because the first appeal was not made until May 1943, for naval volunteers in the 18–35 age group.

If the Netherlands was considered a Germanic nation by the Nazis, then the situation in Belgium was not as straightforward. Belgium is really two countries and a German region, all joined together in a single political unit. One part, Flanders, is Germanic in language and racial origin. The other, Wallonie, is French speaking whose racial origins are a mixture of Celtic and Roman. The only strong bond between the two is a common religious faith: Roman Catholicism. The quiet town of Eupen, only 10km (6 miles) from the German border, had a population of 17,000 citizens in the 1930s, most being ethnic Germans. It is the capital of German-speaking Belgium, a region

where about 65,000 people lived in the 1930s. Control of the territory has shifted many times between France, Germany and Belgium throughout history. After escaping the clutches of the Burgundian dukes in the fifteenth century, it was a German princedom, before being annexed by France after the revolution in 1789. It reverted to German control after the Napoleonic wars, but then switched back to Belgium in 1919 as part of the Versailles settlement. After the invasion of 10 May 1940, Hitler declared it to be part of the Reich. The Nazis always drew a clear distinction between the two ethnic peoples of Belgium, who initially favoured the Flemings, their racial "cousins". However, they eventually came to view the Walloon leader, Léon Degrelle, as being a more valuable asset to their cause.

A feeling of resentment had been nurtured by the people of Flanders against the French-speaking state created in 1830 and dominated by the Walloons. The German occupation of Belgium in World War I gave Flemish nationalism, which until then had been mainly intellectual, the impetus to become a political movement in its own right. Under German patronage, a Council of Flanders was set up in Brussels in February 1917. It consisted of some 200 Flemish autonomists, and was granted the status of a provisional government. The *Frontbeweging* or Front Movement, an influential separatist faction, was founded which later became the *Frontpartij* or Front Party. The leaders of the Council of Flanders were tried for high treason after the war, though none was executed and all were set free by an act of clemency in March 1929. The ranks of the *Frontpartij* began to rupture in the early 1930s as the new ideology of fascism increased the demand for autonomy and manifested itself with the formation in October 1931 of a breakaway party known as the *Verbond van Dietsche Nationaal Solidaristen* (Union of Netherlandish National Solidarity). This was abbreviated to *Verdiaso* or simply *Dinaso*. Joris van Severen, a young lawyer, was the leader of *Dinaso*. He was a former army officer who had been stripped of his commission when his nationalist sympathies became apparent. *Dinaso*'s first demand was that the Flemish part of Belgium should join Holland in a Greater Netherlands community, but in 1934 van Severen discovered that the Walloons shared a common Frankish descent with the Flemings. There was thus a complete reorientation of policy, and he now favoured the continued existence of the Belgian state. *Dinaso* had its own stormtroopers known as the *Dinaso Militie* until 1934, when they were renamed the *Dinaso Militanten Orde* (DMO).

Belgian volunteers

Belgium was attacked by Germany on 10 May 1940, and in little more than two weeks was overrun and occupied. Before this happened, many "fifth column" suspects were arrested and transported by the Belgian police to northern France. The German incursion was rapid, causing widespread panic and confusion. This resulted in 22 of the "fifth columnists" being summarily executed at Abbeville on 20 May. Joris van Severen was among the victims, thus dealing *Dinaso* a mortal blow. No replacement of his standing could be found. And following the Nazi occupation, the party was deeply divided over how far it should cooperate with the Germans.

The *Vlaamsch Nationaal Verbond* (VNV – Flemish National Union) emerged as the leading movement regarding collaboration with the Germans, and those wanting to court favours with the Germans had to do so within the framework of this party. Gustave de Clercq assumed the leadership of the party after several Flemish national parties came together in October 1933. In general terms, the party's political goals were not unlike those held by *Dinaso*, i.e. the creation of a Greater Netherlands embracing all those of Dutch/Flemish stock. The region was to encompass an area from French Flanders in the south to German Friesland in the north. The main difference between the VNV and *Dinaso* was over religion. The VNV was staunchly Catholic while van Severen was anti-clerical.

Probably the most important part of the VNV was the *Dieische Militie* (DM), the uniformed militia. It was formed by an amalgamation of the VNV's *Grijze Werfbrigade* (Grey Defence Brigade) and the DMO from the disbanded *Dinaso*.

In 1935, a harmless "cultural" body was founded that aimed for the promotion of better artistic contacts between Flanders and Germany. This small group styled itself the *Duitschen–Vlaamsche Arbeidsgemeenschap* (German-Flemish Working Community), which was abbreviated to *Devlag*, the Flemish word for "flag". However, the group's objective was but a smokescreen as its leader, Jef van de Wiele, held the grandiose view of himself as the Führer of a National Socialist Flanders under the benevolent protection of the Germans. This fanatical apostle of Adolf Hitler ensured that the wholesale incorporation of Flanders into the German Reich became *Devlag*'s aim. On 11 May 1941, the German occupation authorities issued an edict stating "all authorized political parties in Flanders must merge with the VNV or face dissolution". The reference to "authorized" meant collaborationist parties, so in effect all pro-Nazi factions in Belgium were now under one umbrella. An exception, which allowed *Devlag* to escape the net, was made for "cultural" bodies. Although before the war it was only on the fringe of politics, it was now to drop its "cultural" camouflage and emerge as a serious rival to – and even an enemy of – the VNV.

September 1940 witnessed the creation of the equivalent of the German Allgemeine-SS in the city of

Right: Members of the Freiwilligen Legion Niederlande on parade. Note the arm shield in the Dutch colours of red, white and blue below the sleeve eagle. The legion was disbanded in May 1943, having earned itself a reputation for being a dependable combat formation.

Antwerp. The founding fathers were two pro-German Flemings, Ward Herman and René Lagrou. They began by enrolling 130 supporters into the "New Order", and by November 1941 the ranks had swollen to 1580 members with a further 4000 "sponsoring members". The corps was originally titled *Algemeene Schutscharen Vlaanderen* but was more commonly known as the *Vlaamsche SS* or the *SS–Vlaanderen*. In September 1941, it reached regimental strength and was then known as 1. SS-Standarte *Flandern*. In October 1942, with Himmler's policy of bringing all non-German General SS formations together, it became the *Germaansche SS in Vlaanderen* or Germanic SS in Flanders. *Devlag* maintained a close relationship with the

Flemish SS, and *Devlag* leader Jef van de Wiele held an honorary commission in its ranks. Both were openly pro-Nazi, advocating much greater German control in Flanders. The VNV's cautious attitude was thus very much at odds with the policy of the Flemish SS.

Soon after the occupation of Belgium, the Germans began recruitment, which was fairly successful for the NSKK. The age limits were set at 18 to 45 years. The physical standards for volunteers were lower than those required for the legion or for the Waffen-SS. Recruits could also sign on for a specified period of service, the minimum being 12 months. German sources of the time note 2500 Flemings recruited in 1941, and a further 1500 the following year. The whole of the DM/DMO was virtually absorbed into the NSKK as the NSKK Transportbrigade *Flandern*. Flemish volunteers were allowed to wear a shield on the left upper arm with the black lion of Flanders on a yellow background

Below: *A political rally in Flanders proclaiming the Flemish state of Holland. The VNV had always advocated the break-up of Belgium, with the Germanic Flemings forming a "Greater Netherlands" with the Dutch.*

Above: *A dinner held in honour of the 27th SS Panzergrenadier Division Langemarck, a Flemish unit that was expanded from a brigade to a division in September 1944. Note the trident sun wheel insignia on the collar patch and the black lion of Flanders worn by the nurse.*

within a black frame. Later, in July 1943, the Flemish NSKK volunteers combined with Walloon, Dutch and French NSKK volunteers to form the NSKK Transportgruppe Luftwaffe. Like many other German formations, this went under a variety of designations: NSKK Regiment Luftwaffe, NSKK Transportregiment Luftwaffe, NSKK Gruppe Luftwaffe and NSKK Motorgruppe Luftwaffe.

Recruitment of civilian workers in Flanders had begun practically with the start of the occupation, and if German sources are to be believed it was highly successful. In the autumn of 1941, recruiting started for the defence forces of the Organization Todt (OT) in the so-called Schutzkommando. The OT Schutzkommando took on 4–5000 Flemings to protect its property and doubtless also to keep watch over their compatriots, though service could be in any part of occupied Europe.

A recruiting office was opened in Antwerp (later moved to Brussels) for the Kriegsmarine to recruit

Right: *Two Flemish soldiers serving with the Luftwaffe, one of whom shoulders a flag depicting the black lion of Flanders on a yellow background. Note the Luftwaffe eagle on their helmets, and compare the two styles of Flemish arm shields in the pictures on this page.*

Flemings in July 1943. Volunteers had to be between 17 and 45 years of age, and had to sign on for either a period of two years or for the duration of the war. However, as in other occupied countries, private enlistment had certainly taken place before this authorized date. All recruits, whether former members of the Belgian Navy or not, had to go through a 12-week period of training. In November 1943, it was announced that 300 Flemings had enlisted. In all, there may have been about 500 Flemings in the Kriegsmarine, seeing service usually in either E-Boats or U-boats. Although German naval regulations allowed foreign volunteers to wear a shield in their national colours, there is no evidence that any Fleming wore such an emblem in the German Navy.

Above: *Léon Degrelle, leader of the Walloon fascist Rexist Party and commander of the 28th SS Panzergrenadier Division* **Wallonien.** *He survived the war to die in Spain in 1994, being unyielding in his view that Adolf Hitler was the greatest statesman of his age.*

As stated above, in Wallonie the Germans discovered a far more dependable and charismatic collaborator than could be found elsewhere in Flanders: Léon Degrelle. In 1935, he founded a political movement called *Christus Rex*, popularly known as the Rexist Party. Its fortunes, however, were in steep decline in the months immediately preceding World War II, but the German conquest and occupation provided the catalyst for its revival. The only authorized political party in Wallonie was declared to be the Rexists in May 1941. Rexism was a "one-man show", unlike the VNV, and enjoyed a much narrower base of popular support in Wallonie than the VNV did in Flanders. *Rex* had its own stormtroopers known as the *Formation de Combat*.

Among the people of Wallonie, recruitment into the NSKK was a much more attractive proposition than service with the legion. Manpower sources were *Rex* and another Flemish party, *Amisdu Grande Reich Allemand* (AGRA – Friends of the Great German Reich), which was founded in 1941 and escaped suppression by claiming it was a non-political party (though the fact that it was the most outspokenly pro-German party in Wallonie probably had more to do with its continued existence). Both parties were rewarded for their efforts by being granted the right to wear their respective party emblems on the NSKK uniform. The NSKK absorbed most of the Brigade Vollante *Rex*, which became known as NSKK *Rex*. After merging in July 1943, NSKK *Rex* and NSKK AGRA formed part of the larger NSKK Motor Group Luftwaffe, and was then known simply as NSKK *Wallonie*. The minimum period of engagement was for 12 months, but, like their Flemish compatriots, many found themselves eventually drafted into the Waffen-SS. Possibly about 6000 Walloons served in the NSKK.

The conquest of Western Europe meant that it was possible for the Waffen-SS to recruit directly among the Nordic peoples, especially from Norway, Denmark, Holland and Flanders. The collaborationist parties were the instruments that would provide the manpower of the "correct" calibre, and special units were set up to absorb volunteers from these racially approved regions. SS Standarte (Regiment) *Nordland*, for example, was established within weeks of Norway and Denmark being occupied to enable young men from these two countries to train "for police duties" in their respective homelands. After the defeat of France, Alsace-Lorraine was reincorporated into Germany. Sennheim in Alsace housed a French Army barracks, which the SS took over for the initial selection and basic training of the Norwegians along with other Western European volunteers. Those who passed were then posted on for more advanced instruction elsewhere – in the case of the Norwegians, to Austria. In January 1941, recruitment intensified for the *Nordland* Regiment. Quisling made a radio appeal for 17-

and 25-year-olds to come forward "to help our Germanic brethren fight English despotism". It was hoped this call would yield 3000 volunteers, but the response was not encouraging, being numbered only in the hundreds. Jonas Lie, the chief of the Norwegian police who although strongly pro-German was not a member of NS, was among those who did volunteer, as did Axel Strang, Minister of Sport and Chief of Staff of the *Rikshird* (a sub-organization of the *Hird*, the NS's party militia; it comprised a flying section, naval section and an armed section – the latter provided a cadre for the Freiwilligen Legion *Norwegen*). The age limit for volunteers was then raised to 40 years, and a minimum engagement of two years was called for, at the end of which recruits would receive joint German citizenship. Nebenstelle Nordsee in Copenhagen acted as the recruiting agency for the Danes.

The *Nordland* moved to Heuberg in northern Germany and then to Vienna and Klagenfurt in Austria in February 1941. There, the *Germania* Regiment of the *Das Reich* Division was to be the cadre around which a new division of the Waffen-SS was to be formed. The Danish-Norwegian *Nordland* and the Dutch-Flemish *Westland* Regiments were to be incorporated into this new unit. This fresh division was now given the name *Wiking* and numbered the 5th division of the Waffen-SS

Norwegian volunteers

A number of "green" personnel were seconded to the *Das Reich* Division to provide them with combat experience before they joined *Wiking*. They took an active part in the invasion of Yugoslavia in April 1941, among them being Jonas Lie and Axel Strang. After his return as a war-decorated hero, having won the Iron Cross 2nd Class, Lie immediately engaged in intriguing with Reich Commissioner Terboven against their mutual enemy Quisling. Within the *Rikshird*, Lie founded the equivalent of the Norwegian Allgemeine-SS with the complicity of the German authorities. On 16 May 1941, the immediate establishment of a Norwegian political SS unit was proposed by him at a secret meeting of the 7th *Hird* Regiment in Oslo, with some 130 of its members enrolling at once. This was announced in the press on 21 May. Not forewarned or consulted, Quisling was furious but impotent. In fact, the Norwegian SS had already been given Himmler's blessing and the Reichsführer-SS arrived in Oslo to preside over the oath taken by the new recruits the very

same day. The unit was called *Norges SS* (Norway's SS). Elverum was the destination for the new Norwegian SS men, where they began their six-week basic training course following Himmler's departure. However, a dramatic event occurred before its completion which changed the whole direction of the war as well as their part in it. Hitler invaded Russia on 22 June 1941.

Little success had been gained by Quisling's call to his fellow countrymen to join in the fight against "English despotism". However, a much more effective propaganda weapon lay in Hitler's self-styled "crusade against Bolshevism". Stalin's unprovoked attack on Finland (November 1939 to March 1940) had already angered the Norwegians, who responded with a call for assistance in the struggle against Russia. It was answered by the formation of a legion of Scandinavian volunteers. Unfortunately for the Finns, it made no significant contribution to the war as it arrived too late.

An announcement was made on the formation of a Norwegian legion on 29 June 1941. It was under the control of the SS from the very beginning, with precautions being taken to conceal this fact from the Norwegian public. The legion was portrayed as a Norwegian expeditionary force fighting against Bolshevism rather than as an SS body in Hitler's pay. The NS paramilitary formations such as the *Rikshird* responded well, and 85 percent of the recently formed *Norges SS* volunteered for service in the legion. Promises were made to the volunteers that existing ranks would be retained by serving soldiers, that they would be subject to

Right: SS-Oberscharführer Alfred Seehagen, a Danish member of the Totenkopf Division. On his left breast he wears the Germanic Proficiency Runes Badge Bronze Class. Seehagen was killed fighting the Red Army in Hungary in the spring of 1945.

Norwegian not German military law, and that the raised right-armed Nazi salute employed by the SS would not be used. These promises were not honoured, however.

The legion was officially christened Freiwilligen Legion *Norwegen* (Volunteer Legion Norway) on 1 August, with its strength being listed as 1218 men by the end of 1941. In Norway, recruiting continued unabated with two new companies being raised, one drawn from cadre personnel of the labour service and the other raised from the police.

The Germanic SS, as devised by Himmler, encompassed all non-German Allgemeine-SS formations in occupied Western Europe. This meant the *Norges SS* became the Germanic SS Norway on 21 July 1942. The Germanic SS Norway severed all connections with its *Rikshird* parent, and membership of both organizations was no longer possible. Its prime allegiance was now to Germany and not to its local collaborationist leader: a new oath of loyalty was taken to Hitler, not Quisling.

The Danish Government announced its intention of raising a corps of volunteers to fight against the Soviets

Above: *A soldier of the 11th Panzergrenadier Division Nordland, a unit made up of Danes, Dutch, Norwegians, Estonians, Finns, Swedes and Swiss volunteers. Many of its members came from the remnants of the national legions raised by the Germans.*

Below: *The front gate of the Norwegian SS police camp. In Norway, all police formations came under the control of the SS through SS-Obergruppenführer Willhelm Rediess, and many Norwegian police members were committed to action on the Eastern Front.*

within a week of the invasion of Russia. The Freikorps *Danmark*, as it was to be known, was proclaimed on 28 June 1941. Volunteers between the ages of 17 and 35 who had either completed their period of conscript service within the previous 10 years or who had been in the Danish armed forces at the time of the German invasion, were called on to enlist. Career soldiers were promised equivalent ranks in the new unit. Freikorps *Danmark* was very definitely an official body sponsored by the Danish Government, not the protégé of any political party, and from the start was part of the Waffen-SS. In its homeland, like the Norwegian legion, this fact was concealed from the public. The Freikorps *Danmark* had a strength of 1164 men by the end of 1941 and was attached to the *Totenkopf* Division. It went into action in May 1942 and took part in the celebrated action in the Demjansk Pocket. This action took place in the northern sector of the Eastern Front. The division was encircled for several months, taking heavy casualties but holding out and eventually being relieved in April 1942. Having suffered 78 percent casualties by August, the Freikorps was brought back to Denmark for four weeks' leave in September. In October 1942, it again returned to the Eastern Front and saw heavy combat in December and January 1943. In April 1943, it was finally

withdrawn, being disbanded the following month. Most of those Danish volunteers left alive were transferred to the SS-Panzergrenadier Regiment 24 *Danmark* of the Waffen-SS *Nordland* Division.

After the Freikorps was disbanded, Himmler ordered a Danish branch of the Germanic SS to be set up. The so-called Germanic Corps was changed to *Schalburg* Corps in memory of the most popular commander of the Freikorps, Count Christian Frederik von Schalburg, who was of Baltic German origin. A one-time leader of the DNSAP youth, he went on to become an SS-Sturmbahnführer with the *Wiking* Division. In some sources he is referred to as Frederik-Christian von Schalburg, the second out of seven commanders of the Freikorps *Danmark* who was killed in action on 2 June 1942 at Demjansk, and was given a state funeral by the Nazi authorities in Denmark.

Several ex-Freikorps soldiers formed themselves into the new cadre of the *Schalburg* Corps, which was divided into two groups: the first made up of "regular" soldiers; and the second group, which came to be known as the *Dansk Folke Vaern* (Danish People's Defence), was made up of civilians, some of whom were expected to provide financial backing. Many of Clausen's former supporters were drawn away by the *Dansk Folke Vaern*. For example, Max Arildskov's *Nye Danmark* (New Denmark), which had been formed after Clausen's poor results in the March election, broke away from the DNSAP, and started its own SA known as the Landstormen (200 men with a further 500 civilians as back-up). In December, Arildskov put his men at the disposal of the *Schalburg* Corps, but only around 50 were accepted. The others remained as a form of reserve group, still keeping the Landstormen title.

In July 1944, the *Schalburg* Corps was incorporated into the SS as SS Training Battalion *Schalburg*. Six months later it was renamed the SS Guard Battalion *Zealand*. It was officially disbanded on 28 February 1945.

Dutch and Flemish males between the ages of 18 and 25 were encouraged to volunteer in the Standarte *Westland*, which had been established by the SS in May 1940. Recruiting did not get under way until that autumn, though, when the volunteers were told they were being trained "for police duties" in their respective homelands. The regiment was up to full strength in a matter of weeks due to the large numbers of volunteers who presented themselves for service. *Westland* was incorporated into the Waffen-SS during the winter of 1940–41. Himmler was encouraged by his success in finding Dutch and Flemish volunteers to raise a second volunteer regiment on 3 April 1941, to be known as the Freiwilligen Standarte *Nordwest*. It was for young men from Flanders, Holland and also Denmark. But *Nordwest* shrank to such an extent that it was no longer able to carry on as a regiment, due to the fact that the Flemings, Dutch and Danes were being drawn off into ethnic legions of their own. It was therefore disbanded on 21 September 1941.

The formation of a Flemish Legion, open to men between the ages of 17 and 40, was then announced. In September 1941, it was officially christened the Freiwilligen Legion *Flandern*, having previously been known variously as the Verbond *Flandern*, Landesverband *Flandern* and Bataillon *Flandern*. Ex-regular soldiers, especially officers and NCOs, were particularly sought after. Those below the age of 23 could sign on for a specified period, the minimum being 12 months, while for other candidates enlistment had to be "for the duration". The unit was sent to the front at Leningrad in November 1941, having been deemed ready for active service, as part of the 2nd SS Motorized Infantry Brigade. It was pulled out of the line after six months' active service at the front in June 1942 after suffering heavy casualties, returning in August 1942. In May 1943, the unit was renamed the 6th SS-Sturmbrigade *Langemarck* (6th SS Volunteer Assault Brigade *Langemarck*). The honorary title *Langemarck* had been conferred on the SS Infantry Regiment *Langemarck* of the *Das Reich* Division on 20 April 1942. This regiment now became the cadre around which the Flemish brigade was to be constructed. Throughout Belgium, the SS had by this time no fewer than 23 recruiting offices, but there were still insufficient numbers of volunteers coming forward, and it was only by adding a Finnish SS battalion that the brigade could be brought up to the required strength.

Walloon volunteers who came from Léon Degrelle's Rexist movement were grouped by the German military administration in the 373rd Infantry Battalion and

Below: *Léon Degrelle with his Walloon volunteers on the Eastern Front. This photograph is dated before February 1944, as Degrelle is not wearing the Knight's Cross at his neck and he is in German Army uniform. The Walloons were not taken into the SS until June 1943.*

Above: *A ceremony to honour the foreign fallen in the service of the Third Reich. The flag on the far left is the cross emblem of the Walloon Rexist Party. When asked after the war if he had any regrets, Degrelle replied: "I am only sorry I didn't succeed."*

assigned to the army. They fought in this army unit in the Eastern campaign; then, in 1943, an agreement was reached between the supreme command of the Wehrmacht, the head of the General Staff of the army and the Reichsführer-SS that the Walloons should be assigned to the Waffen-SS on 1 June 1943. The Legion *Wallonie* was then converted into the SS-Sturmbrigade *Wallonien*. In July 1944, it was reorganized and enlarged to become the 28th SS Volunteer Panzergrenadier Division *Wallonien*.

The division's commander, Léon Degrelle, was the archetypal Nazi foreign volunteer. He spent most of the war on the Russian Front with his legion of Walloon volunteers. In January 1944, the Walloons were cut off in the Cherkassy Pocket, 2000 men out of 56,000 German troops trapped. Degrelle and his men cut their way through Soviet lines to reach safety, though 1300 of them died doing so. Following a period of rest in Germany, the brigade was posted back to Russia, this time to the north at Narva in April 1944. Degrelle and his Walloons put up an heroic defence against heavy odds in the subsequent Battle of Narva, his leadership being so exemplary that he was awarded the Oakleaves to his Knight's Cross by

Hitler personally in August 1944. The Führer had earlier remarked to him: "If I had a son I would want him to be like you."

In December 1944, Degrelle and his men were in the Rhine area, the "division" having a strength of 3000 men. Meanwhile, the Belgian Government, having been reinstated by the Allies, sentenced Degrelle to death in absentia. Between January and May 1945, he and his men were again fighting the Russians, this time on German soil. Following the fall of Germany, Degrelle escaped to Spain where he lived until 1994. Asked if he had any regrets about the war, his reply was: "Only that we lost!"

Degrelle was perhaps an exception among the volunteers who staffed the legions, but there is no doubt that the first draft of West European volunteers who fought for the Germans in Russia did so with great enthusiasm, and needed little encouragement to take part in the anti-Bolshevik crusade. The casualties the legions suffered in Russia in late 1941 and early 1942 is perhaps testimony to the old adage that enthusiasm does not compensate for proper training. However, the figures also indicate the level of commitment and bravery displayed by the foreign legions fighting their ideological foe: Legion *Niederlande* – 80 percent losses; Freikorps *Danmark* – 78 percent losses; and Legion *Norwegen* – 50 percent losses. Such enthusiasm would be a defining factor among the West European foreign volunteers fighting for the Third Reich for the rest of the war.

Chapter 7

NEUTRALS AND ALLIES

The campaign against the Soviet Union attracted a number of foreign nationals of neutral countries. In addition, Finland and Italy committed troops to the war against Russia. Mussolini actually sent a whole army to the Eastern Front, while Spain's Franco sent enough troops to show Hitler his good faith.

This chapter concerns those foreign volunteers from the neutral states who fought for the Third Reich, plus the units raised from Finnish and Italian recruits. The inclusion of the latter two categories in this chapter might at first appear strange. However, the Italian force that was committed to the war in Russia was very much an ideological deployment, containing as it did fascist blackshirt units. And when Italy left the Axis in July 1943, the Germans raised several units of loyal Italians to continue the battle against the Allies.

Left: The flags of Finland and Nazi Germany side by side at a ceremony to welcome Finnish volunteers to the SS. Finland contributed a battalion to the Waffen-SS.

Finland is a unique case with regard to its relations with Germany during World War II. When tensions between Germany and the Soviet Union increased during the spring of 1941, Finland made overtures to Germany but did not conclude a formal agreement. That said, she did allow the transit of German troops, and Finland participated in Operation Barbarossa in June 1941. Helsinki termed this campaign the "War of Continuation", an important title as the Finns wanted to retake all their territory lost in the earlier Winter War. But the Finnish population had no desire to join Nazi Germany in an ideological crusade; those Finns who were committed fascists made their way into the Waffen-SS. First, however, let us look at the neutrals.

Switzerland was the only country of Central Europe that managed to remain neutral in World War II. There were several reasons for this: she was well defended and the mountainous terrain gave her certain advantages. More importantly, perhaps, Switzerland had a long tradition of neutrality and was also useful to both sides as an informal meeting place. But the most important reason for the Germans not molesting the Swiss was that the latter were virtually surrounded by Axis territory anyway. From the German-speaking part of Switzerland, about 700 to 800 volunteers found their way into the Waffen-SS. Considering the long border around Lake Constance, on the border of Germany, Austria and Switzerland, and the natural exchange between the two countries, it is surprising that the number was not larger. The greatest concentration of Swiss volunteers was in the *Wiking* Division, which had its own all-Swiss company. In the course of the war, 33 Swiss SS men were commissioned as officers. Swiss volunteers could also be found in the *Kurt Eggers* Regiment of the Waffen-SS. This

Below: *Many Swedes found their way into the Waffen-SS' war correspondents' Kurt Eggers unit, which started out as a company but was expanded to a regiment (Himmler was determined to publicize the SS's achievements). Its was named after its first commander.*

war correspondents' unit was the first truly "Germanic" formation of the SS, since it included not only Swiss but also British, Danes, Norwegians, Finns, Dutch, Flemings, Swedes and Icelanders. It was named after its first commander, SS-Standartenführer Kurt Eggers. Not all Swiss volunteers served in the Waffen-SS; some fought in the Wehrmacht. In all, it is reckoned that 300 Swiss men were killed during the war.

The neutrality of Sweden during World War II was both precarious and questionable for, in many ways, the Germans dominated the country. During the 1940 invasion of Norway, for example, Sweden was forced to allow trainloads of German soldiers to travel through her territory on their way to and from the Narvik area, although this was agreed only after the British and Norwegian troops had finally left the area. Sweden also allowed some rescued German seamen to pass through her territory; a clear if insignificant breach of international law which she had little option but to permit. Officially, Sweden did not permit recruiting by belligerents within her neutral frontiers, and this policy was successfully upheld until the start of the Nazi campaign against the Soviet Union in June 1941. Thereafter, German pressure and Swedish anti-communist

Above: *The Spanish dictator Francisco Franco (centre) sent the Blue Division and other units to fight with the Germans on the Eastern Front. This aid was the extent of his help to Germany, however. He refused to declare war on the Allies.*

sentiment caused the government to turn a blind eye to clandestine recruitment by the German Legation in Stockholm and by the German Auslands Organization (the Nazi Party agency concerned with the care and supervision of Germans living in foreign countries). Volunteers interested in serving proceeded via occupied Norway to Germany. A supposedly top secret questionnaire was circulated among senior officers of the Swedish Army seeking to discover how many would be prepared to serve actively in the German armed forces should recruitment be made legal. The response was decidedly negative, and thereafter neither the Swedes nor the Germans sought to pursue the matter. The Swedish Government, however, took a more relaxed line with regard to its nationals joining the Finnish Army. This occurred on a sufficient scale to make possible the creation of an all-Swedish battalion, the *Hangö* Battalion, within the 13th Infantry Regiment of the Finnish Army. This unit saw action against the Soviets on the Svir Front. There was even an official "Finland Volunteers" department within the Swedish High Command.

The precise number of Swedes who served in the German forces may never be known accurately, but the SS Statistical Department lists only 39 Swedish volunteers in 1942. By the end of the war, this figure may have increased to 130, of whom perhaps 30 were killed in action. There were certainly never enough men for a Swedish legion, although the Germans would have liked to have founded one.

Swedish volunteers were trained at Graz and Klagenfurt in Austria, as well as at the international SS camp at Sennheim in Alsace. When the *Nordland* Regiment was separated from the *Wiking* Division to form a new *Nordland* Division, only about 40 Swedes remained in the *Wiking* Division, the bulk being transferred to the *Nordland*. The closest to an all-Swedish unit was the 3rd Company, Reconnaissance Abteilung (Battalion) 11, of the *Nordland* Division. Since the use of mortars was a speciality in the Swedish Army, and many of the volunteers were ex-army soldiers skilled in this

Above: *The Blue Division Medal Spanish Government Issue. The example on the left is a Spanish-made model, while on the right is the German-made model. This medal was introduced by the Spanish Government on 9 November 1943 for those Spaniards who served in Russia.*

art, some Swedes were formed into a motorized heavy mortar platoon, the Schwedenzug, within the division. Swedes were scattered throughout the other sections of this division, as well as serving in the supposedly all-Dutch 23rd SS Volunteer Panzergrenadier Division *Nederland*. They had their first "blooding" against the partisans in Yugoslavia, and then they were dispatched to the Leningrad Front. There they participated in the Battle of the European SS at Narva in Estonia in mid-1944. They suffered heavy losses before finally taking part in the last-ditch defence of Berlin in April 1945.

Some 20 Swedes graduated from the SS officers' school at Bad Tölz, in two instances at the top of their class. Swedes were also prominent in the multi-national Kurt Eggers Regiment of the Waffen-SS, in which at least five Swedes of officer grade served. Although almost all of the Swedish volunteers who served with the German forces did so in the Waffen-SS, and enlistment continued until February 1945, there are two recorded instances of Swedes serving in other branches of Hitler's armed forces. One was in the 3rd Panzer Division of the army, the other in the 8th Field Division of the Luftwaffe.

Spain was also a neutral country, though one much closer ideologically and politically to Nazi Germany than was Sweden. Hitler was desirous that Franco's Spain

should join the Axis. For his part, the Spanish dictator was not unwilling, but his price was high. He wanted Gibraltar, French Morocco and Oran, the former Spanish province that was part of French Algeria. Following the German armistice with France in the summer of 1940, Hitler was unwilling to take any action that might jeopardize the agreement. That said, he was prepared to grant French Morocco to Spain in return for German bases and mining rights in the area, a request Franco refused. He also refused a request for one of the Canary isles as a German base. Hitler forcefully reminded Franco of the debt he owed Germany for the military support she had supplied him during the Spanish Civil War, but this had little effect.

However, with the outbreak of war in the East, Franco willingly allowed Spaniards to serve as volunteers in the "crusade against Bolshevism". Within hours of the German invasion of Russia, for example, Minister for Foreign Affairs von Ribbentrop received a Spanish offer

Above: Members of the Spanish Blue Division on parade prior to their departure for training in Germany. The division was named after the colour of the Spanish fascist Falange movement.

of aid, and on 24 June 1941 he secured Hitler's approval for the participation of a Spanish volunteer legion in the campaign.

In Spain there was no lack of recruits, although initially only 4000 volunteers were called for. However, 10 times that number, most of them veterans of the civil war, presented themselves for enlistment in the legion. It was quite apparent to the Spanish authorities that they could do much better than a mere token legion and that they would have no difficulty in raising a full division which, in Spanish terms, meant in the region of 19,000 men. This response suited Franco, who saw it as tangible evidence of his good faith and support for Hitler's aims, without being drawn into the Axis proper.

Right: The Bravery and Commemorative Medal of the Spanish Blue Division. The medal was introduced on 3 January 1944 to reward the services of Spanish volunteers who had fought on the Eastern Front between 1941 and October 1943.

tunic with a blue collar and cuffs. Before being sent to the front, though, the Spanish troops were obliged to dress in the field-grey German Army uniform. On the right upper arm they wore a shield in the Spanish national colours surmounted by the word "Espana".

On 13 July 1941, the first batch of volunteers left Madrid for Grafenwöhr in Bavaria, where they became officially the 250th Infantry Division of the German Army, with a strength of 17,924 officers and men divided into four infantry regiments. This presented immediate problems as it was Spanish practice to have four regiments to a division, but German organization specified only three, which meant that one of the Spanish regiments had to be disbanded and its personnel reallocated among the three remaining regiments. The three resultant regiments were numbered the 226nd Infantry Regiment, with its members being mainly from Barcelona; the 263rd Infantry Regiment, with members drawn from the Valencia region; and the 269th Infantry Regiment, with its personnel being predominantly from Seville. Each regiment had three battalions, each of which had four companies. The 250th Artillery Regiment was also attached. It consisted of three batteries of 105mm guns and one battalion equipped with 150mm heavy guns.

The Blue Division in Russia

On 20 August 1941, the division was considered adequately trained after its five weeks at Grafenwöhr and it was transported by train to the German-Soviet border. At this time, the frontline was more than 1000km (625 miles) to the east, and to reach it the division had to proceed on foot. Upon arriving at Smolensk, where it had expected to join Army Group Centre in its offensive against Moscow, it found itself instead redirected north to Leningrad where it became part of the German Sixteenth Army. The Spaniards saw their first action on 12 October 1941 when they were put into the line between Lake Ilmen and the west bank of the River Volkhov. A major German offensive against Leningrad opened four days later. Both the fighting and the bitter cold took their toll on the Spaniards. Death, wounds and frostbite so seriously depleted the Spanish ranks that there was alarm in Madrid that the Blue Division was about to disintegrate. Since the honour of Spain rather than just the fate of one division was at stake, replacements were rapidly rushed to the front.

The division was to remain as part of the force besieging Leningrad for the rest of its time in Russia. At times, the Soviets mounted counteroffensives and then the Germans would launch another assault in an attempt to break into the city. The Spaniards were always in the vanguard of these actions, but as the war situation deteriorated for the Axis the British put increasing

Above: The Blue Division in Russia. The fighting northwest of Novgorod was severe, and soon the Spanish were suffering heavy casualties. First in action in September 1941, for example, the 269th Infantry Regiment had lost 120 dead and 440 wounded by December.

Volunteer regiments were raised in Madrid, Barcelona, Seville and other main cities. With the legion thus formed, it was announced on 27 June 1941 that the commander would be General Augustin Munoz Grandes, later described by Hitler as a "man of energy". Since Spain was not at war with any nation, let alone the Soviet Union, there was a problem of how the volunteers should be dressed. What uniform should they wear, as it would not be possible to be attired in the dress of the Spanish armed forces? This gave Franco the opportunity to produce what was to be a symbolic Spanish uniform consisting of the red beret of the Carlist movement (Spanish traditionalists of the nineteenth century), the blue shirt of the Falangist movement (an extreme nationalist political group founded in Spain in 1933 by José Antonio Primo de Rivera) and the khaki trousers of the Spanish Foreign Legion, while officers wore a khaki pressure on Franco to declare Spain's absolute neutrality and remove his forces from Russia.

By the spring of 1943, the Spaniards had begun negotiations with the Germans for the withdrawal of the Blue Division, although the order to do so was not given to General Emilio Esteban-Infantes until 14 October 1943 (he had replaced Munoz Grandes as the division's commander in December 1942). With repatriation of the division under way, officers called for volunteers from the single men to remain with the so-called Volunteer Legion, or Blue Legion as it was unofficially known. The Spanish Ministry of Foreign Affairs and the Ministry of the Army were unable to agree on the size of the proposed legion. In desperation, Esteban-Infantes despatched Lieutenant-Colonel Diaz de Villegas by aircraft to Madrid where, on the morning of 4 November, he was granted a meeting with General Franco who gave him a decision within 20 minutes. To mollify the resentment of the Germans, and indeed of many of the volunteers themselves, it was announced that a "Spanish Legion" consisting of some 1000 to 1500 men would be allowed to stay on and continue the battle against communism. This meant that there were volunteers to spare.

The legion was commanded by Colonel Navarro and known as the *Legion Espanola de Voluntarios* (LEV), and was assigned to the 121st Division of the German Army. Leaving Diaz de Villegas in command of the remnants of the division, Esteban-Infantes flew to Berlin on 16 November to conclude arrangements with the German High Command regarding the division, the legion and the many Spanish service organizations in Russia. By 20 November 1943, while the Blue Division was continuing its process of repatriation, the 1500 volunteers for the Blue Legion had assembled in barracks at Yamberg on the Latvian frontier.

The legion was commanded by Colonel Antonio Garcia Navarro and consisted of a headquarters staff, the 1st and 2nd Infantry *Banderas* (battalions) commanded by Comandantes Ibarra and Navarro respectively. There was also a 3rd Mixed *Banderas* with three companies of artillery, anti-tank guns, plus sappers, signallers and reconnaissance elements under the command of Comandante Virgili. Following initial operations against partisans either side of the roads leading to Narva, the

Below: *Spanish soldiers in a bunker on the Eastern Front. The war in Russia came as a nasty shock to many Spanish volunteers, not least because the Red Army executed any Spaniards they captured. At Udarnik, for example, the Spanish prisoners were killed by pickaxes.*

Above: *The Italian dictator Mussolini leads a detachment of blackshirts during a parade in Rome. When he learnt of Hitler's attack on the Soviet Union in June 1941, on his own initiative he despatched the Italian Expeditionary Corps to take part in the crusade against Bolshevism.*

legion was transported eastwards to Begolovo, Schapki and Kostovo where it was attached to the German 121st Division. Manning an 11km (6.8-mile) front, the Spanish repulsed two strong Soviet assaults on 24 and 25 December in bitter winter weather.

Earlier, on 23 December, General Esteban-Infantes flew home to Madrid, and the following morning Lieutenant-Colonel Diaz de Villegas boarded a Junkers Ju 88 at Nikolayevka — the last soldier of the Blue Division to leave the front.

During the latter period of its service on the Eastern Front, the Blue Division was not made up entirely of volunteers. Conscription had to be applied to keep up the numbers. Although the nominal strength of the division was 18,000 men, the system of regular rotation of troops

and replacements for battle losses meant that as many as 45,000 Spaniards may have seen service with the 250th Infantry Division between June 1941 and October 1943. In just over two years of war, the Blue Division had suffered a total of 12,726 casualties comprising 3934 dead, 8466 wounded and 326 missing, together with many invalided out of Russia with frostbite or taken prisoner by the Soviets.

As 1944 began, the entire northern front was collapsing under relentless Red Army pressure. The encirclement of Leningrad was abandoned and a general retreat westwards began. On 19 January, the legion was ordered to withdraw southwards, and commenced a slow, hard march through freezing wind and snow, fighting off partisan attacks as it did so. Passing through Ljuban, Sapolgje and Oredesch, the legion's retreat continued until it reached Luga on the last day of January. From Luga the unit left by train for the Taps-Aiguidu zone in Estonia. There, the Spaniards were re-equipped to defend the Narva coast against possible Soviet landings, only to find that an agreement had been reached between the Spanish and German governments to repatriate the legion to Spain. On 21 March, the legion departed in trains towards Königsberg from where it continued by rail until, on 17 April 1944, the Blue Legion crossed the frontier into Spain. So ended the official Spanish participation in Hitler's war against Russia. In April, General Franco closed the frontier with France to deter any would-be volunteers enlisting in the German armed forces.

Even after Spain had declared her neutrality, some former members of the Blue Division and Blue Legion could not forget the struggle being waged in the East by their erstwhile German comrades-in-arms. Spanish volunteers thus continued to fight in the German forces. These were both members of the LEV who refused to return home after the official withdrawal of the legion, together with fresh volunteers who managed to get across the Pyrenees to Lourdes in France, where Sonderstab F, a special army unit, collected these illicit warriors and passed them on to the Waffen-SS. In June 1944, the Spaniards were formed into a special unit at the Stablack Camp near Königsberg. Taking its name from the camp, this formation was known as Volunteer Unit Stablack. At this time, it was only company strength, but by March 1945 a second Spanish SS company had been formed. These two units were then known as SS Freiwilligen Kompanie 101 (span.) and SS Freiwilligen Kompanie 102 (span.). In addition, a Spanish volunteer battalion commanded by SS-Hauptsturmführer Miguel E. Sanchez served with the Waffen-SS to the bitter end, taking part in the final defence of Berlin in April and May 1945.

Hitler's assessment

In general, the Spanish volunteers fought well, though their leadership often left a lot to be desired. Hitler provided a succinct summary regarding Spanish soldiers: "Extraordinarily brave, tough against partisans but wildly undisciplined. What is lamentable with them is the difference in treatment between officers and men. The Spanish officers live in clover, and the men are reduced to the most meagre pittance."

The Blue Division was not the only Spanish military unit to serve on the Russian Front. One of Spain's leading civil war fighter aces, Comandante Salas Larrazabal Salvador, formed a fighter formation from veterans of the civil war. It consisted of five squadrons, which relieved one another consecutively at the front. Not surprisingly, this unit was promptly nicknamed the Blue Squadron. It left Madrid on 27 July 1941, two weeks after the departure of the Blue Division. The Spanish pilots flew Messerschmitt Bf 109 fighters until the end of 1942, when the 3rd Squadron was supplied with Focke-Wulf Fw 190s. The Blue Squadron was numbered 15/JG 27, i.e. the 15th Squadron of Jagdgeschwader (Fighter Group) 27 and later JG 51. The

squadron operated in support of Army Group Centre, its principal mission being the protection of German bombers. The most outstanding action of the 1st Squadron was in the advance on Moscow and the subsequent retreat, while the 4th Squadron fought in the retreat from Kharkov and the fighting at Kursk and Smolensk in 1943.

In March 1942, most of the Spanish aircrews were replaced by a fresh batch of volunteers from the homeland. In October of the same year, a further exchange of personnel took place. In general, the morale and effectiveness of the Spanish pilots remained high. For example, they shot down a total of 156 Soviet aircraft. Comandante Salas Larrazabal personally scored 7 kills; and Comandante Cuadra, 10. But, like the Blue Division, the Blue Squadron was pulled out of frontline service before the end of 1943 and returned to Spain in the early months of the following year. A total of 22 squadron

Below: Cannon fodder for the Eastern Front: Italian fascist recruits strike a suitably warlike pose during a summer camp for the fascist militia. Mussolini committed Italian troops to the war in Russia to earn a share of the spoils of an Axis-occupied Soviet Union.

Above: The Military Training in Germany Badge for Italian Personnel. This badge was produced in recognition of those Italians who underwent military training in Germany. Most of these individuals did not return to the Italian armed forces but were taken into the Waffen-SS.

personnel were reported dead or missing, one of whom was eventually repatriated as a prisoner of war.

As well as the "teeth" arms, the Spanish sent a large number of support personnel to the Eastern Front. In 1937, General Franco had appointed Mercedes Mil Nolla inspector general of women auxiliaries of the *Sanidad Militar* (the Spanish Army's medical branch). Lieutenant-Colonel Pellicer was appointed inspector of hospitals. The Spanish Army nurses of the *Sanidad Militar* in Germany wore a uniform that comprised a khaki blouse which had an unusual pocket design, dark brown leather buttons, and white collar and cuffs. Displayed at the throat was the emblem of the Spanish Red Cross, while other nursing badges and decorations could be worn on the pocket. They also wore a black belt with a silver-grey *Sanidad Militar* buckle-plate, a pleated khaki skirt, light brown stockings and dark brown shoes. Headdress consisted of a khaki wimple and white coif, upon which was pinned a silver-grey metal badge of the *Sanidad Militar*.

The Blue Division's seriously sick and wounded were treated at hospitals in Mestelevo, Riga, Vilna, Königsberg, Berlin and Hof (Saale), which were operated principally by Spanish medical staff, who included many volunteer nurses from the Spanish Army and the Falange's feminine section. Foreign volunteers in general were cared for in the regular German Army reserve hospitals, and they usually received the same care given to Germans. When artificial limbs were required, for example, the German Government supplied them. When going on convalescent leave in their homelands, volunteers received some monetary assistance from the Wehrmacht money service office located in their country of origin. Most of the travel costs, however, were borne by the volunteers themselves. While on convalescent leave in Germany, the German Government augmented their leave money, but when they left Germany they could take only 10 Reichmarks with them. The notable exception were Spanish volunteers returning to Spain, who were allowed

Right: The reality of the war in Russia. Italian troops on the retreat from the Don in January 1943. When it was hit by the Red Army November 1942 offensive, the Italian Eighth Army collapsed. It had little motor transport, so its men had to make their way to safety on foot.

Right: *A soldier of the Italian Expeditionary Corps poses for a photograph on the Eastern Front. Though Mussolini sent 227,000 troops to Russia, they were ill-equipped to fight in the vast expanses lacking anti-tank guns, heavy artillery and adequate air support.*

to carry twice as much as the normal allowance for other foreign volunteers.

As Europe's first fascist dictator, it was inevitable that Mussolini would commit troops to the "anti-Bolshevik crusade". However, up to June 1941, World War II had gone badly for Il Duce. He had nothing to show in comparison with Hitler's territorial gains. In May 1940, Mussolini's frustration was further heightened when the German armies drove the British forces off the continent and brought France to her knees. It now seemed certain that Germany would win the war. Desperate to share in the spoils of war, Mussolini announced on 10 June 1940 to an enormous crowd gathered in the Piazza Venezia that Italy was at war with Britain and France. Unfortunately, Il Duce was caught in what his Foreign Minister Ciano ironically called "an outbreak of peace" which left Mussolini in a state of limbo. His ego and thirst for power drove him subsequently to invade the Balkans. The Italians invaded

Greece in October 1940, only to be militarily humiliated by the Greeks. However, fascist honour was restored by the German Blitzkrieg in the Balkans in April 1941. Greece and Yugoslavia were quickly conquered, and a British expeditionary force was expelled from the mainland. It found refuge on Crete, which was then taken by a German airborne assault in May. This was followed by Turkey signing a formal treaty with Berlin that granted the Germans passage through the Dardanelles.

These factors convinced Mussolini of the Führer's invincibility and that the impending German attack on the Soviet Union would be an unqualified success. He was convinced he would gain the prestige that he longed for, and Italy would share in the spoils of war. He thus joined the war against Russia and committed a force of 60,000 men to the struggle, known as the *Corpo di Spedizione Italiano* (CSI – Italian Expeditionary Corps in Russia). This force comprised three divisions: *Pasubio* and *Torino*, which were 1938-type binary divisions (two infantry regiments and an artillery regiment each plus support services), and the 3rd Mobile Division *Principe Amedeo Duca d'Aosta*. The latter had two mounted cavalry regiments, a Bersaglieri cycle regiment, a light tank group with obsolete L-3s, an artillery regiment and service units. Later, he sent the 63rd Assault Legion *Tagliamento* to represent his fascist Blackshirts.

The CSI on the Eastern Front

In July 1941, the supposedly motorized CSI followed the German Army through the Ukraine, mainly on foot. Morale was high at the prospect of an easy campaign, and the Germans were impressed with their Italian allies. Unfortunately, this initial euphoria soon disappeared. Inadequate leadership, armour and transport, plus shortages of artillery and anti-tank weapons, revealed the corps to be ill-equipped for the fighting it was to encounter. Undeterred, in March 1942, Mussolini sent II Corps comprising the *Sforzesca*, *Ravenna* and *Cosseria* Infantry Divisions, together with the élite Alpine Corps comprising the *Vicenza* Infantry and *Tridentina*, *Julia* and *Cuneense* Alpine Divisions. Further Blackshirt units were also sent, formed into the 3 Gennaio and 23 Marzo Groups to reinforce the CSI, now designated XXXV Corps. This force of 227,000 men became the Italian Eighth Army. In August 1942, it was guarding the Don Front north of Stalingrad with German liaison officers and formations attached to ensure its reliability. Although a Russian attack had been expected, the Italians were unable to resist the massive armoured thrust that was hurled against them on 11 December 1942. II and XXXV Corps crumbled almost immediately, leaving the Alpine Corps stranded and resulting in a huge gap in the Don defences. The lack of anti-tank guns and medium tanks

was keenly felt in this rout. The Italians were left to fend for themselves during their retreat, in which they were harassed continually by the Red Army. In January 1943, the survivors regrouped in the Ukraine but the Italian Eighth Army had ceased to exist. The disillusioned Germans sent the survivors back to Italy.

The fall of Mussolini

Once in Italy, the survivors bitterly blamed both Mussolini and Hitler for the suffering they had endured. This, in part, influenced the events that were to follow in Italy when, on 25 July 1943, Mussolini was voted out of office by his own Fascist Grand Council and subsequently placed under arrest. On 8 September, Italy officially quit the war. After the fall of the fascist regime, the liberated areas of the country turned to the Allies. On 12 September, Mussolini was rescued from captivity on Gran Sasso by a German commando unit under the leadership of Otto Skorzeny and then evacuated to Germany. Later, in the town of Salo on the shores of Lake Garda, Il Duce set up a puppet fascist state, the so-called Italian Social Republic or, as it is sometimes referred to, the Republic of Salo. The official foundation of the armed forces of the *Repubblica Sociale Italiana* (RSI) was on 28 October 1943.

A virtual civil war had broken out in Italy after Mussolini's deposition and Italy's exit from the Axis camp. Some of the Italian forces actively resisted the Germans and were defeated and made prisoner; others deserted to swell the ranks of the resistance; and a few remained loyal to fascism. The Germans were anxious to utilize the pro-fascist elements in the struggle against the now greatly augmented resistance. Above all, they were determined to keep open the vital lines of communication between Austria and northern Italy. Mussolini's republic cannot be considered anything but a puppet state of the greater German Reich. Four infantry divisions were formed and trained in Germany: the *Italia*, *Littorio*, *San Marco* and *Monterosa* Divisions. These and other units were under German control. For example, a unit that was formed in France after the fall of Mussolini from two battalions of the Blackshirt militia wore Italian Army uniforms with the Wehrmacht eagle and swastika above the left breast pocket and as a cap badge. It returned to Italy in October 1943 to fight the partisans and later the Allies at Anzio. It was granted the title, 1st Battaglione *9 Settembre*, by Mussolini in August 1944. In October 1944, it was attached to the German

Right: *The myth of Axis fraternal friendship. An Italian soldier between two Germans on the Eastern Front. In general, the Germans had a very low opinion of their Italian allies. They effectively left them to their fate when the Eighth Army was retreating in early 1943.*

Above: *Soldiers of the CSI in action on the Eastern Front during the winter of 1942–43. Up to 60,000 Italian soldiers were captured by the Russians during the war, and nearly 50,000 of them died from abuse, starvation and disease in Russian prison camps.*

Brandenburg Division and, as part of this unit, fought against the Red Army on the Eastern Front from October 1944 to January 1945, when it was brought back to Italy to take part once again in anti-partisan fighting.

The Germans also raised a unit composed of Bersaglieri personnel. Before the RSI was proclaimed, this formation was called the Voluntary Battalion of the Waffen-SS. It should not be confused with the 29th Grenadier Division of the Italian SS, which appeared later and was formed by more than 15,000 Italian recruits who joined the Waffen-SS.

From September 1943 to the end of February 1944, a separate SS battalion was being formed at the SS Heidelager Training Centre at Debica, Poland. Major Fortunato, a former Bersaglieri officer who had served in Russia, was tasked in the selection of new recruits loyal to the Germans. Most of the volunteers came from the

Italian 31st Tank Battalion of the *Lombardia* Division and the élite alpine *Julia* Division.

The formation, which had 20 officers and 571 men, was referred to as the SS Battalion *Debica*. For the most part, these troops were considered as Waffen-SS men; and by early March 1944, the men of the SS Battalion *Debica* had been kitted out in German paratrooper uniforms.

On 21 March 1944, the SS Battalion *Debica* was deployed to carry out anti-partisan operations around the Pellice Valley, southwest of Turin. On 12 April, the SS Battalion *Debica* was incorporated into SS Battle Group *Diebitsch*. However, it was not deployed to the Anzio frontlines. During April and May, the battalion fought around Nocera Umbra, Assisi and San Severino Marche against Italian partisans, suffering 50 casualties. New volunteers were able to keep the battalion's strength at 500 men and 20 officers.

In early June 1944, SS Battalion *Debica*, now subordinated to the German I Parachute Corps, was in action to the north of Rome along the Tyrrhenian coast. It suffered heavy losses while fighting American tank units in this area and against partisans behind the German lines. The 200 or so survivors were then dispersed among small battle groups. On 16 June, the SS

Battalion *Debica* was ordered to Florence to help guard the defensive positions of the Gothic Line under Army Group von Zangen. Because the battalion was understrength, it was sent to Pinerolo for refitting. By August, the battalion was back to full strength and ordered to take part in Operation Nightingale against partisan strongpoints in the Chisone and Susa Valleys. On 7 September the SS Battalion *Debica* became part of the new Waffen Grenadier Brigade der SS (Italian nr. 1), being converted into the new 59th Waffen-SS Reconnaissance Battalion.

The 24th Waffen Gebirgs Division *Karstjäger* was a mixed German Volksdeutsche and pro-fascist Italian formation. To combat Tito's partisans in the Carso and Julian Alps, the SS Karstwehr Company had been formed in the summer of 1942, initially to combat partisans in the Karst alpine regions bordering Austria, Italy and Slovenia. Out of this special anti-partisan mountain combat company grew a division (after Mussolini's removal made Himmler decide that the Karstwehr Battalion should be strengthened with locally recruited Volksdeutsche from the South Tyrol, and subsequently by Italian fascist "loyalists"). A divisional headquarters was set up in the town of Moggio in the province of Udine. The division consisted of two mountain infantry regiments and one mountain artillery regiment. Apart from one brief encounter with the British in the latter stages of the war, all the actions fought by this unit were against the partisans. General Paul Hausser, a Waffen-SS corps commander, referred to the non-German part of the division as, "a mixture of Italians, Slovenes, Croats, Serbs and Ukrainians". The division began to fall apart in the closing weeks of the war, with only the German component fighting on to the end. The remnants surrendered to the British 6th Armoured Division in Austria at the beginning of May 1945.

Below: Two members of the CSI in Russia. The Italian troops had almost no motor transport, inadequate supply lines (which stretched all the way back to Italy) and poor equipment. Little wonder, then, that they suffered a terrible fate on the frozen steppes.

SS-Brigadeführer Gottlob Berger, head of the SS recruiting office, once stated: "If a minority is even passably well led, all will volunteer; those who do not volunteer will have their houses broken up." He could not send his SS thugs into Finland to break up the houses of locals, but he still coveted Finnish men for the Waffen-SS. In December 1940, more than 100 Finnish subjects had come forward to show their willingness to join the German armed forces. This whetted Berger's appetite, but he had a problem: these Finns were not strictly Germanic. He thus had to find another source of volunteers and so he concentrated on the minority of Finns of Swedish origin who passed Himmler's racial requirements for entry into the SS.

Recruitment in Finland

The German military attaché in Helsinki reported to Berger at the start of 1941 that potential volunteers were available. There was one overriding problem, though: two sovereign powers were implicated. However, Hitler agreed to the recruitment programme and the German Foreign Office opened negotiations with Finland on 22 February 1941 for its approval. Berger was anxious to begin recruitment immediately, but the lack of urgency on the part of the German Foreign Office forced him to seek out the Finnish ambassador to Germany in Berlin directly. He suggested an SS recruiting team be dispatched to Finland immediately with the objective of finding 700 volunteers. As agreeable as the Finnish ambassador was, he was impotent because Berger had circumnavigated normal diplomatic channels. Undeterred, Berger pursued another avenue of endeavour and persuaded a German Foreign Office Scandinavian expert to draft an instruction to the German ambassador in Helsinki, which was given Ribbentrop's blessing. The document stated that 1000 Finns were to be recruited as workers for German industry, of whom at least half must have military experience. This was a cover to disguise the fact that they were to be recruits for the Waffen-SS, with officers and NCOs being accorded an equivalent rank in the SS and granted dual nationality.

The Finnish Government had grave misgivings about the undertaking, but had to consider it against the desire of keeping Germany's friendship in case of a Soviet attack. The Finnish Government insisted that it was inappropriate for Finns to serve alongside volunteers from countries that had been occupied by the Germans. In addition, it was eager for Finnish volunteers to serve in the German Army as opposed to the Waffen-SS.

These issues caused further delays but were eventually resolved. It was agreed that a Finnish committee should handle recruiting, assisted by an SS doctor. The recruiting, as far as practicable, was to be clandestine, with "idlers and adventurers" being weeded out at the earliest opportunity. It was thought that in two months a target of 1000 volunteers with previous military experience would be feasible. The Finnish SS Committee laid down three further conditions in April. First, no Finnish volunteer was to fight against Britain or Greece in Africa or against any other state at war with Germany, except the Soviet Union. Second, no Finn was to swear loyalty to Adolf Hitler (a compromise was reached whereby an oath to the Führer of the Greater Germanic Reich was taken). Finally, in the event of another Russo-Finnish war in which Germany did not participate, the volunteers were to be returned home.

These additional conditions were agreed, and the German ambassador in Helsinki was informed on 29 April 1941. As far as practicality allowed, they would be honoured in their entirety, thus signalling that recruitment could begin. The first draft of 1251 Finns had been shipped to Germany by the end of May 1941. Most were of Finnic rather than of Swedish stock and also included 33 Estonians, veterans of the Winter War.

The Finns in Russia

On 5 June 1941, the fifth and final draft of volunteers set sail for Germany accompanied by members of the Finnish SS Committee. When they arrived, they met up with the first contingent, many of whom were veterans of the Winter War who had been assigned to units of the *Wiking* Division. This gave cause for some alarm, which was to some extent mollified by the sympathetic attitude extended to the Finns by Felix Steiner, the divisional commander. He gave them his personal assurance that once the Finns had mastered German tactics, they would join their compatriots in an all-Finnish battalion. This did the trick, and the 400 Finns in the *Wiking* Division advanced into the Soviet Union with the rest of their formation on 22 June 1941. In the subsequent fighting they acquitted themselves well. Meanwhile, the later drafts had gathered at Wien-Schönbrunn where, on 15 June 1941, they had been formed into the SS Freiwilligen Battalion *Nordost* under a German commander, SS-Hauptsturmführer Collani. At the beginning of August, it was transferred to Gross-Born, Pomerania, and was organized into three motorized infantry companies and a motorized machine-gun company.

Rumours of inconsiderate treatment meted out to the Finish and other foreign volunteers almost immediately reached Berger's ears. The disproportionate quantity of Finnish officers and NCOs gave rise to a situation where many had not been given equivalent SS rank. To exacerbate the matter, the SS Führungshauptamt (the operational headquarters of the SS responsible for the training, organization and non-tactical employment of Waffen-SS divisions in the field) had discharged a number

of superfluous Finnish officers, who then complained about their treatment at the hands of the SS on their return home. Added to this, inexperienced SS instructors were treating veteran Finnish NCOs like raw recruits at a time when their colleagues in Finland were training German officers in the art of winter warfare. The Finnish Government learnt of the situation and demanded the immediate return of its citizens, which did not bode well for future recruitment. Thus, a rapid improvement in the lot of foreign volunteers in the SS had to be achieved, and quickly. Berger made sure the improvements were carried out, and the Finnish battalion was permitted to continue its service.

On 6 May 1941, the 3rd Battalion of the *Nordland* Regiment received its first contingent of 116 Finnish volunteers, with the second of 257 men following on 15 May. Among them were 10 regular officers, 66 reserve officers and 29 regular NCOs of the Finnish Army. These first two contingents were trained at Heuberg and were

Above: *Italian Bersaglieri parade past Mussolini on 17 July 1944. These must be part of the Voluntary Battalion of the Waffen-SS that was formed from Bersaglieri personnel. A further 15,000 Italian recruits were later formed into the 29th SS Grenadier Division.*

then distributed among practically all units of the *Wiking*, seeing service in Russia from the first day of Operation Barbarossa. Three further contingents – 326 men on 23 May 1941, 289 men on 2 June 1941 and 219 men on 5 June 1941 – were sent to Vienna to form the Finnish Volunteer Battalion. From September 1941, the Finnish unit was known as the Finnish Volunteer Battalion of the Waffen-SS, being sworn in on 15 October 1941. Despite the anti-Christian ideology of the SS, from the beginning the Finns had chaplains to look after their spiritual needs. The first was SS-Untersturmführer Ensio Pihkala and then, after his death, SS-Hauptsturmführer Kalervo Kurkiala.

Above: *A parade attended by Finnish and German officers to welcome Finnish volunteers to the SS. There were initial problems with Finnish SS recruits, which the Finnish Government was unhappy about. However, these were resolved by the intercession of Gottlob Berger.*

After training at Gross-Born, the Finns were dispatched to the Mius Front in February 1942. Here, they joined the *Wiking* Division and became the third battalion of the *Nordland* Regiment. They subsequently served in the Caucasus on the Terek, on the Mius in the western Caucasus, in the oil-bearing area of Grossny in the Kalmuck steppes and at Krasnoarmeyskoye. They fought well and as a result suffered heavy casualties, which to some extent were made good by replacements recruited by a new committee in Finland. On 16 September 1942, for example, a replacement battalion numbering 200 Finnish volunteers arrived. After their training in Vienna, the replacement company, commanded by SS-Obersturmführer Schröder, was distributed among the existing companies on 7 December 1942.

By the end of 1942, as it became apparent to the Finns that Germany was not going to win the war in the immediate future, Helsinki began to look for an opportunity to conclude a separate peace with the Soviet Union. However, the existence of several hundred Finns in the Waffen-SS made it difficult to put out peace feelers to the Soviets. At the same time, the Finnish Government was having difficulties in making good the heavy losses sustained on the Eastern Front, but Berger struggled and intrigued to keep the unit up to strength even though many of the two-year engagements were about to expire.

The battalion spent from 11 to 27 May 1943 in the Bavarian health resort of Ruhpolding for a period of rest and relaxation. On their arrival at the station, the Finns were cordially received by a big crowd and welcomed by the mayor of the town. They took up private quarters, and soon were making friends with the locals. They also made excursions into the beautiful alpine countryside. The director of the health resort, Dr Dengener, invited the officers of the battalion to a drinks function, which was recorded for propaganda purposes. On 1 June 1943, the Finnish volunteers started on their return home. The Finnish Government then explained that it could not continue to provide replacement personnel for the battalion. Moreover, Marshal Mannerheim, Finnish commander-in-chief, himself made it quite clear that he did not wish the volunteers to re-enlist. Rather than employ a

Above: A Finnish SS recruit on the Eastern Front. The scruffy attire hides an experienced soldier. Many Finns were already proficient in winter warfare before they joined the SS, having served in the Finnish Army and fought the Russians in the Winter War.

force of considerably less strength than a battalion, therefore, the German authorities decided to put the best possible face on the matter. When the Finnish battalion reassembled, its members were informed that their unit had been disbanded. Its personnel were subsequently distributed among units of the Finnish Army.

While serving on the Eastern Front, 222 Finns were killed and a further 557 wounded. A few Finns continued in German uniform after the Finnish armistice of September 1944, but SS efforts to form a new Finnish volunteer regiment met with no success – only 5 Finnish officers and 60 other ranks volunteering.

Right: A Finnish SS-Scharführer of the Finnish Battalion of the 5th SS Panzer Division Wiking. This unit, until its recall by Helsinki, was one of the division's most effective. The Finns were skilled fighters, and their loss was greatly felt by the division.

Chapter 8

BRITISH VOLUNTEERS

The total number of British nationals who fought for Germany during World War II was derisory. In the grandly titled British Free Corps there were no more than 60 members, and very few saw any frontline service. Nevertheless, the unit was useful for propaganda purposes, and allowed the SS to claim that British troops were taking part in the campaign against Bolshevism. In truth, the British volunteers were more of a liability than an asset.

The number of British volunteers who fought for Germany during World War II was derisory. The main reason for this was that fascism was never a large-scale movement before the war, and was thus an ideology that was perceived as un-British. British prisoners of war (POWs) held in German camps during the war displayed zero enthusiasm for Hitler's crusade against Bolshevism, hence recruiting drives by the Germans fell on deaf ears.

The only fascist party of any real significance in Britain in the 1930s had been Oswald Mosley's Black Shirts, the British Union of Fascists (BUF). It was formed on 1 October 1932 and had 40,000 members at its height. In Germany, in contrast, the Nazi Party had eight million members, 1 in 10 of the population, at its height. As result of the German invasion of Western Europe in May 1940 and the "fifth column" threat, 800 members of the BUF and others on the fascist fringe of British politics were interned as security risks for varying lengths of time. This action, together with the proscription of the BUF in July 1940, effectively closed down British fascism.

Ironically, the first British citizens who ended up fighting with the Germans did so almost by accident, and via a very circuitous route. The British Communist Party at first approved of the war as an anti-fascist crusade, and

Left: Berry (left) and Minchen (centre), two members of the British Free Corps in SS uniform. Clearly visible is the Union Jack arm shield and unit cuffband.

Above: *The participants in a boxing match held in a British prisoner-of-war camp in Germany during the war. The individual sitting in the centre of the front row, with the cup between his legs, is Eric Pleasants, who became the British Free Corps' physical training instructor.*

then a few weeks later reversed its attitude on orders from Moscow. This only served to discredit the party, and its membership fell by a third. Actually, most British communists were against the war and took every opportunity to obstruct the war effort. There was a real fear within the government that an invasion could be aided by the communists, who were known to have political cells secreted throughout the country. The communist "threat" gave rise to a bizarre British decision. On 14 February 1940, the British Government announced that volunteers would be permitted to go from Britain to Finland to fight in the Finnish Army against the Red Army (the Winter War having broken out in November 1940). Sir John Anderson, the Home Secretary, answered a question tabled in the House of Commons by Mr D.N. Prill on the position of volunteers under the Foreign Enlistment Act 1870. This act had been resurrected when volunteers went to Spain at the time of the Spanish Civil War. Under the act, King George VI issued a decree permitting British subjects to take part in a conflict in another country if they wished to volunteer. It was this legislation that enabled men to go to Finland under a scheme organized by the Finnish Legation in London. They were to go as private citizens and be formally enlisted when they arrived in Finland. As the League of Nations resolution on the Russo-Finnish War made it clear that Russia was the aggressor, British help for Finland would thus not violate international law. Male applicants over the age of 27 were to be granted exit permits by the Foreign Office. It was stated: "In view of the Cabinet's decision, it is expected that the office in Westminster, near the Finnish Legation, which deals with those wishing to volunteer, will be kept very busy during the next few weeks." Some volunteers who went to Finland actually fought under German orders during the war.

In addition to these individuals, a small number of Britons were serving in various German units during the early part of World War II. These men enlisted individually and were not part of a specific recruitment campaign. In May 1940, for example, seven Britons were serving in the *Totenkopf* Division. Other Britons served in the *Leibstandarte* Division and the *Kurt Eggers* unit. Two Britons served as *Hiwis* (see Chapter 10) in the flak detachment of the *Leibstandarte* Division, both being awarded the Iron Cross, 2nd Class. Most of these individuals had left Briton before the war had started.

Amery's recruiting efforts

With Britain still undefeated after the fall of France, albeit isolated, there was clearly no way that British volunteers could be raised through indigenous fascist parties. However, following the end of the campaign in France in June 1940, there were around 150,000 British POWs in German hands. The idea that these POWs could be persuaded to fight in an anti-Bolshevik legion was formulated in the mind of a scion of a distinguished British political family. John Amery, a Conservative Party diehard, was the eldest son of Leo Amery, Churchill's Minister for India. Born on 14 March 1912, he was a pre-war Mayfair playboy who left Britain after becoming bankrupt. During the Spanish Civil War he had been a gun-runner for Franco, and had served as an intelligence officer with Italian volunteer forces. He had also met with Jacques Doriot, the French fascist leader. Between 1940 and 1942, he lived in Vichy France. Captain Werner, a German liaison officer, spoke with Amery in 1942 and forwarded a report through official channels about the Englishman's desire to speak on the radio and form a renegade legion. Shortly afterwards, the young man and his girlfriend Jeannine Barde left for Berlin via Paris, where they received identity documents from the German Embassy. At this time, the German Army was lukewarm about the idea, as it was opposed to the recruitment of prisoners. A change of heart occurred, though, when Hitler himself became interested in the notion. The Führer stated, however, that only British fascists should be recruited, along with those of a "similar" ideology. As a result, Amery undertook a recruiting tour of POW camps.

In his rhetoric he begged members of the audience to discard the idea that Britain favoured the continuance of the struggle between two brother nations. Amery claimed to be speaking on behalf of a committee in the motherland. Reasons of security prohibited any mention of actual names, but in order to unite the two countries within a Nordic block the committee had approved the foundation of a so-called Anti-Bolshevik League, which was the executive political board for a fighting force to be called the British Legion of Saint George. He embellished the fantasy by stating it was already 1500 strong and counted among its recruits not only ex-POWs and ex-internees but also sailors, soldiers and airmen. The latter, after hearing in England about the project, had flown to Europe by aeroplane or sailed in boats in order to do battle with Soviet Russia. British privates and noncommissioned officers (NCOs) were already training in field-grey uniforms with distinctive flashes at special barracks just outside Berlin under the orders of German officers. It was all lies and fooled nobody: Amery's recruiting tour yielded one volunteer.

Right: Thomas Hellor Cooper (left), the only Englishman to win a German combat award in World War II. He ended the war as leader of the British Free Corps. After the war he was tried by the British and sentenced to death for treason, which was commuted to life imprisonment.

Left: *Vivian Stranders, the Free Corps' liaison officer, one of the few members of the unit who was actually pro-Nazi. Most of the others were opportunists and criminals who were out to further their own ends. The Germans viewed them as propaganda pawns.*

commensurate with his abilities. He made numerous applications to join the police, only to be rejected (he was unsuitable due to his mother's birth). Embittered, he subsequently went to Britain for work and joined the BUF. In 1939, he sought the help of the German academic exchange organization in London and was eventually sent to Stuttgart. The RAD offered him a job teaching languages at a school in the Taunus Mountains, where he started work on 20 August. With the outbreak of war, he was dismissed from his post as an enemy alien, and had to report to the police and register. He was now alone and destitute. He managed to find work as a private tutor, though following a suggestion that he might join the German Army he was eventually presented to Gottlob Berger, head of Waffen-SS recruiting, who enrolled him in the SS.

The Germans decided to drop Amery thereafter but not the idea of a British volunteer corps. The propaganda campaign was therefore heightened and further recruiting drives were undertaken. A new recruit for the undertaking was found: SS-Unterscharführer Thomas Hellor Cooper.

Cooper was the son of a British soldier who had become a photographer and in 1908 started a business in Berlin, where he met and married a German girl, Anna Maria Simon. After World War I they returned to England, where Thomas was born. He was a solitary youth, much under the influence of his mother. Cooper was a bright pupil, but had to leave school after matriculation in 1936 as his parents could not afford to send him to university. Thereafter, he had difficulties in finding work

Right: *SS-Rottenführer Hundrupe of the British Free Corps. Clearly visible is the distinctive three heraldic "leopards passant guardant" worn on the right collar. His uniform is the 1944 field blouse based on British battledress, although in German field-grey.*

sent to the Russian Front due to the collapse of the Spanish Blue Division.

Once at the front, the unit was in heavy combat. In the face of a heavy barrage and onslaught by infantry and tanks, Cooper collected his unit together and withdrew. Having travelled only a few yards, he fell, his legs severely wounded by shrapnel. Cooper was awarded the Wound Badge in Silver – the only Englishman to receive a German combat decoration.

The second recruiting drive among British POWs raised 58 volunteers who were assembled at Hildesheim. Himmler's original name for the unit was the British Legion, though this was dropped when it was discovered that it was also the title of a British World War I veterans group. It was thus changed to British Free Corps. While recovering from his wounds, Cooper learnt of the fledgling unit and contacted his superiors. He seemed a

On 1 February 1940, he reported to the *Leibstandarte* for basic training (it is quite amazing that he should be accepted into Hitler's bodyguard unit). He found life difficult, and had disagreements with members of the formation. He was moved to a new unit of the SS-Totenkopfverbände based at Radolfzell where he repeated his basic training. In July 1940, Cooper was transferred to the 8th company of the 5th Totenkopf Infantry Regiment. He received temporary NCO rank and acted as an instructor. He remained with the regiment until 1941, holding the rank of SS-Rottenführer. He left the regiment to go to the SS NCO school at Lauenburg, undergoing a course until May 1941. He was moved yet again to the Wach Bataillon Oranienberg, and in January 1943 was moved from Debica with his unit, reaching Schablinov on 7 February. Three days later, the NCOs were called to a company briefing and were informed they were being

Right: *Eric Pleasants in his British Free Corps uniform. After the war he lived in Dresden entertaining occupying Russian troops, until he was arrested in early 1946 on suspicion of spying. He served seven years in a Russian prison camp before returning to the West a free man.*

Left: *An English NCO – Courlander – of the British Free Corps. An indication of the value placed on the unit by the Germans was that though its members were armed, they were not issued with ammunition. Felix Steiner, commander of Nordland, wanted nothing to do with them.*

collaboration between the two great Germanic peoples.

4) The British Free Corps will neither make war against Britain or the British Crown nor support any action or policy detrimental to the interests of the British people.

Despite the efforts of the SS, the "corps" only reached a strength of 60 men in the spring of 1944. The British Free Corps was sent to Dresden with the intention of training it as an assault engineer unit. During the morning of 4 September 1944, the corps, under the command of Captain Jupp, travelled to Dresden, collected personal and other effects and proceeded to the nearby barracks, where the captain lined up his men on the parade square and reported to the commandant the arrival of his unit. There stood SS-Unterscharführer Thomas Cooper, Sergeant Montgomery and NCOs Bartlet, Davies, Hundrupe and Milton, and privates Beckwith, Brown, Cameron, Clyde, Durin, Johnson, Jordan, Kingsley,

logical choice to aid its formation, and was thus ordered to join the project.

The ideological aims of the corps were expounded by one of its members, Frank Wood, a member of the BUF. His recruiting leaflet stated:

1) The British Free Corps is a thoroughly British volunteer unit, conceived and created by British subjects from all parts of the Empire who have taken up arms and pledged their lives in the common European struggle against Soviet Russia.

2) The British Free Corps condemns the war with Germany and the sacrifice of British blood in the interest of Jewry and International Finance and regards this conflict as a fundamental betrayal of the British people and British Imperial interests.

3) The British Free Corps desires the establishment of peace in Europe and the development of close friendly relations between England and Germany and the encouragement of mutual understanding and

Right: *John Leister was a friend of Eric Pleasants who joined the British Free Corps. At the end of the war, he escaped to Italy and surrendered to the Americans. He was handed over to the British, who tried him at the Old Bailey. He received three years' penal servitude.*

Right: *SS-Hauptsturmführer Hans Werner Roepke, the English-speaking German officer who commanded the British Free Corps between January and November 1944. The scar on his face and the ribbon of the Iron Cross indicates he saw much more combat than his charges.*

Nicholson, Owens, Reeves, Snell, Taylor, Thrush and Voysey. Other men perhaps present were Bryant, Giffard, Jackson, Walters and White. These numbers indicate that the unit had halved in size. The disillusioned members who dropped out were quietly returned to their former POW camps.

In welcoming the assembly, the commandant informed them that soldiers from many European nations were being trained there as pioneers and expressed his assurance that the new intake would soon acclimatize. Upon dismissal, the men were conducted to their new billets. Once there, the treasured picture of King Edward VIII was hung on the wall of their classroom. The unit must have been there for some time, for in the course of the infamous "fire storm" raid on the city in February 1945 the British Free Corps ironically suffered its first casualties when two of its members were killed. The British recruits underwent training but the Germans seemed at a loss about how to employ them. The small size of the unit meant it was militarily useless, and its propaganda value (if it ever had any) was zero at this late stage of the war.

The British Free Corps was sent to Berlin in February 1945 and then assigned to the *Nordland* Division in March. On 13 April, Cooper, the senior NCO in charge, went to the headquarters of the division to discuss the corps' duties with the commander, SS-Brigadeführer Ziegler. Cooper briefed Ziegler on the background to the corps, emphasizing that most of its members had been press-ganged into joining and that its combat value was dubious. Ziegler agreed, and Felix Steiner, the commander of II SS Panzer Corps, gave his formal consent to withdraw the British Free Corps from the frontline. Although withdrawn from a combat role, the corps still had tasks to do: driving trucks, directing traffic and helping with the evacuation of civilian refugees. On 29 April 1945, Steiner told his staff of his decision to break contact with the Russians and then ordered his forces to head west into Anglo-American captivity. The British Free Corps was duly captured and returned to Britain.

The first commander of the British Free Corps from the summer of 1943 until January 1944 was SS-Hauptsturmführer Johannes Roggenfeld of the *Wiking* Division and a decorated veteran of the Eastern Front. It is reported that he had lived in the United States before World War II and spoke fluent English. From January 1944

until November 1944, another English-speaking German officer, SS-Hauptsturmführer Hans Werner Roepke, commanded the corps. From November 1944 until February 1945, the leadership of the corps was in the hands of SS-Obersturmführer Dr Walter Kühlich, who was replaced in the last few weeks of the war by SS-Hauptsturmführer Dr Alexander Dolezalek.

Following their capture, the members of the corps faced the death penalty for treason or long prison sentences. In fact, most received minor punishments and some were only fined. The British authorities accepted that the majority had been coerced or fooled into joining the unit. They made an exception for Amery, who was hanged for treason in December 1945.

Chapter 9

THE INDIAN LEGION

The Indian Legion was one of the more unusual units raised by the Germans in World War II. Formed from prisoners of war captured in North Africa, its chief use was as a propaganda tool to be used against British rule in India. The Indian nationalist Chandra Bose had high hopes of the legion but, following German reverses in North Africa and southern Russia in 1942–43, the Germans had little use for it. Bizarrely, it ended the war as part of Himmler's Waffen-SS.

The Indian Legion must surely be among the strangest of all the non-German units in the German armed forces. As such, it has a unique place among the foreign volunteer formations of the Third Reich. The very presence of turban-wearing, brown-skinned men caused alarm among the racially indoctrinated German population in the early 1940s. Leo Bech, for example, who lived on Insel Reichenau on the Bodensee, reminisced years later that the one thing that stayed with him vividly from the war years was seeing this unit in his village.

Left: One of the volunteers for Germany's Indian regiment – probably not what Hitler had in mind when he talked about the Aryan master race.

Clearly, the Indians had no place in a future post-war Third Reich of a Germanic master race. However, as agitation for an end to British rule in India had existed for decades prior to the outbreak of World War II, it made sense for Nazi Germany to capitalize on anti-British sentiments by attempting to recruit a military force from disaffected Indian prisoners of war (POWs) captured while serving with British Commonwealth forces in the North African campaign.

The story of the Indian Legion, unsurprisingly, begins in India. The Free India movement, the *Azad Hind*, had grown out of the Indian Congress Party (a broad-based political party which dominated the Indian movement for independence) and against the will of its leader Mahatma Gandhi. Subhas Chandra Bose, an Indian revolutionary,

Above: *The Indian nationalist leader Subhas Chandra Bose. He was created head of the Provisional Government of India by the Japanese on 21 October 1943, but his Indian National Army was disbanded when the Allies overran Burma. Bose died in a plane crash in August 1945.*

was a Cambridge-educated lawyer; a one-time Mayor of Calcutta and at one point President of the Indian Congress Party, he was one of the most influential figures in the struggle for Indian independence. He saw himself as the Führer of India, and used the title *Netaji* (Respected Leader). Between 1933 and 1936, Bose had lived in Europe, spending much of his time in Italy and Germany, whose systems of government he came to admire and wished to use as models for a future administration in India. He had briefly visited Berlin in 1939 looking for support, then returned to India.

Because of his politics, Bose had been under house arrest at the start of the war. He escaped, despite British surveillance of his house in Calcutta, on 17 January 1941 and with the assistance of the Abwehr (Wehrmacht Military Intelligence) made his way to Peshawar on India's northwest frontier with Afghanistan. There, supporters of the Aga Khan helped him across the border into Afghanistan where he was met by an Abwehr unit posing as a party of road construction engineers from the

Organization Todt. The Germans aided his passage across Afghanistan via Kabul to the border with Soviet Russia. Once in Russia, the NKVD transported Bose to Moscow, where he hoped that Russia's traditional enmity to British rule in India would result in Soviet support for his plans for a popular uprising in India. However, Bose found the Soviets' response disappointing, and he was rapidly passed on to the German Ambassador in Moscow, Count von der Schulenberg. He had Bose flown on to Berlin in a special courier aircraft at the beginning of April 1941.

Bose admired Hitler, and was rather peeved when he found the Führer did not reciprocate the sentiment. His ego was further dented when he found out that few Germans outside the Foreign Ministry knew of him. Foreign Minister Ribbentrop received him, and he was subsequently introduced to Nazi Propaganda Minister Goebbels. The latter was conscious that Bose had some propaganda potential, and thus allocated him a personal allowance, car and residence.

Almost immediately, Bose commenced broadcasting for the Germans from the *Azad Hind* transmitter at Nauen. No objections were raised when he set up a Free Indian Centre in Berlin. Hitler granted him an audience where issues were discussed and gifts exchanged, Bose receiving a silver cigarette case. Nothing concrete was to materialize from the meeting, though, i.e. no recognition

prisoner by Rommel's Deutsche Afrika Korps at Mechili in Cyrenaica (Libya).

The Italians attempted, unsuccessfully, to exploit anti-colonial feelings among these POWs and raise a *Battaglione Hazad Hindoustan* (Free Indian Battalion) themselves. The project had to be abandoned when the Indians refused to serve under Italian officers. The Germans now ventured down the same road and proved more successful. On 15 May, a Luftwaffe major was sent to interview English-speaking members of the prisoners with a view to recruiting men for a proposed German Army unit made up of Indian troops. The Germans were helped in their efforts by the self-appointed "President" Subhas Chandra Bose, whose name was well known among the captives, if not to the Germans themselves. This initial approach led to 27 officers being flown to Berlin four days later, together with the establishment of a special camp for about 10,000 Indian POWs at Annabert in Saxony.

that the Free Indian Centre would be accorded the status of a provisional government. Yet Bose, who now styled himself "President of the Provisional Government of India", was convinced that his credentials had at least been tacitly acknowledged by Hitler.

The Free Indian Centre produced a number of stamps, and also banknotes for the INA (Indian National Army – see below). Bose also instituted an *Azad Hind* decoration in 1942 in four grades, each of which could be awarded with or without swords in the German fashion. Both Indian and German members of the legion were eligible to receive the decoration (almost half of the Indian Legion's members received one or more of these awards). The Order of *Azad Hind* Grand Star in four classes comprised the *Sher–e–Hind* (Tiger of India) 1st Class Star; *Sardar–e–Jang* (Leader of Battle) 2nd Class Star; *Vir–e–Hind* (Hero of India) Medal; and *Shahid–e–Bharat* (Martyr of the Fatherland).

Chandra Bose was permitted to promote the idea that the freedom of India would be achieved through a German military victory. The self-appointed "President" repeated this message on tours of POW camps where Indians who had been captured in North Africa were held. Bose was handed a golden opportunity almost immediately when, in April 1941, most of the members of the British 3rd (Indian) Motorised Brigade were taken

Right: *One of the awards instituted by Bose in Germany. This is the Azad Hind "Tiger of India" Grand Star with Swords. It was instituted in 1942 by Bose, and was awarded to both German and Indian personnel for their valour on the battlefield.*

Above: *Bose addresses members of his legion in Germany in 1942. The Indians were officially incorporated into the German Army in September of that year, becoming the 950th Infantry Regiment (Indian) and having a strength of 2593 men in three battalions.*

Below: *Two members of the Indian regiment practise fighting with the staff, or Bo, a traditional Eastern weapon. Such training perhaps indicates that the Germans had little intention of considering the Indians as a frontline combat unit.*

Right: *A section of Indians in German Army uniforms. Their breeches narrow below the knee to button tightly around the calves and are tucked into high lace-up boots. Apart from the Sikhs, the men are sporting standard-issue peaked field caps.*

Bose visited the camp where he made an impassioned appeal to the Indian prisoners for them to enlist in the proposed unit, variously referred to as the Indian Legion, *Azad Hind* Legion or the more exotically sounding Tiger Legion. The first group of volunteers, recruited both from POWs and Indian civilians resident in Germany, left Berlin's Anhalter railway station on Christmas Day 1941 for a camp at Frankenburg, near Chemnitz, in order to receive future groups of released Indian POWs. Despite the recruitment of only eight committed volunteers, in January 1942 the German Propaganda Ministry felt able to announce the establishment of the rather grandly titled Indian National Army or *Jai Hind*.

Training and uniforms

Further efforts by Bose produced some 6000 volunteers, who were segregated from the others and moved to Frankenburg where they were formed into an arbeitskommando (work commando). However, only 300 of these were selected to form the nucleus of the new army. These were transferred to a special training camp at Koenigsbrueck, near Dresden, where they were kitted out in German Army field-grey uniforms. The recruits received training in a mixture of English, German and Hindi, but it was Bose's wish that Hindi should be the language of command, to which end a 228-page command and recognition book was printed. However, because English was the language that both instructors and trainees had in common, it became common usage in the unit. Interpreters came from a variety of backgrounds. Sonderführer Frank Chetwynd Becker, for example, was born in England to an English mother and a British-naturalized but German-born father. He was posted to the Indian Legion in July 1942.

Difficulties with communication and German insensitivity in dealing with people whose culture and customs they were largely ignorant of led to the legion suffering from poor discipline throughout its existence. Indeed, in one instance it led to the shooting, by one of his own men, of the Indian Legion's most enthusiastic member, Unteroffizier Mohammed Ibrahim.

On 26 August 1942, the volunteers undertook an oath of allegiance to Adolf Hitler. The Germans never succeeded in fully standardizing the dress of the legion. Some members wore their former British uniforms. However, this could have been until such time as they were issued with standard army field-grey uniforms. In practice, German tropical uniforms in various shades of khaki were worn. The standard Hoheitszeichen (eagle and swastika badge) of the army was worn by all personnel above the right breast pocket. As a sign of recognition, a cloth badge depicting a springing tiger over the Indian national colours, headed by the German words *Freies Indien* (Free India), was sewn on to the right upper arm. As with the many other German badges, it could be either printed or machine-woven.

Headgear proved a problem. Sikhs, by their religion, are not permitted to cut their hair or to remove their turbans. The turban itself was, from photographic evidence, khaki, but as a sign of caste it could be black, white, orange, green, dark red, light red or violet. The German authorities respected these religious requirements. Where a turban was not obligatory, the Indians and the German cadre wore the tropical soft peak cap – a lightweight brown version of the Bergmuetze – though volunteers were also seen wearing the forage cap. The steel helmet had the German colours of red, white and black on the right, and on the left the Indian colours of green, white and orange.

The regimental flag comprised an upper quarter of orange with the word "AZAD" in white, a lower quarter of green with the word "HIND" in white, and a centre of half-white with a springing tiger coloured as per the arm badge. The flag was fringed in silver. It is interesting to note that at the ceremony of swearing-in and presentation of the colours in 1942, there was a contingent of high-ranking Japanese officers present – no doubt in recognition of Bose being commander of the

Japanese-raised Indian National Army (INA). The INA was formed by the Japanese from Indian POWs taken after the fall of Singapore in February 1942. It was commanded by a former Indian officer, Mohan Singh, and numbered 45,000 men. The Japanese then arrested Sing for complaining about their lack of commitment, and handed over command of the INA to Bose.

Conditions for an intensive recruiting drive of Indians at this time could not have been better. In Russia, the German summer offensive continued to gain ground, and the Grand Mufti of Jerusalem was in Germany. Amin al-Husseini had been imprisoned by the British for inciting an attack against Jews in Jerusalem in 1920. The first Palestine High Commissioner, Sir Herbert Samuel, had granted him a full pardon in 1921, and appointed him Mufti of Jerusalem. But Amin immediately took the title "Grand Mufti" and then instigated a programme of insurrection against the British and incited his Moslem followers to massacre Jews. The British were eventually forced to issue an order for the Grand Mufti's arrest, whereupon he escaped to Syria disguised as a beggar. He then established cordial relations with Mussolini and Hitler. In 1941, he met with Mussolini and offered to lead

Above: The Indians are presented with their colours at the swearing-in ceremony in 1942. A number of high-ranking Japanese officers were present at the occasion, no doubt reflecting Bose's status as head of the Japanese-raised Indian National Army.

another anti-Semitic revolt in Palestine if the fascists would subsidize him. From Italy he went to Germany and conferred with Hitler. The Grand Mufti's championing of Hitler's cause was to convince many Moslems not only in India but also in the Balkans that the Nazi cause was honourable and to the betterment of the Islamic world. SS chief Himmler was very enthusiastic about harnessing the zeal of the Moslems, seeing their hatred of the Jews as being compatible with his racial ideology (see Chapter 9 for foreign volunteer units in the Balkans). Indeed, he began forming a Moslem SS division. Thus, in late 1943, Indian Moslems were also considered for recruitment into the 13th SS Freiwilligen Gebirgs Division *Handschar*, which was recruited chiefly from Bosnian Moslems. However, SS-Obergruppenführer Gottlob Berger, chief of SS recruitment, pointed out to Himmler in November 1943 that the Indian Moslems "perceive themselves primarily as Indians, the Bosnians as Europeans". The idea of integrating Indians into the division was therefore dropped.

Hitler did not know how to employ Bose, so the Führer decided to send him by submarine to Japan. Through the Japanese ambassador in Berlin, General Oshima, Bose was named as leader of a Japanese-sponsored Indian government-in-exile. He departed Germany on 8 February 1943, leaving behind a German wife and a five-month-old daughter. The submarine *U–180* commanded by Fregattenkapitän Musenberg took him, his adjutant Dr Habib Hassan and two officers of the Indian Legion from Kiel to a rendezvous near Madagascar in the Indian Ocean, where he was transferred to the Japanese submarine *I–29*. By 6 May, he was in Sumatra.

Singapore at this time was under Japanese control, where Bose found the INA. Subsequently, he travelled to Tokyo for talks with the Japanese Government. In the wake of these successful negotiations, he returned to his Japanese-provided residence in Singapore where his aides

Below: In early 1943 the legion's officer corps and best men were shipped off to Singapore to join up with Bose and his INA. The operation involved the use of four specially prepared blockade runners. This photograph was taken just before their departure from Germany.

had assembled other like-minded Indians to form the "Provisional Government of Free India". Bose, commander of the European and Asian wings of the organization, recruited troops from among POWs held in Japanese hands and raised an additional three regiments. The INA, he declared, would fight beside the Japanese in Burma, from where they would invade India and liberate it from British rule. The INA went into India with the Japanese and got to Imphal in March 1944. It subsequently suffered terrible losses and had to retreat.

On the German home front, armed with propaganda films of the swearing-in of the Indians, the Nazis instigated a more aggressive recruiting programme, which resulted in a larger number of volunteers coming forward. Indeed, Indians from South Africa were transported to German-occupied areas by the ultra right-wing South African Purified National Party for the purposes of volunteering.

The Abwehr had envisaged the Indian Legion being part of an Axis campaign that would advance into India via the Caucasus through Iran to end British rule. By the end of August 1941, the Abwehr had instituted a plan shared with Bose that included parachute landings in India by the Indian Legion to start an anti-British revolt. To this end, some Indians were recruited into the Special Purpose Construction Training Division Brandenburg and quartered at a training camp near Meseritz.

In preparation for the anticipated Indian national revolt, Operation Bajadere was launched in January 1942: 100 Indians were parachuted into eastern Persia with the aim of infiltrating Baluchistan to reach India, and thereafter to commence sabotage operations against the British. Unfortunately for Bose, an attack into India by the European Axis powers appeared increasingly unlikely following the reverses at Stalingrad and El Alamein in late 1942.

However, in the Far East the seemingly unstoppable Japanese Army was master of Burma and stood poised to devour India. With Bose's departure for Singapore and success with the Japanese Imperial Government, the German Foreign Ministry entered discussions with the Abwehr to move the Indian Legion's leadership to the Far East. Together with the operations staff of the Brandenburg Division and the German Naval High Command, Department II of the Abwehr organized the plan which required the use of four blockade-runners to transport the officer corps and best men of the legion to

Below: A group of Indians in Germany prior to their posting to the Netherlands. Some of the men are wearing the arm shield depicting a springing tiger over the Indian national colours, headed by the words "Free India" in German, on their upper right arms.

Singapore. The proposed operation was extremely audacious considering Allied naval power. Careful planning was required, resulting in one blockade-runner being converted to resemble a neutral Swedish iron ore carrier, the *Brand III*. It was crewed by Swedish-speaking Brandenburgers and some Indians with experience as seamen. A specially constructed space at the bottom of the hold concealed the majority of the Indians. This was covered with iron ore to give the impression of a full hold when viewed from above.

Leaving Germany the *Brand III* travelled to Malmö in Sweden, refuelled and took on cargo. The "neutral" vessel then sailed through the English Channel to Gibraltar where she was stopped and her cargo manifest examined. Verification checks by the British authorities showed everything to be in order. The *Brand III* steamed through the Suez Canal and into the Indian Ocean. In the Bay of Bengal she was inspected again, this time by US warships. Having survived this inspection, she steamed just west of the Sunda Strait to rendezvous with a Japanese cruiser, which escorted her to Singapore. A second blockade-runner fared less well, taking the longer sea route around the Cape of Good Hope. She was intercepted at dusk just west of the Cape by British warships, whereupon the captain decided to generate a smokescreen and make a run for it at top speed into the gathering darkness. In

order to avoid the inevitable search, the blockade-runner was forced to make course for the far southern latitudes and was not heard of again. The fate of the other two blockade-runners is also unknown.

In September 1942, the Indians were officially incorporated into the German Army as the 950th Infantry Regiment (Indian). All of its officers and most seniors NCOs were German. It eventually reached a strength of 2593 men and was formed into three battalions, each of which consisted of four companies. With further recruiting, its strength increased to more than 3000, and by October 1943 the first Indians had been granted officer rank. One interesting aspect of the religious breakdown of the unit was that only 516 were Sikhs (the traditional Indian warrior caste, perhaps they were less willing than others to renounce their allegiance to the British King-Emperor). The rest comprised two-thirds Moslem and one-third Hindu. The unit was partially motorized, being equipped with 81 motor vehicles and 700 horses, and was later referred to as Panzergrenadier Regiment 950 (Indische) to reflect this.

In April 1943, the regiment was posted to the Zeeland area of the Netherlands for garrison duties, where it came under the command of the 16th Luftwaffe Field Division. It remained there as part of the Atlantic Wall garrison until September of that year. Despite being a quiet duty, 47 of the Indians refused the posting and were quietly returned to their POW camps. Had the deteriorating fortunes of war for the Axis powers or the seeming loss of Indian independence with Bose's departure made them change their minds? During the winter of 1942–43, the

Above: Garrison duty on the Atlantic Wall in the Netherlands, spring 1943. By this time many Indians were feeling disillusioned. They had lost Bose and there seemed little hope that they would return to India, at least not as part of the German Army.

German Army had suffered disaster at Stalingrad, in North Africa the British had won a victory at El Alamein and "President" Bose, had, inexplicably, disappeared from the scene.

Legionskommandeur Oberstleutnant Kurt Krappe, who had been in the German Colonial Service, arrived in the Netherlands on 13 April 1943 in order to prepare for the transfer of the Indian Legion from Königsbrück. The 1st Battalion arrived at Truppenübungsplatz (Military Training Ground) Beverloo in Belgium on 30 April, and was followed by the 2nd Battalion from 1–3 May. The 3rd Battalion left Germany somewhat later and arrived at Truppenübungsplatz Oldebroek on the night of 13/14 July together with the regimental support companies numbered 13, 14 and 15. However, the 12th Infantry Company was left behind in Germany as a replacement unit. On 5 May, the 1st and 2nd Battalions were inspected at Beverloo by General der Infanterie Hans Reinhard, General Officer Commanding LXXXVIII Army Corps and Commander of the Army Troops in the Netherlands, who later remarked that the Indian troops should not be stationed in the Netherlands beyond the end of October because the cold climate on the North Sea coast would be detrimental to their health. Thus, on 17 September 1943, the regimental headquarters left Haarlem and

Left: *Four members of the Indian Legion manning a 28mm PzB 41 anti-tank gun. This photograph was probably taken in the winter of 1944–45. If so, the legion had become part of the Waffen-SS, which had assumed control of all non-German volunteer units.*

redeployed to St André de Cubzac in southwest France. This was the beginning of the legion's redeployment to the southwest of France, which had been completed by April 1944. During that month, it was tasked with coastal defence duties in the area of Lacanau, near Bordeaux, where it was inspected by Feldmarschall Rommel.

In the autumn of 1944, Hitler placed Himmler in charge of the Replacement Army. The SS now assumed command of all non-German volunteer formations. Thus, on 8 August 1944 at Heuberg, the Indians became the Indische Legion der Waffen-SS. It received a new commanding officer: SS-Oberführer Heinz Bertling. The transfer of non-German units to SS command was often a paper exercise only, and though a special tiger's head collar patch was designed for the SS Indian Legion doubts have been raised as to whether it was ever worn, or even manufactured (one Waffen-SS officer's tunic with the tiger's head collar patch with twin runes worn below the breast pocket exists, though it might be of modern

Below: *Two members of the Indian Legion relax in camp. Hitler was scathing about their combat value, remarking towards the end of the war: "I imagine that if one were to use the Indians to turn prayer wheels they would be the most indefatigable soldiers in the world."*

manufacture). German SS personnel entitled to wear the runes on the collar wore them instead in this manner when the runic patch was replaced by an "ethnic" one. Oberleutnant Rolf Schackert of the legion, who became SS-Obersturmführer, was photographed wearing the arm shield and with the right collar patch blank, providing further proof. In reality, it was the German officers who wore SS uniforms and insignia – none of the Indian personnel did.

On 6 June 1944, the long-anticipated Allied invasion took place in Normandy. The legion remained at Lacanau for more than two months, but following the Allied breakout from the Normandy bridgehead and with the growing threat of Allied landings on the Mediterranean coast of France, it was at risk of being cut off. Thus, on 15 August 1944 (the same day that Allied landings took place on the French Riviera), the legion left Lacanau to move back to Germany. The French resistance was not prepared to allow the withdrawal to proceed unhindered, though. The first part of their journey was by rail to Poitiers where they were attacked by French FFI (*Forces Françaises de l'Interieur*) units, resulting in a number of Indian wounded. The French resistance continued to harass the legion when, at the end of August, it moved again to Allier via Chatrou, this time moving by road. The legion reached the town of Dun on the Berry Canal by the beginning of September where it came up against French regular forces. In the resulting street fighting, the Indian Legion suffered its first combat death: Leutnant Ali Khan, who was later interred with full military honours at Sancoin cemetery.

The legion continued its withdrawal through Luzy, marching at night, but suffered more casualties in ambushes including Unteroffizier Kalu Ram and Gefreiter Mela Ram. The River Loire was crossed and the Indians headed for Dijon. In the course of the transfer to Dijon, some 40 members of the legion were killed, while another 250 either surrendered or defected. After a rest of several days, the Indians continued on to Remisemont then to Oberhofen near the garrison town of Hagenau in Germany. During Christmas 1944, the legion was billeted in the private houses of German civilians before moving in bitterly cold weather to the vacant Truppenübungsplatz at Heuberg. One company is said to have been transferred to Italy, but this remains unverified.

By this stage of the war, the Indian Legion was just another foreign volunteer unit in the rapidly shrinking German order of battle. Its propaganda value had long since vanished, and Nazi racial prejudices meant it was abandoned. The Germans always had a very low opinion of the fighting qualities of the Indian Legion. Hitler is reputed to have commented: "The Indian Legion is a joke. There are Indians that can't kill a louse, and would prefer

Above: *SS-Obersturmführer Rolf Schackert of the Indian Legion. Just visible is the legion's arm shield on his right arm in the bottom left-hand corner of the photograph. In addition, his right collar patch is blank. Only the German officers of the legion wore SS uniforms.*

to allow themselves to be devoured. They certainly aren't going to kill any Englishmen ... it would be ridiculous to commit them to a real blood struggle." Nevertheless, the Indians still had a number of weapons. An official report of 25 March 1945 quotes its strength as 2300 men and its equipment as: 1468 rifles, 550 pistols, 420 submachine guns, 200 light machine guns, 24 heavy machine guns, 20 medium mortars, 4 light field howitzers, 6 infantry howitzers, 6 anti-tank guns, 700 horses, 61 cars, 81 other vehicles and 5 motorcycles. Hitler ordered the weapons to be handed over to the 18th SS Volunteer Panzergrenadier Division *Horst Wessel*.

The Indian Legion remained at Heuberg until the end of March 1945, when it was transferred to Radolfzell on the shores of the Bodensee on the Swiss border. The Indian SS men then happily turned themselves over to the US Army and French forces in April 1945. Before their delivery into the custody of British forces, it is alleged that a number of Indian soldiers were shot by French troops. The survivors were repatriated to India at the end of 1945, held in captivity but finally released in 1946.

Chapter 10

RUSSIAN NATIONALS

It is truly ironic that the most numerous units of foreign nationals raised by the Germans during World War II came from among the "sub-human" Slavs of the Soviet Union. Faced with waging war in a country of vast distances and infested with enemy partisans, the Germans had no choice but to recruit Russians to ease the strain on their own manpower. Even the "Aryan élite", the Waffen-SS, raised Russian formations.

It is impossible in one chapter to present a detailed analysis of all the Russian nationals who served with the German armed forces in World War II. Instead, a general summary of the main units raised by the Germans from the different ethnic groups in the Soviet Union will be presented.

Before analyzing the Russian nationals who served the Third Reich, it is important to stress the unique nature of the Nazi war in Russia. It was, above all, an ideological conflict, and was waged in varying degrees as such by the German Army, Waffen-SS and the Nazi administrators in

Left: *A Cossack serving with the Wehrmacht in the 1st Cossack Division, photographed with his balalaika during operations against Yugoslav partisans.*

the occupied territories. If Western Europe was viewed by Berlin as being populated mainly by Aryans, the peoples of Russia were seen largely as "sub-human" Slavs. Himmler and his cronies may have singled out some ethnic groups, such as the Latvians, as being "racially acceptable", but even in Latvia the Germans treated the local population atrociously.

On the eve of the campaign in Russia, Hitler informed his commanders: "We must depart from the attitude of soldierly comradeship ... we are talking about a war of annihilation ... commissars and members of the GPU [secret police] are criminals and must be dealt with as such." Just before the attack in June 1941, he signed the Commissar Order instructing his generals to have captured commissars shot forthwith. To carry out these instructions, four SS Einsatzgruppen (Special Action

Left: *Russian prisoners during Operation Barbarossa, the German attack on the Soviet Union in June 1941. By October, the Germans had two million prisoners, and Wehrmacht commanders were determined to make use of them to relieve demands on their own manpower.*

Squads), composed of SS, criminal police and security police, operated behind the German lines. Although Reinhard Heydrich, chief of the Einsatzgruppen, specified to the higher SS and police officers in charge of captured Russian territory that only "Jews in the service of party and State" were to be shot, it seems very likely that the action squads were encouraged to execute all the Jews they could lay their hands on – which is exactly what happened.

Nazi racial publications stressed the ideological nature of the war in the East: "The most dangerous opponent of our worldview at present is Marxism, and its offspring Bolshevism. It is a product of the destructive Jewish spirit, and it is primarily Jews who have transformed this destructive idea into reality. Marxism teaches that there are only two classes: the owners and the propertyless. Each must be destroyed and all differences between people must be abolished; a single human soup must result. That which formerly was holy is held in contempt. Every connection to family, clan and people was dissolved. Marxism appeals to humanity's basest drives; it is an appeal to sub-humans.

"We have seen first-hand where Marxism leads people, in Germany from 1919 to 1932, in Spain and above all in Russia. The people corrupted by liberalism are not able to defend themselves against this Jewish-Marxist poison. If Adolf Hitler had not won the battle for the soul of his people and destroyed Marxism, Europe would have sunk into Bolshevist chaos. The war in the East will lead to the final elimination of Bolshevism; the victory of the National Socialist worldview is the victory of Aryan culture over the spirit of destruction, the victory of life over death." (Official Nazi pamphlet outlining racial theories, Berlin 1943.)

Hitler and his General Staff anticipated that the Blitzkrieg against Russia would last a maximum of 10 weeks, during which time the Red Army would be smashed. Afterwards, the defeated Soviet Union would be organized into a series of provinces. As part of the Lebensraum policy, the conquered population would be resettled, Germanized or exterminated.

Against this background, it was inconceivable to Hitler and the Nazi hierarchy that the Wehrmacht should raise foreign volunteer units from among "sub-human" Slavs. As the German Army groups rolled east following the invasion of 22 June 1941, it appeared that the war would indeed be over quickly. But then the offensive ran out of steam at the end of November, and the Wehrmacht was faced with at least another year of fighting in Russia. In the face of military necessity, therefore, the Germans were forced to enlist the assistance of indigenous Slavs in their fight against the Soviet Union.

The first Russian units

The first volunteer units raised in Russia were created in the autumn of 1941 by individual German Army commanders. On their own initiative, they organized auxiliary units made up of Soviet deserters, prisoners (the Germans had taken two million prisoners by mid-October 1941) and volunteers from the local population. The German Army greatly underestimated the number of prisoners it would take. As a result, many prisoners of war (POWs) ended up dying of disease or starvation in overcrowded POW camps. This was a huge waste of potential manpower, especially given the dissatisfaction towards Moscow among many non-Russian ethnic minorities. The so-called *Hilfswilligen* (volunteer helpers), or *Hiwis*, were employed as sentries, drivers, store keepers, depot workers and so on. Hundreds of *Hiwis* also carried out combat roles. In July 1941, for example, the 134th Infantry Division began openly enlisting Russians. By the spring of 1942, there were 200,000 *Hiwis* in the rear of the German armies, and by the end of the same year their number was allegedly one million.

The reasons for this rapid expansion are not hard to find: German Army commanders realized that because of the wide expanses under their control and the general shortage of German manpower, they would have to resort to local recruits. *Hiwis* served either as individuals or as members of a group (up to company size) attached

Above: *Potential Hiwi recruits. To thousands of Russian prisoners, service with the invader, which meant pay and rations, was preferable to rotting in a prison camp. What is interesting with regard to the prisoners taken during Barbarossa was their lack of any allegiance to Stalin.*

Right: *SS-Obergruppenführer Reinhard Heydrich was the ultimate Nazi racial warrior, and viewed the Russians as akin to slaves. He commanded the Eisatzgruppen during Operation Barbarossa, and these roving death squads killed more than 630,000 Jews in Russia up to 1943.*

to German units, mainly in the rear. The *Hiwi* experiment, undertaken without the authorization of either Hitler or the High Command, was a success, and so the Germans gradually expanded the range of jobs *Hiwis* carried out, their conditions of service were formalized, they were given German uniforms, and their food rations and pay almost achieved parity with those of German soldiers.

The next step taken by the Germans was the organization of voluntary military troops, called *Osttruppen*. These troops, dressed in German uniforms, guarded roads and railway lines, fought Soviet partisans in the German rear (Nazi brutality towards the local population had created high partisan activity behind the German frontline, which army commanders did not have the manpower to deal with) and occasionally held sectors of the front. *Osttruppen* were usually organized in

Above: *A cuffband of an SS Turkistani unit. The so-called Eastern Legions were raised by the Germans from late 1941 in response to an appeal from General Erkilet of the Turkish General Staff to raise units from Red Army prisoners of Turkic origin.*

battalions, and by the middle of 1942 there were six such battalions in the rear of Army Group Centre alone. Each battalion was drawn from a single ethnic group, with liaison and certain command positions being occupied by German officers and noncommissioned officers (NCOs). Each battalion numbered around 750 men, with recruits being drawn from POW camps, recently captured prisoners, conscription by the Germans and men already serving as *Hiwis*.

What was the motivation of *Hiwis* and *Osttruppen*? Decades of inhumane social, ethnic and religious policies had alienated huge groups of the Soviet population. If in central Russia the state through terror had annihilated or kept under tight check any opposition, in the recently "liberated" Baltic republics, the Ukraine, Belorussia and Bessarabia the harshness of the Soviet regime was still fresh in the memory. Brief acquaintance with the gulag system, NKVD and collectivization in agriculture had shown the true nature of Stalin's regime. As a result, ethnic minorities in the Soviet Union were more than happy to be liberated and even join the fight against Bolshevism. However, it is doubtful that there was a substantial number of pro-Hitler supporters among these peoples. Some were pure opportunists, criminals and adventurers who did not care which side they fought on. Many secretly hated Stalin for collectivization, labour camps and the reign of terror, while others were disillusioned with the Soviet system after the initial collapse of the Red Army. The majority, however, simply did not want to rot in German POW camps. Others, of course, wanted to win independence

Right: *One of the recruiting leaflets posted by the Germans in the Ukraine. They yielded sizeable numbers of deserters from the Red Army, to the great surprise of the Germans. Today, such items are rare due to the Russians using them as toilet paper during the war!*

for their own homelands, i.e. to be free of both German and Russian rule.

As well as German-organized units, there were other more ad hoc formations that were briefly independent before the Germans took them over. The most infamous of these was the Kaminski Brigade. This was a locally raised militia group whose members gathered on the verges of the Bryansk Forest in the small Belorussian town of Lokot in late 1941 to protect themselves from Russian partisans. It was commanded by Bronislav Vladislavovich Kaminski, who spoke fluent German and had spent five years in the gulag for being an "intellectual". By mid-1943, with the encouragement of

До Української Молоді
округи Бережани!

Надійшла довгоожидана хвилина, в котрій патріотична і сміла молодь з оружжям в руці може розправитися з нашим найбільшим ворогом, большевизмом. В кого бадьоре серце, хто знає геройські подвиги Козаччини, хто дорожить світлими споминами Січових Стрільців, хто з пошаною переживає спомини Галицької Армії 1918-1920 рр., кому дорогі чини юнацтва під Крутами і Базарем, — той має нині можність вступити в ряди СС Стрілецької Дівізії - Галичина.

Юнаки! Усі найкращі з вас, маєте нагоду на вістрях багнетів широко рознести добру славу українського народу, взяти в руки його судьбу, заговорити гуком гармати про його будучину. Одним словом, можете юнаки бути тим, чим ви повинні бути і чим ви є як наслідники наших великих предків, - будучою силою народу.

Наші вороги пускають різні поголоски, щоби до того недопускати і вас зневірити. Може знайдуться часом і між вами лежні, що люблять лише теплий запічок, боягузи і труси, котрі будуть вам відраджувати вступати в ряди СС Стрілецької Дівізії Галичина. Тямте, що перші роблять це на те, щоби за вас ніхто не знав і не чув, та щоби ми попали в непамять в отсих бурхливих часах.

Другі будуть робити це на те, щоби покрити і оправдати свою трусливість, а в дійсності на те, щоби таких, як вони було більше та щоби і на правдивих юнаків, а не тільки на них, могли люди показувати пальцем, що це труси й боягузи. Уся ідейна молодь, якого б напрямку вона не була, розуміє, що творення СС Стрілецької Дівізії Галичина є зворотною точкою в нашому збірному житті і згідно з тим ставиться до цієї справи прихильно.

Усі великі діла починаються малими чинами. Січові Стрільці починали свою курінем (баталіоном), а дійшли до Галицької Армії. Творення великого лежить у ваших руках, тому всі вписуйтеся в ряди добровольців до СС Стрілецької Дівізії Галичина.

Український Окружний Комітет.

the Germans, his brigade numbered 10,000 men in 14 rifle battalions, an anti-aircraft battery and support companies. Each battalion consisted of four rifle companies, plus mortar and artillery platoons. It also had an armoured element which had eight tanks (a KV-1, two T-34s, three BT-7s, two BT-5s), three armoured troop carriers (a BA-10, two BA-20s), two tankettes and cars and motorcycles. Kaminski called himself the "Warlord of the Bryansk Forest" and was given a free hand to clear partisans from the area. He called his force the *Russkaya Ovsoboditelnaya Narodnaya Armija* (RONA – Russian Army of National Liberation). The RONA enforced security during harvesting, escorted special food trains, guarded railways and mounted "punitive" operations in partisan zones.

By the end of August 1943, the situation in the Lokot district was deteriorating so Kaminski evacuated the RONA and its civilians to the town of Lepel in the Vitebsk region. The mission of the brigade in Belorussia was to guard the rear of the Third Panzer Army. In addition, because of high partisan activity at the beginning of 1944, the RONA was moved to the town of Djatlovo in western Belorussia.

Below: Members of the Kaminski Brigade during the 1944 Warsaw uprising. The behaviour of Kaminski's troops was appalling as they went on an orgy of death and destruction. They killed anyone who got in their way, including Germans. Kaminski was later shot by the SS.

In spring 1944, the Germans conducted some anti-partisan operations in the region between Minsk and Lepel. The RONA took part in these missions as part of a group headed by SS-Obergruppenführer Gottberg, and had the status of assault brigade. By this time, it had been officially accepted into the Waffen-SS as SS-Sturmbrigade RONA, and Kaminski was made a Waffen-Brigadeführer. The brigade acted with great ruthlessness, and Kaminski was decorated with the Iron Cross, 1st class, for his efforts. In July 1944, the brigade became the 29th SS Waffen Grenadier Division (Russische Nr 1).

At this juncture, it would be useful to say something about anti-partisan operations as many Russian units in German pay undertook these unpleasant missions. On the Eastern Front, the area from the frontline towards the rear up to a depth of 160km (100 miles) was under German Army control. Then came the Reich Commissariats, which were under the control of the SS. Units were under SS or army control depending on the areas in which they were operating. At first, partisan activity in German-occupied areas was light, but due to Nazi excesses, by mid-1942 it had grown enormously. There were no military or political guidelines for the German occupying forces on the treatment of civilians in partisan-infested country. This meant many innocent civilians were arrested and shot merely on suspicion of being partisans.

Regions that contained partisans would first be cordoned off, and then the area would be de-populated

Above: *A Georgian recruit in the German Army in September 1944. By this time, there were more than 20,000 Georgians serving with the army. Georgians were organized into either battalions or companies, and were scattered throughout the various armies in the East.*

Kottbus, for example, conducted between mid-May and 21 June 1943, an attempt was made to seal off the partisan-infested area between Borissow and Lepe. It involved 16,000 German soldiers and Russian allies. The result was a total failure, with only 950 enemy small arms taken but 12,000 civilians killed.

In August 1944, two battalions of RONA volunteers, headed by SS-Obersturmbannführer Fromov, were despatched to Warsaw to help crush the Polish uprising. They were sent to the district of Wola and committed so many atrocities, including the rape of German girls, that there were widespread demands (even from some SS commanders) for their withdrawal. It was reported that in one day alone – 5 August 1944 – they murdered 10,000 Polish civilians. Kaminski was later shot by the SS, being tricked by the Germans to leave his men and his death made to look like a motoring accident. The division was disbanded, with the personnel being sent to Vlassov's army (see p134) and others to the 30th SS Division. The less desirable elements of the division were either sent to concentration camps or shot. The 29th Division was dropped from the rolls of the Waffen-SS, and the title given to the new Italian division that was being formed.

The RNNA

Alongside the RONA was the *Russkaya Natsionalnaya Narodnaya Armiya* (RNNA – Russian Nationalist National Army) led by a "White" Russian émigré called S. N. Ivanov. The unit was formed at Ossintorf near the Orsha-Smolensk rail line. It was organized along Russian lines, being equipped entirely with captured Soviet arms. Its personnel wore Red Army uniforms with tsarist-type white, blue and red cockades. The unit's Russian members, along with many other Russian units in German service, wrongly assumed that they were the nucleus of a future great Russian "liberation" army. They therefore decided (without prior German approval) to name their embryonic formation the RNNA. By the end of 1942, the formation numbered 7000 men organized into four infantry battalions, an artillery battalion and an engineer battalion. Recruits came mainly from POW camps, the volunteers joining to escape starvation. Some émigrés also decided to join the RNNA, including Lieutenant V. Ressler, Lieutenant Count G. Lamsdorff and Lieutenant Count S. von der Pahlen.

The formation's first major engagement took place in May 1942, in the Yelnia area east of Smolensk. Some 300 RNNA men were assigned the task of probing the positions of the encircled Soviet Thirty-Third Army, an operation that took several weeks. By December 1942, the RNNA was approximately the size of a German brigade and was a well-trained formation. Feldmarschall Hans von

and all livestock removed. Men and women who were not shot as partisans were deported to Germany as POWs, and the women taken to work in German factories. Unfortunately for the Germans, partisan areas were often located in swamp or forest terrain, which was difficult to penetrate and clear. In addition, mines and booby traps took a toll on attackers, which resulted in harsh and indiscriminate treatment being meted out to anyone unfortunate enough to fall into German hands.

The Germans used locals and Russian national units to assist them in anti-partisan work. Foresters and game-keepers were especially useful, as were dogs, though many German commanders believed that Russian hounds had been bred with anti-German instincts! Local units, especially Cossacks and *Hiwis*, were unreliable and often deserted to the partisans. Bearing all the above in mind, it is no wonder that most anti-partisan missions ended in failure.

This caused frustration among the Germans, who often committed atrocities in response. During Operation

Kluge, commander of Army Group Centre, having personally inspected the unit, was impressed by what he saw but issued an order that stipulated that the formation be divided into individual battalions and assigned to separate German units. These actions were in line with Hitler's order to keep all the units of Russian nationals no larger than battalion size.

The RNNA almost mutinied in protest, since the order destroyed any idea that they were an embryonic Russian army of liberation. The matter was resolved when several RNNA officers were promoted and the formation was not broken up (though neither was it sent to the front). However, the damage had been done and the RNNA soldiers no longer trusted the Germans. Those who remained were later incorporated into the ROA formation (see below).

In parallel to the RNNA were the so-called Eastern Legions (*Ostlegionen*). In late 1941, Hitler was visited by General Erkilet of the Turkish General Staff, who urged the Führer to intervene on behalf of Red Army POWs of Turkic nationality. Hitler, eager to recruit Turkey as an ally, granted permission in November for the creation of a Turkistani legion. The experiment was such a success that by the end of the year three more Eastern Legions had been formed, the Caucasian Moslem Legion (later split into the North Caucasian Legion and the Azerbaijani

Legion), Georgian Legion and Armenian Legion. In addition, by mid-1942, the Crimean Tartar and Volga Tartar Legions had been raised. Hitler, wary of this rapid growth, stipulated that the legions be organized into units no larger than a battalion and then widely dispersed among German Army formations to prevent them being a security hazard. An exception, as a gesture to court the Turks, was the formation of the Turkistani 162nd (Turkish) Infantry Division in May 1943 to serve as the parent unit for the various legion battalions.

The most interesting legion was the Sonderverband Bermann, formed by Abwehr chief Admiral Canaris and composed of Georgians, Armenians, Azerbaijanis and other Caucasian POWs. The plan was to parachute the unit behind Soviet lines to act as a "fifth column". Nothing came of the idea, though, and its two battalions ended up fighting at the front.

In August 1942, General Ernst Köstring was made Inspector General of Turkic and Caucasian Forces; by September 1944, he had thousands of legion members

Below: *Soldiers of the 162nd (Turkish) Infantry Division, which was formed on 21 May 1943 from the Turkistani, Azerbaijani and Georgian Legions. It originally had two infantry regiments, an infantry battalion, artillery regiment and support arms. It ended the war in Austria.*

under his command. In the legions and replacement battalions were 11,600 Armenians, 13,000 Azerbaijanis, 14,000 Georgians and 10,000 North Caucasians. These nationalities formed a further 21,595 men in pioneer and transport units, 25,000 in German Army battalions and 7000 in Luftwaffe and Waffen-SS formations. This gave a total of 102,195 men.

The legion movement was a success in that large numbers of recruits were raised, which freed up regular German units to undertake combat duties. However, when it came to frontline combat duties they were less useful. Often poorly armed, trained and motivated (especially when they were located away from their region of origin), they were unreliable and next to useless. For example, the 797th Georgian Battalion simply refused to fight when ordered to do so.

No study of Russian units in German service would be complete without mention of the Cossacks. Contrary to popular legend, and despite anti-communist sentiments nourished by many Cossacks and the cracking-down on many aspects of Cossack traditions by the communist regime, the overwhelming majority of

Above: *Casting the net ever wider. A North Caucasian recruit fighting for the Thousand Year Reich. Hitler was always suspicious of his Eastern volunteers; indeed, he had thousands of them redeployed to the West because he believed their loyalty was suspect.*

Below: *Crimean Tartars in German service. The Soviets exacted a heavy revenge on the Tartars once the Crimea had been recaptured. Some 400,000 of what the Red Army labelled "traitors to the fatherland" were deported from their homes; up to 200,000 died as a result.*

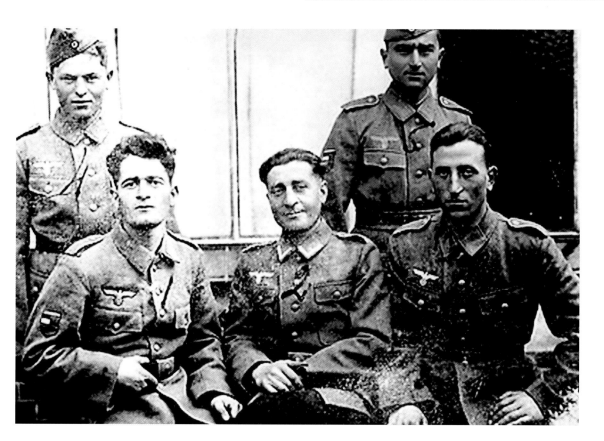

Cossacks remained loyal to the Soviet Government. That said, substantial numbers of Cossacks did fight for the Germans in World War II.

On 22 August 1941, while covering the retreat of Red Army units in eastern Belarus, a Don Cossack major in the Red Army named Kononov (a graduate of Frunze Military Academy, veteran of the Winter War against Finland, a Communist Party member since 1927 and holder of the Order of the Red Banner) deserted and went over to the Germans with his entire regiment (the 436th Infantry Regiment of the 155th Soviet Infantry Division), after convincing his regiment of the necessity of overthrowing Stalinism (among the few incidences of a whole Soviet regiment going over to the Axis during World War II). He was permitted by local German commanders to establish a squadron of Cossack troopers composed of deserters and volunteers from among POWs, to be used for frontline raiding and reconnaissance missions. With encouragement from his new superior, General Schenkendorff, eight days after his defection Kononov visited a POW camp in Mogilev in eastern Belarus. The visit yielded more than 4000 volunteers in response to the promise of liberation from Stalin's oppression with the aid of their German "allies".

Above: These are Azerbaijanis in Wehrmacht service. By September 1944, there were 18,000 Azerbaijanis fighting for Germany. They were organized into battalions and companies in different armies, as part of Hitler's policy to prevent them becoming a security threat.

However, only 500 of them (80 percent of whom were Cossacks) were actually drafted into the renegade formation. Afterwards, Kononov paid similar visits to POW camps in Bobruisk, Orsha, Smolensk, Propoisk and Gomel with similar results. The Germans appointed a Wehrmacht lieutenant named Count Rittberg to be the unit's liaison officer, in which capacity he served for the remainder of the war.

By 19 September 1941, the Cossack regiment contained 77 officers and 1799 men (of whom 60 percent were Cossacks, mostly Don Cossacks). It received the designation 120th Don Cossack Regiment; and, on 27 January 1943, it was renamed the 600th Don Cossack Battalion, despite the fact that its numerical strength stood at about 2000 and it was scheduled to receive a further 1000 new members the following month. The new volunteers were employed in the establishment of a new special Cossack armoured unit that became known as the

Above: *Members of an unidentified German Eastern legion. This photograph, captured from the Germans, is from Russian NKVD files, and Soviet security had identified each man, hence the numbers above their heads. Any who fell into Soviet hands would meet a swift end.*

17th Cossack Armoured Battalion, which after its formation was integrated into the German Third Army and was frequently employed in frontline operations.

Kononov's Cossack unit displayed a very anti-communist character. During raids behind Soviet lines, for example, it concentrated on the extermination of Stalinist commissars and the collection of their tongues as "war trophies". On one occasion, in the vicinity of Velikyie Luki in northwestern Russia, 120 of Kononov's infiltrators dressed in Red Army uniforms managed to penetrate Soviet lines. They subsequently captured an entire military tribunal of five judges accompanied by 21 guards, and freed 41 soldiers who were about to be executed. They also seized valuable documents in the process.

Kononov's unit also carried out a propaganda campaign by spreading pamphlets on and behind the frontline and using loudspeakers to get their message to Red Army soldiers, officers and civilians. Unfortunately

for Kononov, the behaviour of the Germans in the occupied territories worked against his campaign. But Kononov's Cossacks continued to serve their German "liberators" loyally, and were particularly active with Army Group South during the second half of 1942.

Aside from Kononov's unit, in April 1942, Hitler gave his official consent for the establishment of Cossack units within the Wehrmacht, and subsequently a number of such units were soon in existence. In October 1942, General Wagner permitted the creation, under strict German control, of a small autonomous Cossack district in the Kuban, where the old Cossack customs were to be reintroduced and collective farms disbanded (a rather cynical propaganda ploy to win over the hearts and souls of the region's Cossack population). All Cossack military formations serving in the Wehrmacht were under tight control; the majority of officers in such units were not Cossacks but Germans who had no sympathy towards Cossack aspirations for self-government and freedom.

The 1942 German offensive in southern Russia yielded more Cossack recruits. In late 1942, Cossacks of a single *stanitsa* (Cossack settlement) in southern Russia revolted against the Soviet administration and joined the advancing Axis forces. As the latter moved forward,

Cossack fugitives and rebellious mountain tribesmen of the Caucasus openly welcomed the intruders as liberators. On the lower Don River, a renegade Don Cossack leader named Sergei Pavlov proclaimed himself an *ataman* (Cossack chief) and took up residence in the former home of the tsarist *ataman* in the town of Novoczerkassk on the lower Don. He then set about establishing a local collaborationist police force composed of either Don Cossacks or men of Cossack descent. By late 1942, he headed a regional *krug* (Cossack assembly) which had around 200 representatives, whom he recruited from the more prominent local collaborators. He also requested permission from the Germans to create a Cossack army to be employed in the struggle against the Bolsheviks, a request that was refused.

The Cossack movement

The leading figures in the Cossack movement tried to bring about the creation of a Cossack nation, but were always thwarted by Nazi policy in the East. For example, a former tsarist émigré general named Krasnov, based in Berlin, with Hitler's blessing backed the foundation (in German-occupied Prague) of a Cossack Nationalist Party. It was made up of Cossack exiles who had fled abroad after the White defeat in the Russian Civil War. Party members swore unwavering allegiance to the Führer as "Supreme Dictator of the Cossack Nation". Simultaneously, a Central Cossack Office was established in Berlin to manage and direct the German-sponsored party. The ultimate aim was to create a "Greater Cossackia": a Cossack-ruled German protectorate extending from eastern Ukraine in the west to the River Samara in the east.

Though the idea of a Cossack state had no part in Nazi plans, the Germans did agree to enlarge the hitherto existing autonomous Cossack district in the Kuban and to enroll additional Cossacks into the ranks of the Wehrmacht in order to placate the progressively more dissatisfied Cossacks. By the beginning of 1943, though, the Axis was retreating following the disaster at Stalingrad and thus these plans came to nought. Due to the sudden military reverses suffered by the Germans in southern Russia, many Cossack collaborators were forced to join the retreat west in order to escape reprisals from the Soviets. In February 1943, the Germans withdrew from Novoczerkassk, taking with them Ataman Pavlov

and 15,000 of his Cossack followers. He temporarily re-established his headquarters at Krivoi Rog in the spring of 1943, and shortly afterwards the Wehrmacht allowed him to create his own Cossack military formation. Numerous Don, Kuban and Terek Cossacks were called to the colours, but many turned out to be so unsuitable for combat duties that they were sent to work on local farms instead.

Soon the horde of Cossack refugees was on the move again, eventually ending up at Novogrudek in western Belarus, from where five poorly equipped Cossack regiments were dispatched into the countryside to operate against Soviet and Polish partisans. By this time, much of Belarus was controlled by partisans, and the Cossacks took heavy losses with Pavlov being killed. Domanov was appointed as his immediate successor. As a result of the successful Soviet offensive in Belarus and the Baltics undertaken in the summer of 1944, codenamed Operation Bagration, the Cossack column was once again forced to retreat, this time westwards to the vicinity of Warsaw. By this period, any semblance of discipline had disappeared and the Cossacks left a trail of rape, murder and looting. From northeastern Poland they were

Right: Two Volga Tartar volunteers outside their rest barracks on the Eastern Front. Before the war, the Tartars had their own autonomous republic in the Soviet Union, but most Tartars yearned to be rid of Stalinism and establish their own state.

Above: *The German-produced Young Cossacks' Badge. This rare award was taken from a captured Cossack who ended up in a prisoner-of-war camp in England (no doubt captured during the fighting in Normandy in 1944).*

Below: *The original German caption to this photograph read "Cossacks fight against Stalin". The Germans were to enlist their support because of their knowledge of the terrain and the enemy.*

transported across Germany to the foothills of the Italian Alps where they ended the war.

It was only when the military situation in the East had turned against them that the Germans enticed the Cossacks with promises of greater independence. For example, in mid-1943, the High Command deemed it appropriate to create a Cossack division under the leadership of Oberst Helmuth von Pannwitz. The division was formed at a recently established Cossack military camp at Mlawa in northeastern Poland from Kononov's unit and a regiment of Cossack refugees. Following its formation, the 1st Cossack Division comprised seven regiments (two regiments of Don Cossacks, two regiments of Kuban Cossacks, one regiment of Terek Cossacks, one regiment of Siberian Cossacks and one mixed reserve regiment). As was customary, the Cossack officers were replaced by German ones, with the sole exception of the most notable Cossack commanders who retained their posts (Kononov being one of them). Nazi racial prejudices resulted in the German officers and NCOs mistreating the Cossacks, who retaliated by assaulting and even killing some of their more arrogant superiors. In September 1943, the division was transported to France to assist in the guarding of the Atlantic Wall. However, the Cossacks requested to be assigned frontline responsibilities outside France. The German High Command thus transferred the division to Yugoslavia to take part in anti-partisan operations.

By the end of 1943, the Germans had retreated from the Cossack homelands in Russia. As a result, the Cossacks in German service became disillusioned, and so, in November, Alfred Rosenberg, Nazi Minister for the Occupied Eastern Territories, and Chief of Staff of the OKW, Feldmarschall Wilhelm Keitel, assured the Cossacks that the German Army would retake their homelands. However, as the military situation made such promises unrealistic, arrangements were made to set up a so-called "Cossackia" outside the Cossack homelands. Eventually, the foothills of the Carnic Alps in northeastern Italy were selected for the purpose of providing the wandering Cossacks with a new home.

In March 1944, an organizational/administrative committee was appointed for the purpose of synchronizing the activities of all Cossack formations under the Third Reich's jurisdiction. This "Directorate of Cossack Forces" included Naumenko, Pavlov (soon replaced by Domanov) and Colonel Kulakov of von Pannwitz's Cossack Division. Krasnov was nominated as the Chief Director, who would assume the responsibilities of representing Cossack interests to the German High Command.

Above: *Cossacks employed on rear-area security duties. When the Germans invaded Russia, they established a Nazi Party in the autonomous "Cossack District" in the Kuban under Vasili Galzkov. The latter acknowledged Hitler as the supreme defender of the Cossack nation.*

In June 1944, Pannwitz's 1st Cossack Division was elevated to the status of a corps and became XV Cossack Corps, with a strength of 21,000 men. In July, the corps was formally incorporated into the Waffen-SS, which allowed it to receive better supplies of weapons and other equipment, as well as to bypass notoriously uncooperative local police and civil authorities. Interestingly, the Cossacks retained their uniforms and German Army officers.

The granting of SS status to the Cossack corps was part of Himmler's scheme to limit the Wehrmacht's influence over foreign formations. The Reichsführer-SS was quite happy to accept Cossacks into the SS, as Alfred Rosenberg's ministry came up with the theory that the Cossack was not a Slav but a Germanic descended from the Ostrogoths. A replacement/training division of

Above: In Nazi eyes, the ideal use for foreign volunteers was fighting an unpleasant anti-partisan war. This is a soldier of either the 1st or 2nd Cossack Division in action against partisans in Yugoslavia. At the end of the war, both divisions surrendered to the British.

15,000 men was also formed at Mochowo, southwest of Mlawa. The corps fought in Yugoslavia; and at the end of the war, 50,000 strong, retreated to Austria to surrender to the British.

In all, around 250,000 Cossacks fought for the Germans in World War II. The Germans used them to fight Soviet partisans, to undertake general rear-area duties for their armies, and occasionally for frontline combat. But they were held in scant regard by most German Army commanders.

A far more important pro-German Russian force was the liberation army under the command of the former head of the Thirty-Seventh and Twentieth Soviet Armies, and later deputy commander of the front on the River Volkhov: General Andrei Andreyevich Vlassov. The son of a Russian peasant born in Nizhni Novgorod, in the spring of 1919 he was recruited into the Red Army and fought against the Whites as an officer. He did not join the Communist Party until 1930 but thereafter his rise was rapid: a major-general by 1938 and a divisional commander

by December 1939. During Operation Barbarossa, he commanded a tank corps then an army, taking part in the Battle of Kiev and the defence of Moscow. In March 1942, he became deputy commander of the Volkhov Front but was taken prisoner at the end of June.

He immediately aroused the interest of the 4th Propaganda Section of the Wehrmacht (WPrIV) and was transferred to a special, comfortable camp for important Russian prisoners. There he was subjected to a subtle propaganda campaign which played on his aversion to the Soviet system (of which the Germans must have been aware before his capture). His personal charm, effective manner of speaking, gift of inspiring confidence and high rank earmarked him to head the Russian liberation movement. The persuasion worked, as in September 1942, still in the POW camp, Vlassov wrote a leaflet calling on the officers of the Red Army and the Russian intelligentsia to overthrow the Stalinist regime.

The leaflet was dropped by the thousand from Luftwaffe aircraft, and the response was good. Day after day, the German High Command received reports from all the army groups that thousands of Red Army deserters were coming over to the Germans and asking for General Vlassov.

These reports infuriated Hitler, though, who prohibited any talk of General Vlassov and Russian

Right: *The price of fighting for the losing side. These are Cossacks who surrendered to the British at the end of the war. Under the terms of the Yalta Agreement, all Russian nationals were to be returned to the Soviets. The British sent 22,502 Cossacks to be shot or to rot in the Gulag.*

formations (there was to be no collaboration with the "sub-human" Slavs). However, by January 1943, the leaflet campaign had yielded such good results that the higher echelons of Army Groups Centre and North invited General Vlassov, on their own initiative, to go on a tour of their areas and deliver speeches to POWs and the local population. In March, Vlassov visited Smolensk, Mohylev, Bobruisk, Borisov, Orsha and other places, and later toured the areas of Army Group North. His reasons for taking up the fight against Bolshevism were listed in a letter to a German newspaper in March 1943:

Vlassov's statement

"I realized clearly that Bolshevism had dragged the Russian people into the war in the alien interests of Anglo-American capital. England has always been an enemy of the Russian people. It has always striven to weaken and harm our motherland. But Stalin saw a chance to realize his plans for world domination by following Anglo-American interests. In order to realize these plans he tied the fate of the Russian people to the fate of England, and plunged the Russian people into war, condemning it to countless disasters. These calamities of war crown all the other miseries which the peoples of our country have suffered under 25 years of Bolshevik rule.

"Would it not therefore be criminal to continue shedding blood? Is not Bolshevism, and Stalin in particular, the main enemy of the Russian people? Is it not the primary and sacred duty of every honest Russian to fight against Stalin and his clique?"

Hitler and Feldmarschall Keitel remained deeply hostile to the whole idea, and suggested in June 1943 that Vlassov's recruits should be sent to Germany to work in coal mines as replacements for Germans.

The result was that by the middle of 1944, Vlassov's formation, the *Russkaia Osvoboditelnaia Armiia* (ROA — the Russian Army of Liberation) was not an army in the sense of a military organization. Units that bore its name were mostly commanded by German officers, and were dispersed all over Europe. General Vlassov and his Russian

Right: *The Cossacks' women and children were returned as well. The British 6th Armoured Division handed back the Cossacks throughout May 1945. Not all scenes were as peaceful as this one – the British soldiers had to use their rifles and bayonets on the Cossacks.*

National Committee had no influence whatsoever, and were not recognized by the German Government. In July 1944, however, Himmler, seeing the dire situation the Reich was in, decided to meet with Vlassov (the Reichsführer-SS at this time had great power, being Chief of the SS, Chief of the Police, including the Gestapo, Minister of the Interior and, since the attempt on Hitler's life on 20 July 1944, also Commander of the Reserve Army). Because of the attempt on Hitler's life, the meeting did not take place until 16 September 1944. Himmler agreed to the creation of a new committee called the *Komitet Osvobozhdeniia Narodov Rossi* (KONR – Committee for the Liberation of the Peoples of Russia), and to the creation of the KONR Army under General Vlassov's command. The committee and army were to embrace all Soviet citizens living under German rule, in order to unite their political and military activities in the fight against Bolshevism. To begin with, five divisions were to be organized from among POWs and workers brought to Germany from the occupied territories in the East (by this time, the Red Army had entered Poland, reached East Prussia and was at the Yugoslav border).

The representatives of the non-Russian nationals, who wanted to sever all ties with Russia and create their own independent states, were against the idea of the KONR Army. Despite Himmler's threats, the Ukrainians, White

Above: *Andrei Vlassov (second from left), the commander of the Russkaia Osvoboditelnaia Armiia (ROA – the Russian Army of Liberation) and a genuine Russian patriot. He stated: "There can be no greater crime than the forced enslavement of another nation."*

Ruthenians (a former province in eastern Czechoslovakia), Georgians and Cossacks refused to join the KONR.

On 14 November 1944, the Committee for the Liberation of the Peoples of Russia held its inaugural meeting in Prague. The Prague Manifesto was proclaimed detailing KONR's aims: the overthrow of Stalin's tyranny, the liberation of the peoples of Russia from the Bolshevik system, and the restitution of those rights to the peoples of Russia which they had fought for and won in the people's revolution of 1917; discontinuation of the war and an honourable peace with Germany; and the creation of a new free people's political system without Bolsheviks and exploiters.

All decisions and instructions had to be "coordinated" with the appropriate German commissar. Nevertheless, the publication of the Prague Manifesto made a deep impression on many Russians. First of all, it brought forth a great number of voluntary applications for service in the KONR Army, a number that surpassed all expectations. On 20 November, for example, 60,000 applications were received. Large numbers of volunteers from among POWs and Soviet refugees who had left their native lands voluntarily with the retreating German armies, preferring a wandering life in strange and perhaps unfriendly lands to a return under the NKVD yoke, were received. Bizarrely, desertion from the Red Army to the Germans increased after the publication of the manifesto, despite the looming defeat of Nazi Germany.

The KONR Army had begun to form in November 1944, accompanied by shortages of arms and equipment. As a result of the deteriorating military situation in the East, the five divisions were reduced to two. Despite his difficulties, Vlassov formed an army headquarters, two motorized divisions, one reserve brigade, an engineer battalion and support units – a total strength of 50,000 men. On 28 January 1945, he officially took command of the army.

The 1st KONR Division, under the command of General Sergei Kuzmich Bunyachenko, was given the name 600th Panzergrenadier Division. Its organization began in November 1944 at Muensingen, and operational

Below: Some of Vlassov's Russkaia Osvoboditelnaia Armiia (ROA – POA in Cyrillic). The POA attracted thousands of recruits, but Hitler remained deeply suspicious of a movement that he believed would undermine Germany's ambitions in the East.

readiness was reached in mid-February 1945. The nucleus of the division consisted of the remnants of the 30th SS Waffen Grenadier Division (Russian No 2), which had been greatly reduced during the fighting in France, and the remnants of the infamous Kaminski SS division. When the rabble of the latter formation arrived at the camp where the division was being formed, gangs of armed and unarmed men in all kinds of uniforms, accompanied by women in gaudy dresses, spilled out of the railway carriages. At the sight of them, Bunyachenko exclaimed in anger: "So this is what you're giving me – bandits, robbers, thieves. You'll let me have what you can no longer use!" Amazingly, despite acute shortages of arms, equipment and supplies, at the beginning of April the division reached the front on the River Oder.

The 2nd KONR Division, under the command of General G. A. Zveryev, was named the 650th Panzergrenadier Division. Its formation began in January 1945 in Baden, some 69km (43 miles) from the camp of the 1st Division. Owing to the shortages in arms and equipment, it never really reached operational readiness. The nucleus of the division consisted of a few battalions withdrawn from Norway, and some recently captured Russian prisoners. In addition, the KONR Army's headquarters, the reserve brigade, the engineer battalion, the officers' school and other units, in all some 25,000 men, were being formed in the same area as the 2nd

Right: *A recruit in the POA. Like his commander, he probably joined the army because he was sick of the Soviet system that treated human life with utter contempt and threw thousands of soldiers into battle inadequately trained, and then called prisoners traitors.*

Division. The organization of the 3rd Division was begun in Austria, but its strength apparently never exceeded 2700 men.

In mid-April 1945, the 1st Division was given the task of capturing the Soviet bridgehead in the area of Frankfurt-on-Oder. This bridgehead had been previously attacked by the Germans, but without success. The attack of the 1st Division also failed, with heavy losses owing to lack of adequate artillery and air support. After the failure of this attack, Bunyachenko withdrew the division on his own authority, and a few days later began the march towards the frontier of Czechoslovakia, together with other Russian volunteers — more than 20,000 men in all. On the way, the Germans tried in vain to induce him to obey their orders. At the end of April, the division reached the frontier of Czechoslovakia where Vlassov himself joined it.

The saga of the KONR army

On 2 May, they stopped short of Prague where they were informed that the army's headquarters, 2nd Division and the remaining formations of the KONR were on their way through Austria to Czechoslovakia.

At this time, Prague seemed to be the objective of both the American and Soviet armies which were approaching from two directions. This induced the Czechoslovak National Council to call for an uprising against the Germans, which began on 5 May. On the same day, the Czechs implored the Allies by radio to come to their aid because Prague was threatened by the Germans. Receiving no reply to its appeal, the council turned for help to General Bunyachenko. On the morning of 6 May, the 1st Division joined the fight, and by the evening had cleared Prague of SS troops. The Czechs greeted Vlassov's men joyfully, but the next day Bunyachenko was informed that Prague would be occupied by the Red Army, not by the Americans as he had expected, and that the Czechoslovak National Council was being replaced by a pro-Soviet government headed by Eduard Benes. The latter demanded that the forces of General Vlassov were either to await the Red Army's entrance in order to surrender, or leave Prague as soon as possible. On the morning of 8 May, General Bunyachenko's troops began to march towards the same area from where they had come only four days before.

A few days after leaving Prague, the 1st KONR Division laid down its arms in the Czech village of Schluesselburg in

the American zone. On 12 May, Bunyachenko was informed that Schluesselburg would be included in the Soviet zone, and that the local American commander did not consent to letting the division march beyond the new demarcation line. The only possible solution, suggested the Americans, was that the soldiers of the KONR might try to cross over to the American zone individually. General Bunyachenko immediately disbanded the division, advising his subordinates to try their luck on their own. During the flight, however, many were shot by Soviet troops and the majority were captured by the Red Army. Some 17,000 of them are said to have been deported to Russia, where they suffered death or life imprisonment. General Vlassov himself fell into Soviet hands on 12 May.

The 2nd KONR Division split into two parts; the greater part, together with the Pannwitz's Cossack corps, surrendered to the British on 12 May in Austria, to be interned in the area of Klagenfurt. One regiment of the 2nd Division and the army's headquarters reached the American zone after a long and weary journey, and were interned at Landau in western Bavaria. Thus ended the saga of the ROA.

One group that deserves special mention with regard to foreign units in German service are the Ukrainians. Ukraine contributed thousands of recruits to the German war effort during the four-year war on the Eastern Front.

Above: The paybook of a Russian pilot in the POA air force. The slip of paper was permission for him to wear German insignia. Despite the best efforts of Vlassov and senior German commanders, Hitler never considered a Russian national army seriously.

In mid-September 1939, in accordance with the Nazi-Soviet non-aggression treaty, western Ukraine (western Wolhynia and eastern Galicia) was handed over to the Soviet Union and incorporated into the Ukrainian Soviet Socialist Republic (SSR). In June 1940, Bessarabia and northern Bukovyna were annexed from Romania and added to the Ukrainian SSR. Western Galicia was under German control.

The aim of Ukrainian nationalists was independence from both German and Russian rule. The *Organizacji Ukraiƒskich Nacjonalistów* (OUN — Organization of Ukrainian Nationalists) was formed in 1929 and headed by Stepan Bandera. Its military wing, the Nationalist Military Detachments, was organized in 1939 under the leadership of Colonel Roman Sushko. It had the support of the Germans immediately before their war against Poland, but existed for a very short time, being disbanded when the Nazi-Soviet pact came into effect. In February 1940, the OUN split into two hostile factions: OUN-M, led by Andriy Melnyk; and OUN-B, led by Stepan Bandera. They and their followers were popularly known as *Melnykivtsi* and *Banderivtsi*.

During Barbarossa, the Germans had captured most of the Ukraine by the end of November 1941. Galicia was attached to the General Government of Poland, while Bukovyna and the area up to the southern River Bug, including Odessa, was handed over to Romania. The remainder was organized as the Reichs Commissariat Ukraine, administered by Erich Koch. With the German armies came Ukrainian nationalists. The Brotherhood of Ukrainian Nationalists was organized with the support of the Germans and fought under the auspices of the

Bandera faction of the OUN (OUN-B). It was divided into two battalions: Nachtigall and Roland. Nachtigall had about 1000 men in Lvov when a Ukrainian state was proclaimed by OUN-B in June 1941 (to the great surprise of the Germans, who arrested both Melnyk and Bandera and the OUN-B leadership). Both battalions were returned to Frankfurt-on-Oder and there organized into Guard Battalion 201, which was sent to Belorussia to combat partisans. Because of various complaints about the Ukrainians' insubordination, almost all its officers were arrested and the unit disbanded. One officer, Captain Roman Shukhevych, escaped and later became commander-in-chief of the *Ukrainska Povstanska Armiya* (UPA — Ukrainian Insurgent Army, a nationalist as opposed to communist organization). He headed the Ukrainian underground until his death in a battle with Soviet MVD troops in March 1950, near Lvov.

The Galician Division

Galicia's governor-general, Otto Wachter, approached Himmler with a proposal to create a frontline combat division from Galician recruits. After speaking with Hitler, Himmler gave Wachter the go-ahead and ordered the creation of the 14th Waffen-SS Grenadier Division *Galicia*. Despite Himmler's position as the head of the SS, he encountered opposition to the idea. Erich Koch, Karl Wolfe (Waffen-SS liaison officer on Hitler's staff) and SS General Kurt Daleuge (Reich Protector of Bohemia and Moravia) believed that the weapons supplied to such a unit would be turned on the Germans. Himmler stood firm, though, and the Galicia division was established. He had two reasons for doing so: the loss of manpower after the defeat at Stalingrad meant the Reich desperately needed new formations; and he had a fear that disaffected Ukrainian youths would join the underground movement, i.e. the UPA.

The 14th Waffen-SS Grenadier Division was formed in mid-1943 from 80,000 applicants. The best 13,000 were selected and the rest were used to form police regiments. From its inception, UPA members infiltrated the unit. Despite this, it was trained and equipped and passed out with a strength of 18,000 men. Like other Slav units, the division's commander, SS-Brigadeführer Fritz Freitag, and his officers were all German. In June 1944, the division was part of Army Group North when it was committed to its first and only major battle — in the Brody-Tarnow Pocket — which almost destroyed it. Following this engagement, the division numbered only 3000 men. After a period of rest and refitting, the division participated in several half-hearted anti-partisan operations in Slovakia and Slovenia before surrendering in Austria in May 1945.

Other Ukrainian units were formed by the Germans from Red Army POWs. This was the case with the Sumy (Ukrainian) Division, created in late 1941 and early 1942, which was nearly destroyed during the fighting at Stalingrad in 1942–43. In 1944, its remnants were attached to Vlassov's ROA.

As a result of Ukrainian complaints, all Ukrainian units were separated from the ROA and reorganized as the Ukrainian Liberation Army in the spring of 1943. Its original strength was around 50,000, but by the end of the war this had increased to 80,000. However, it was short of arms and other supplies, and took heavy casualties fighting the Red Army. The remnants ended up in Czechoslovakia in May 1945.

In a typical German response to the dire situation in the East, in early 1945 all Ukrainian units or their remnants were brought together under one command, when the Ukrainian National Committee, headed by General Pavlo Shandruk, was established in Berlin. In addition, the Germans finally agreed to the creation of the Ukrainian National Army (UNA). The core of the army was to be the reorganized Galician Division, which was to become part of the UNA's 1st Division. Although this plan was never fully realized because of Germany's defeat, the Germans' consent to Ukrainian control of

Above: *Soldiers of the Ukrainian Galician Division give the right-armed Nazi salute in the presence of a bust of their Führer. Such was the legacy of hatred created in the Ukraine by the Stalinist terror of the 1930s that the SS had no difficulty in raising a division of volunteers.*

these units gave the Ukrainians a free hand to negotiate with the Allies at the war's end.

Once removed from the Eastern Front, i.e. for garrison duties in Western Europe, the Ukrainian units were often unreliable. For example, two guard battalions of the 30th SS Infantry Division, composed of Ukrainian forced labourers in Germany who were pressed into service, were sent to fight the French underground. In late 1944 these units deserted to the French and became part of the resistance. The units were first named the *Bohoun* and *Chevtchenko* (*Shevchenko*) Battalions, and later became the 1st and 2nd Ukrainian Battalions. Both battalions were dissolved at the request of the Soviet authorities at the end of 1944. Another unit, led by Lieutenant Osyp Krukovsky and composed of the remnants of three battalions of the Galician Division sent to the West for training, also tried to desert to the French resistance. The attempt was thwarted by the Germans but a small group managed to escape in 1944. The rest were shipped back to Germany.

Above: *Otto Wachter (standing centre right, between the swastika and SS standards), who raised the 14th Waffen-SS Division Galicia. Wachter believed that raising an anti-Bolshevik division would foster closer ties between the Germans and Ukrainians.*

Below: *Reichsführer-SS Himmler (second from left) with officers of the Galician division during a training exercise. On the right is SS-Brigadeführer Fritz Freitag, the commander of the division from 20 November 1943 until 27 April 1945. He committed suicide on 10 May 1945.*

Chapter 11

THE BALTIC STATES

Latvia, Estonia and Lithuania all contributed indigenous units to the German war effort. They were a mixed bunch, but the Latvians and Estonians provided the Waffen-SS with excellent divisions which fought well in defence of their homelands. The police units raised in the Baltic states were less commendable, being responsible for rounding up Jews for execution.

The Baltic states of Lithuania, Estonia and Latvia warrant their own chapter because they were independent nations on the eve of World War II. These former provinces of Russia had been independent only since 1920. Unfortunately, the Nazi-Soviet pact of August 1939 left them to the mercy of the USSR, as it designated them to be in the Soviet sphere of influence. In June 1940, following the collapse of France, Stalin ordered his army into the Baltic states under the pretence that they had, in official Soviet language, "grossly violated their mutual assistance pact with the Soviet

Left: Members of the Latvian 15th SS Waffen Grenadier Division scan the horizon fighting on the Eastern Front in early 1944. Note the knocked-out Russian T-34 tank.

Union". In fact, the move was part of Stalin's aim to advance the Soviet frontier westwards to create a buffer zone to absorb any future German attack.

The subsequent behaviour of the Soviets in the Baltic states – 34,250 Latvians, 60,000 Estonians and 75,000 Lithuanians either killed or deported – should have turned their populations into willing allies of the Germans. Indeed, during the early stages of Barbarossa, the Germans were welcomed as liberators. However, as with the other Eastern peoples, the Baltic states were subject to Nazi ideology, which meant "germanizing" the "racially suitable", German colonization, and deportation or extermination of "undesirables" (usually the latter). The head of Hitler's secretariat, Martin Bormann, put it succinctly: "There are no independent nations in the

Above: *Victims of the Lithuanian police battalions – either Jews or political opponents. They are probably the latter, as most Jews were killed in pits. It is a sad fact that the Nazis were able to tap into a rich anti-Semitic seam in the Baltic states, which they mined greedily.*

East, but only the Sovietized mass of Slavs, who must and will be mastered."

The Germans were able to recruit sizeable numbers of volunteer units, though many of the recruits believed they were fighting to liberate their homelands from the Soviets and restore national sovereignty. In reality, they were just tools to further Nazi aims. Examining each Baltic state in turn, this chapter will show how Nazi ideology, as elsewhere in the Soviet Union, resulted in wasted opportunities that ultimately contributed towards the German defeat in the East.

On 15 June 1940, the Soviets assumed control of Lithuania, including the capital Vilna, which had been part of Poland until October 1939. Seven weeks later, the country was officially annexed by the USSR. In response, underground groups were formed, including the extremist nationalist and German-sponsored *Lietuviu Aktyvistu Frontas* (Lithuanian Activist Front).

On 14 June 1941, tens of thousands of Lithuanians were exiled to Siberia by the Soviets for being "politically or socially unreliable". Eight days later, the Germans invaded the Soviet Union and had occupied Lithuania by the middle of August.

The Soviets had exacted a bloody toll from the Baltic states, and the Lithuanians suffered as much as their northern neighbours, Latvia and Estonia. In the face of such brutal treatment, and with the German invasion providing an impetus for revolt, it is estimated that at least 125,000 Lithuanians rose up to fight the retreating Soviets during the time between the initial German crossing of the eastern frontier and the final evacuation of all Russian troops. At least 4000 Red Army troops are estimated to have been killed during this period and another 10,000 wounded. Numerous Lithuanian cities were also liberated even before the Germans arrived, a sign of the determination with which the Lithuanians were willing to fight for their homeland. On 23 June, the Lithuanian Activist Front led a revolt against the Soviet occupiers. Partisans took over the largest cities, Kaunas and Vilnius, set up a provisional government and declared the restoration of Lithuanian independence.

Most of the Lithuanian population welcomed the Germans, and many subsequently collaborated with them in the hope of restoring Lithuanian independence, a hope that was to be quickly quashed. The provisional government was abolished and Lithuania became part of the Reich Commissariat Ostland and its name was changed to *Generalbezirk Litauen* (General District of Lithuania). The Lithuanian national army was not reconstituted, though some of its former officers and soldiers were incorporated into the Lithuanian police battalions formed by the Germans.

Shortly after the German occupation, a reorganization was carried out of all local Lithuanian units comprising policemen, ex-soldiers, ex-officers and nationalist elements. These disparate elements, which also included schoolboys and university students, had been attacking the retreating Soviet forces and had been harassing and murdering Lithuanian Jews (there existed a rich vein of Baltic and Russian anti-Semitism before the Germans arrived). That July, many of the units in Kovno and elsewhere were incorporated into a paramilitary organization, the *Tauto Darbo Apsauga* (National Labour Guard). In Vilna and other places, the corresponding military organization was named the *Lietuvia Savisaugos Dalys* (Lithuanian Self-Defence).

Anti-Jewish measures in Lithuania

At the end of 1941, these formations were reorganized into battalions by the Germans, and were renamed *Policiniai Batalionai* (Police Battalions). By August 1942, 20 such battalions were in existence with a total strength of 8388 men, of whom 341 were officers and 1772 non-commissioned officers (NCOs). They were commanded by former officers and NCOs who had served in the army of independent Lithuania. But the occupiers had them firmly under control, with German liaison officers assigned to each battalion and all the units being directed by the district SS and police leader headquarters in Lithuania.

Just as the NKVD had rounded up "enemies of the state", so the SS began to clear Lithuania of Jews and political opponents. The police battalions were involved in these actions, and also assisted the German Einsatzgruppen (SS Special Action Groups). The 1st and 2nd Battalions, for example, took a leading part in the mass murder of Jews in Lithuania, as well as in the adjacent territories of Poland and Belorussia.

The first formal Wehrmacht unit composed of Lithuanians to be formed was known as the Lituanische

Hunterschaften, which was later used as a foundation for a series of self-defence units known as Selbschutz Bataillonen (Self-Defence Battalions). These battalions were later brought under the control of the German organization of uniformed frontline police, the Ordnungspolizie, and thus the SS, and renamed as Schutzmannschaft Bataillonen (Security Battalions) or Schumas. The Schuma units were universally renamed and reformed into police battalions in May 1943. Nearly all battalion-sized units consisted of 500–600 men. They were primarily assigned to rear-area security duties, but as the Red Army neared Lithuania they also saw frontline service. These Lithuanian units numbered a total of 35 battalions during World War II, consisting of units numbered 1–15, 251–257, 263–265 and 301–310. These units were also posted to Poland, Belorussia, the other Baltic states and even to the southern Ukraine. The battalions numbered 263–265 and 301–310 were never fully trained and were disbanded before they could be employed in combat.

Right: Feldmarschall Walther Model, commander of Army Group North. On 22 March 1944, he made a request for the formation of 15 Lithuanian units to be employed to guard Luftwaffe airfields. Lithuanian volunteers, thinking they were joining the SS, were far from impressed.

As the Red Army approached Lithuania, the Germans grouped 3–4 Lithuanian police battalions into regimental-sized units known as Lituanische Freiwilligen Infanterie Regimenter (Lithuanian Volunteer Infantry Regiments). Three such units were formed as the Soviets reached the border, and they were sent directly to the front in an attempt to hold back the Red Army advance in late 1944 and early 1945.

Invariably lightly armed and poorly trained for frontline duties, the battalions fared badly against the Soviets. As they served as auxiliaries to the Ordnungspolizei, they often supported the Einsatzgruppen's mass murder operations. The Lithuanian units were often put under the control of the Reichssicherheitshauptamt (RSHA – Reich Security Department) and the Higher SS and Police Leader (HSSPF) in Ostland. This resulted in them taking part in punishment operations against local civilians for partisan attacks, which usually meant murdering all humans and their livestock in a designated area.

Lithuanian SS recruits

In addition to the above units, there were also five Lithuanian battalions formed during 1943 which were attached to German pioneer units and under the control of Army Group North. The commanding officers of these units were all Lithuanians. Their tasks were road and railway construction and the building of defensive works. Initially, the units were not armed, but as partisan activity increased they were given light weapons for protection. Many members of the Lithuanian construction units were later asked to join the Waffen-SS; 40 percent eventually did.

In January 1943, the HSSPF in Lithuania, SS-Brigadeführer Wysocki, was ordered to raise a Lithuanian legion for the Waffen-SS, similar to those raised from the Latvians and Estonians. He failed miserably, with very few volunteers coming forward. As a result, Wysocki was replaced by SS-Brigadeführer Harm, although the results still did not improve. Thereafter, the Germans threatened to put all able-bodied Lithuanians into labour camps until a compromise was reached. The Lithuanians were holding out for an independent formation led by Lithuanian officers and not under the control of the SS. They also requested that the formation only be used internally within Lithuania, and not outside their national borders. The Germans, though, wanted the exact opposite. The wrangling continued until February 1944 when the Germans agreed to all Lithuanian requests. The new formation was known as the Lithuanian Territorial Corps (originally, Himmler had refused to accept Lithuanians on the grounds that they were politically unreliable and racially inferior; however, by early 1944, the military situation in the East forced him to lower SS racial requirements).

Right: Estonian SS personnel on their home territory. Estonia, because pro-German sentiment was stronger there than elsewhere in the Baltic region, was selected to provide the first Eastern Waffen-SS unit. Himmler gave his approval to raise the formation in August 1942.

On 16 February 1944, an appeal was made for volunteers, which yielded more than 19,000 men. The Germans wanted only 5000, and so, much to the Lithuanians' annoyance, plans were put in motion to use the excess volunteers as replacements for Wehrmacht units. This infuriated the Lithuanians, so to avoid further problems it was agreed to use the excess volunteers to form 13 police battalions and 1 replacement unit. The 14 units were formed in March 1944, and immediately began military training.

However, on 22 March 1944, Feldmarschall Walther Model, commander of Army Group North, made a formal request for the formation of 15 Lithuanian units to be employed to guard Luftwaffe airfields. This move once again greatly upset the Lithuanian volunteers; and, to make matters worse, on 6 May, a general mobilization order was issued (in response to the approach of the Red

Army). On 9 May, the Germans went back on their earlier promises of independence from German military control, and all 14 units were placed under Wehrmacht jurisdiction. This caused widespread dissent among the volunteers who refused the new German demands. Thus, all 14 units were formally disbanded in the face of a mutiny. Of the original 19,000 men, about 16,000 deserted while the other 3000 were drafted into Luftwaffe flak batteries.

In June 1944, Operation Bagration, the Soviet offensive that smashed Army Group Centre, resulted in the Red Army entering Lithuania. In response, the Germans formed an emergency formation called the Fatherland Defence Force. This new formation consisted of small groups of retreating Lithuanian troops who were organized into two regiments under German command. It was employed in defensive positions near Papiles where, in early October 1944, it was engaged in heavy combat with Soviet forces. Crippling losses caused the formation

Left: *An Estonian SS man fighting on his home territory at Narva, 1944. It took the Red Army six months to break through.*

Right: *Heinrich Himmler stated of his Estonian SS (seen here): "Racially they could not be distinguished from Germans."*

Above: German troops advance past Narva during Operation Barbarossa in 1941. Narva had been a bastion of the Teutonic Knights in the Middle Ages, and so Himmler looked to recruit members of the local population he classed as "racially suitable".

to pull back and a general retreat ensued. The survivors of the formation, about 1000 men, later regrouped in East Prussia as a new unit known as the Lithuanian Engineer Battalion. This new formation consisted of eight companies, and was tasked with working on defensive emplacements along the Baltic coast. However, it was all but destroyed shortly after formation, and only a very few men managed to escape via the Baltic Sea.

Other units raised by the Germans in Lithuania included an NSKK unit formed towards the end of the war. There were also 1000 young Lithuanian boys and girls drafted into the service of the Luftwaffe to assist with flak, signal, transport and searchlight duties in the last months of the war. In the final analysis, the Germans only trusted the Lithuanians to dig ditches, shoot Jews and communists, and fight partisans. The Germans were more than happy for Lithuanians to undertake these unpleasant tasks. Even when the war had turned against Germany in the East after mid-1943, the Germans were half-hearted and lukewarm in their efforts to raise Lithuanian units.

As a postscript, after World War, II tens of thousands of Lithuanians continued to fight the Soviet occupation forces well into the 1950s. The last of the Lithuanian anti-Soviet partisan forces are thought to have been wiped out in 1956.

In contrast to Lithuania, Estonia was looked on more favourably by Himmler for a variety of reasons. First, Latvia and Estonia was the old territory of the Teutonic Knights, the German warrior monks who had battled the Slavs in the Middle Ages. Racially, as he said himself, "they could not be distinguished from Germans. The Estonians really belong to a few races that can, after the segregation of only a few elements, be merged with us without any harm to our people." He was also careful to stress, however, that "a nation of 900,000 Estonians cannot survive independently, and that as a racially related nation Estonia must join the Reich".

The collapse of Poland, together with almost total political isolation, paralyzed the Estonian Government. On 24 September 1939, Moscow demanded that Estonia hand over its bases to the Red Army; the government accepted the ultimatum, signing the corresponding agreement on 28 September. This resulted in 25,000 Red Army soldiers entering Estonia on 18 October. On 14 June 1940, the German Army marched into Paris; and on 16 June, Moscow presented an ultimatum to Estonia that a new government be appointed and that the occupation of the whole country be permitted. On 17 June, Estonia accepted the ultimatum and the independence of the country ceased to exist. By the end of the month, there were 130,000 Soviet soldiers, NKVD personnel and so-called "specialists engaged in establishing the new administrative apparatus of Estonia" in the country.

The occupation of their country caused great resentment among Estonians. As a result, an unknown number of men went to Finland to fight voluntarily against the Red Army. At sea, when Estonia was proclaimed a Soviet republic, the crews of 42 Estonian ships in foreign waters refused to return to the homeland. These ships were requisitioned by the British and were later used in the Atlantic convoys. Some 1000 Estonian seamen served in the British merchant marine, 200 of them as officers; and a further 200 Estonians served in the Royal Air Force (RAF), British Army and in the US Army.

In June 1940, the 16,800 men of the Estonian Army became XXII Territorial Rifle Corps of the Red Army. Thousands of men escaped from the corps when it was sent to Russia at the beginning of Operation Barbarossa. Of those who remained, 4500 went over to the German side (the corps was destroyed in fighting in September 1941). During Barbarossa, the German Army received help from the Estonian "forest brothers" (partisans). Taking advantage of the disarray of the Red Army, the "forest brothers" liberated south Estonia almost on their own. Their strength was between 25,000 and 35,000 men, of whom 12,000 were well armed. In the liberated territories, a Home Guard was formed from the "forest brothers", which had more than 14,000 men by 1 August and 25,000 men by 1 September. The "forest brothers" and the Home Guard managed to kill 3000 Soviets and took over 25,000 prisoners.

Immediately after the arrival of German troops, the formation of Estonian national units began. First, *Ost* battalions under different names were formed – Security, East, Defence and Police Battalions – in addition to single companies. Under German Army control, they were used to free up Wehrmacht formations for frontline duties by carrying out guard and anti-partisan duties. The police battalions were used to round up Jews, gypsies, the mentally ill and communists, who were systematically

Below: *The shell-pummelled fortress at Narva in 1944. The Battle of Narva, also called the Battle of the European Waffen-SS, lasted six months. The Baltic SS divisions fought tenaciously but in vain to hold back the numerically superior and better equipped Red Army.*

Above: *Jews shot by members of the Latvian police battalions formed by the Germans soon after their occupation of the country. The police battalions were also used for anti-partisan work.*

Below: *In the 1930s, Latvia had its own quasi-fascist organization – the Peasant Union led by Karlis Ulmanis. It had its own badge of merit and membership, shown here. Its self-defence organization was the Aizsargi.*

murdered. Initially, the *Ost* battalions mostly served in the rear of Army Group North. By March 1942, there were 16 Estonian battalions and companies with 10,000 men plus 1500 men in a depot battalion. In total, 54 Estonian battalions were formed, most of them being committed to frontline combat in 1942.

With his regard for the Estonians as racial brothers, it was inevitable that Himmler would raise Estonian Waffen-SS units. The first group of volunteers was raised in July 1941; and in the following months the SS established a number of Schutzmannschaft Bataillonen, which were separate from the army battalions. The next step was the creation of an Estonian legion.

On 28 August 1942, the German powers announced the legal compilation of the Estonian SS legion within the Waffen-SS. SS-Oberführer Frans Augsberger was nominated the commander of the legion, and by the end of 1942 1280 men had volunteered and been sent to the training camp at Debica in Poland. The Estonian Legion had a staff company, three infantry battalions, a heavy mortar company and an anti-tank company.

In March 1943, a partial mobilization was carried out in Estonia, during which 12,000 men were called into service. Of these, 5300 were sent to the legion, and the rest to other units of the German Army. On 23 March, the 1st Battalion was detached and became a motorized grenadier battalion in the *Wiking* Division. At the same time, the legion was designated the 1st Estonisches SS Freiwilligen Grenadier Regiment. During the summer, the regiment expanded into two regiments and became the 53rd Freiwilligen

Brigade with 6069 men. It was renamed the 3rd Estonian SS Freiwilligen Brigade on 22 October 1943.

On 24 January 1944, it was decided to upgrade the Estonian brigade to a division, which was titled 20th Estnische SS-Freiwilligen Division. As the Red Army reached the Narva River at the beginning of February, the division was brought closer to Narva. In April, the battalion that had been attached to *Wiking* returned to join the division; and in May 1944 it was renamed the 20th SS Waffen Grenadier Division (Estnische Nr 1). At this time, the division numbered 10,000 men, which had increased to 15,000 by September.

Estonians were also present in the Luftwaffe (1000, including 140 pilots) and the Kriegsmarine (300) at this time. In total, it is estimated that there were 100,000 Estonians in various units fighting for Germany in the autumn of 1944.

The SS division fought in the six-month battle at Narva, which also involved many other foreign volunteer units of the Waffen-SS. The Estonians, being highly motivated and well trained and equipped, put up a spirited defence and inflicted heavy casualties on the Soviets. At this time, the division's order of battle consisted of the 45th Waffen Grenadier Regiment, 46th Waffen Grenadier Regiment, 47th Waffen Grenadier Regiment and the 20th Waffen Artillery Regiment. Space does not permit a full examination of the division's exploits, but a few examples will be sufficient to illustrate its fighting qualities.

Above: *Latvian arm shield, as worn by members of the Latvian Waffen-SS. It was a white-on-red shield with a scalloped edge and was worn on the left arm. The word Latvija was either in the top corner or across the top.*

Below: *Members of the Aizsargi photographed in 1941. Many later joined the German Army and SS battalions that were responsible for security operations but also saw frontline combat.*

Between 14 and 16 February, one of its battalions (I/45 under Hastuf Harald Riipalu) defeated large Russian forces which had crossed Lake Lammijärv near Meerapalu, inflicting 2000 casualties. On 24 February, the battalion of Hastuf Rudolf Bruus (II/46) destroyed the bridgehead of Riigiküla, and the battalion of Ostubaf Ain-Ervin Meri (I/46) liquidated the bigger bridgehead of Vaasa-Siivertsi-Vepsaküla.

By June, the Estonian division was still in the line at Narva, but no amount of fighting prowess could prevent the impending German defeat (in the Baltic the Germans had two fronts — six to seven armies each — against a weakened Army Group North of two armies). However, the division was still capable of winning local victories, such as stopping the Soviet attack on Auvere, and the division helped to cover the German retreat from Narva in September. The Estonian division was driven from its homeland and forced to retreat along with the rest of Germany's collapsing forces. It fell back to Silesia and then Czechoslovakia. In May 1945, the less fortunate members of the division were captured by the Soviets, most being shot.

Latvian volunteers

Like Estonia, Latvia raised considerable numbers of men for service with the Germans. Before the war, the country had been ruled by Karlis Ulmanis' para-fascist Peasant Union, whose main opponent was the fascist Fire Cross Party, later renamed the Thunder Cross. The latter had its own paramilitary units called Greyshirts. The Thunder Cross extolled the virtues of Latvianness, the peasantry and the land, and it regarded the non-Baltic ethnic minorities in the country, especially the Jews, as a problem. When the Germans occupied the Baltic states in 1941, Thunder Cross members took an active part in assisting the Einsatzgruppen. Viktor Arajs, a former communist, was one such individual. When the Germans took over, he placed an advert in a Riga newspaper for men to assist in "cleansing the country of harmful elements". More than 100 men responded, and their first action was to assist the Germans to massacre imprisoned Jews in July 1941. This marked the beginning of their campaign of murder and rape. On 8 December 1941, they helped to shoot Jews from the Riga ghetto; and by 1942, the so-called Sonderkommando Arajs was conducting anti-partisan operations. The unit numbered 300 men at its height, and many later joined the Latvian Legion.

Following standard procedure, the SS and army formed a number of police battalions for anti-partisan and anti-Jew duties, though those under army command also saw frontline combat. They were raised purely to serve Nazi interests rather than to restore Latvian sovereignty.

Latvian independence was never on Berlin's agenda. Thus, when the Senior SS and Police commander in Ostland, SS-Obergruppenführer Jeckeln, said to Latvian officers, "in a great German empire the Latvian people will have their place in the sun", he received a stiff rebuke from the Ministry for the Occupied Eastern Territories. When Latvian leader and former general Rudolf Bangerskis proposed raising a 100,000-strong Latvian army, the idea received a cool reception. The Germans proposed instead to form a Latvian volunteer legion under the command of the SS. Hitler initially agreed to this, but in their recruitment drive the Germans assured the volunteers they would be fighting for an independent Latvia. The whole idea was therefore quickly scrapped in early February 1943.

The Schuma Battalions

In August 1941, the Latvian urban and country police were formed into units to police the rear areas of the German frontline and also to combat partisan attacks. Called Schuma Battalions, Himmler originally wanted to form them into a Waffen-SS division in late 1941. However, the heavy losses suffered by the German Army meant they were immediately committed as frontline troops. Untrained for such a role and lightly armed, they inevitably sustained heavy losses.

Himmler eventually took control of the Schumas and used them to form the basis of a Latvian SS unit. Despite the initial problems with recruiting a Latvian legion, Himmler was determined to raise a Latvian unit. The job of recruiting was given to Rudolf Bangerskis, who was promoted to the rank of SS-Gruppenführer und General der Waffen-SS and inspector of the Latvian Legion. This proved difficult as he could not draw on the manpower in the police and Schuma units so had to resort to conscription. Males who had been born between 1919 and 1925 were eligible for call-up, but by April 1943 only 2478 of the intended 15,025 men had been enlisted. In September, the Latvian Legion became the 15th SS Waffen Grenadier Division comprising the 32nd, 33rd and 34th SS Freiwilligen Grenadier Regiments, the 15th SS Freiwilligen Artillery Regiment and support units. Recruitment was still incomplete when the division was posted to the Nevel area as part of the Sixteenth Army, Army Group Centre, in late 1943. On 18 November, the Latvians were engaged against the Soviets in the Pstoshka, Majevo and Novosokolniki areas.

In early February 1944, the division left behind two infantry regiments in Novosokolniki and moved northeast to Belebelka, 30km (19 miles) north of Staraya-Russa where it joined X Corps of the Sixteenth Army. It was engaged in defensive fighting until 15 February 1944 when it was forced to withdraw. The division fought a number of rearguard actions until it reached the "Panther Line" position on the

Velikaya River, 40km (25 miles) from Ostrov, on 28 February (the line was a defensive belt constructed from Narva to Ostrov). Once there, it linked up with its sister division, the 19th SS Latvian Division. This had been formed on 7 January 1944 and consisted of the 42nd, 43rd and 44th Waffen Grenadier Regiments, 19th SS Artillery Regiment and support units. It was here that they dug in and prepared for the relentless Soviet advance. Both divisions fought bitterly in the following weeks, but by 19 July 1944, they had been pushed back to Latvia itself. Lack of supplies and the imminent occupation of Latvia by the Soviets prompted some desertions within both divisions, which weakened their strength considerably. Despite this, men still came forward to join the divisions as a result of the lowering of the conscription age to 18.

Both divisions were reformed at Konitz in west Prussia, but during their reorganization Riga fell to the Red Army in October 1944. The 19th SS Latvian Division was cut off in the Courland Pocket, where it fought until the end of the war. As the Germans fell back towards Konitz, the 15th SS Latvian Division was prematurely committed to battle. By early February 1945, what was left of it was engaged in combat at Jastrow and then at Flederborn. Between 14 and 24 February, it conducted a fighting withdrawal from

Above: The 15th SS Waffen Grenadier Division in action in 1944. This formation had the best fighting record of the Baltic SS divisions. Perhaps because of this, when elements of the division surrendered to the Red Army in May 1945 they were shot out of hand.

Peterswalde back to Wusterbarth, though by this time it had been broken up into battle groups.

The division had ceased to exist in an organizational sense, though the battle groups continued to fight. The majority of the division surrendered to the Red Army at Neuruppin in early May 1945.

In all, an estimated 250,000 Lithuanians, Latvians and Estonians served in military units under German command in World War II. Around half of them were killed in action or executed by the Soviets after the war (those captured were executed as traitors, the reasoning being that the Baltic states had been annexed by the USSR and thus their citizens had become Soviet citizens). As in Russia, the police and paramilitary units ably assisted the Einsatzgruppen carry out their grisly work: nearly all the 250,000 Jews in the Baltic states were exterminated during the war. To this figure must be added the tens of thousands of civilians who were murdered by Germany's Baltic legions.

Chapter 12

EXPLOITING BALKAN DIVISIONS

The Germans attempted to exploit ethnic tensions in the Balkans to their own advantage. Initially, they were successful, carving up Yugoslavia and installing a puppet Croat regime. However, units raised in the Balkans were a mixed bunch, and ultimately proved incapable of defeating the partisans.

Nazi attempts to raise volunteer and conscript units in the former Yugoslavia and Albania were moderately successful during World War II, in the sense of numbers of men raised. However, the attempt by Berlin to take advantage of ethnic tensions within the country to further its aims (as part of its objective to transform the Balkans into a satellite region) ultimately proved disastrous, because it resulted in the creation of a large-scale anti-German partisan movement. The Germans had to commit tens of thousands of ground forces to battle these insurgents during a four-year war,

Left: An SS-Hauptsturmführer of the Moslem Handschar Division wearing the unit's fez headdress. The division was raised in the spring of 1943.

troops that could have been better employed elsewhere. For Yugoslavia itself, the war was a tragedy, with Croat fighting Croat, Serb fighting Serb, and both fighting German, Italian, Hungarian and Bulgarian forces.

After World War I, the Paris Peace Conference created the Kingdom of Serbs, Croats and Slovenes, which comprised the former kingdoms of Serbia and Montenegro, Croatia and Bosnia and Herzegovina, plus Austrian territory in Dalmatia and Slovenia, and Hungarian land north of the River Danube. This settlement was much to the annoyance of Italy, which wanted Croatia and Slovenia for herself.

The 1921 constitution of the new country established a highly centralized state in an attempt to keep the fledgling country together, and especially to diffuse any

Above: *Serb Chetniks loyal to the Nazi collaborator General Milan Nedic. The bitter internecine war in Yugoslavia meant that Serbs fought for the Nazis, for the partisans and for themselves. All sides fought for dominance in the multi-national state.*

Serb-Croat hostility. Under this constitution, legislative power was exercised jointly by the monarchy (of the Serbian Karadjordjevic dynasty) and parliament. The king was a powerful figure, as he appointed a Council of Ministers and retained significant foreign policy prerogatives. Indeed, in 1929, King Alexander I prorogued the parliament, declared a royal dictatorship and changed the name of the state to Yugoslavia. Following Alexander's assassination in October 1934 by a Macedonian activist, allegedly with Croat help, Prince Paul became the head of the Council of Regents until the king's young son, Peter, came of age.

In the 1930s, Yugoslavia ostensibly remained neutral, but in fact between 1935 and 1939 moved closer to Nazi Germany under the leadership of Milan Stojadinovic. He was a Serb politician and head of the right-wing Yugoslav Radical Union, a party of Serbs, Bosnian Moslems and

Slovenes. His party had its own stormtroopers, and he adopted the title *Vodja* (Führer). As premier, he negotiated treaties with Italy and Bulgaria with Germany's help. However, he was distrusted by the Croats and in an attempt to preserve national unity Prince Paul accepted his resignation in early 1939. He was replaced by Dragisa Cvetkovic, who maintained the same pro-Axis foreign policy but with fewer fascist trappings.

Events outside Yugoslavia now threatened to suck the country into war. In April 1939, Italy invaded and occupied Albania; while in October 1940, Mussolini invaded Greece, only to receive a bloody nose from the Greeks. To extract his ally, Hitler ordered his General Staff to prepare an invasion of Greece, codenamed Marita. But he needed transit rights through Yugoslavia for his invasion forces to take up position in Bulgaria. Paul had been willing to discuss a three-way, non-aggression treaty with

Right: *Chetniks loyal to Draza Mihailovic, who did more fighting against Tito than the Germans. The Allies at first supported Mihailovic but then realized they were backing the wrong horse and switched to Tito. Mihailovic was eventually executed by the partisans on 17 July 1946.*

Above: *Soldiers of the Croat 369th Reinforced Infantry Regiment in training prior to their deployment on the Eastern Front. The regiment fought valiantly in Russia in 1942–43, being wiped out at Stalingrad. The Germans raised a further two divisions of Croat volunteers.*

Rome and Berlin to maintain Yugoslavia's territorial integrity. But now Hitler wanted him to sign the Tripartite Pact (an agreement signed in Berlin on 27 September 1940 by Germany, Italy and Japan which formalized the Axis powers' partnership) or risk military invasion. Therefore, on 25 March 1941, Prime Minister Cvetkovic and Foreign Minister Cincar Markovic signed the pact. On 27 March, two Serb generals, Bora Mirkovic and Dusan Simovic, led a British-assisted coup in Belgrade against the Cvetkovic government and placed Peter in charge.

Air Force General Simovic was quick to assure Berlin that Yugoslavia was "devoted to the maintenance of good and friendly relations with its neighbours the German Reich and the Kingdom of Italy". He believed that his close personal friendship with several top Nazis, especially Luftwaffe chief Göring, would save the day. He was wrong – the Germans invaded on 6 April. Hitler was particularly enraged by the disruption to his plans, and swore to "wipe Yugoslavia off the map". From the beginning, he wanted to enlist the help of the Croats, stating that "the domestic political tensions in Yugoslavia will be sharpened by political assurances to the Croats".

The Serb-led army quickly withdrew from Slovenia and Croatia to defend Serbia before the Germans appeared, leaving the Croatians and Slovenes without supplies or ammunition. Most Croatian soldiers simply went home. The Yugoslav Army disintegrated in the face of the German invasion: 100 of 135 generals in the officer corps surrendered during the first week. Belgrade was taken by a single platoon of Waffen-SS troops led by a second lieutenant on 12 April. General Simovic and his government fled the country; the fighting was over by 17 April. The Germans were quick to exploit Croatian discontent, presenting themselves as liberators.

After the Axis victory, Yugoslavia was dismembered. The German Army occupied Serbia and Macedonia was given to Bulgaria. Croatia was occupied and divided into German and Italian occupation zones, and the Independent State of Croatia, which was given a slice of Dalmatia and Bosnia and Herzegovina, was established with the consent of Germany though against the express wishes of Italy, which wanted to make it an Italian kingdom. The Serbian province of Kosovo was awarded to the Italian colony of Albania, which became known as Greater Albania.

The Croatian Government was led by Ante Pavelic and his *Ustase* movement (*Ustase* comes from the word *ustanak*, meaning uprising or rebellion), which began as an inter-war terrorist movement before adopting fascist ideology. Pavelic had been an elected deputy in parliament and vice-president of the Croatian Bar Association when Alexander declared the dictatorship and dissolved parliament. He fled to Italy and founded the *Ustase* in exile with the aim of liberating Croatia by force.

Pavelic and the Ustase

When Yugoslavia was invaded, the underground *Ustase* throughout Croatia took control of the government before the Germans arrived. As in the Soviet Union, when the Germans did arrive, they were at first welcomed as liberators. The new Croatian government adopted German racial and economic laws and began persecuting Jews, Serbs, communists, opposition leaders and others. While the majority of the Croatian people favoured an independent Croatian state, many did not support the *Ustase* regime. At its height in 1942, for example, there were only 60,000 in the movement.

Pavelic established himself in Zagreb and immediately unleashed a reign of terror against the local Serb population. Aspiring to form an ethnically pure paradise out of a state in which Croats were, in fact, a minority, he was advised by Hitler not to show too much pity. "If the Croat state wishes to be strong," he told his pupil, "a 50-year policy of intolerance must be pursued, because too much tolerance on such issues can only do harm." Within weeks, Pavelic's bloodiest henchman, Vjekoslav Luburic, began laying the groundwork for Jasenovac, the largest concentration camp in southern Europe. Peasant Party (a popular political movement among the Croats) leader Vladko Macek, who had originally welcomed the *Ustase's* formation of the Independent State of Croatia, found himself among the first internees at Jasenovac; he watched as Croatia's Jewish population, along with untold numbers of Serbs, Roma and political dissidents, passed through the gates on their way to extermination (Macek himself was later released to serve under house arrest).

Above: *The Croat Order of Merit Grand Cross Star. The order was instituted on 10 May 1942 by Pavelic as a reward for meritorious service to the state of Croatia. The star was designed for the Moslems of Bosnia and Herzegovina, who would be averse to wearing a cross.*

Below: *The Croat Order of Merit Grand Cross Sash and Badge. In the centre of the cross can be seen a "U" for Ustase, encompassing the Croat red and white chequerboard shield engraved on a bursting grenade. The sash was also in red and white.*

Above: *Croatia also sent pilots to the Eastern Front. This is the Croat Air Force Legion Badge, whose members achieved some success against their Soviet opponents. Eventually, the unit was withdrawn from the Eastern Front to fight the growing partisan threat in Croatia.*

On 22 July 1941, deputy leader Mile Budak clarified *Ustase* ideology in an official newspaper: "We shall kill one part of the Serbs. We shall transport another third, and the rest of them will embrace the Roman Catholic religion. Our Croatia will become Catholic within 10 years."

Unsurprisingly, *Ustase* atrocities provoked the Serb population in the Independent State of Croatia to rise in arms, flooding the ranks of the monarchist Chetnik and the partisan movements (see below). The state was soon torn apart by internal revolt, and the *Ustase*, for all its violence, was never able to establish full control over the country. Its shocking behaviour even exasperated many hardened German officers, including General Edmund Glaise von Horstenau, German Plenipotentiary General in Croatia, who littered his reports to Berlin with denunciations of the *Ustase* and "unspeakable swineishness of this gang of murderers and criminals". In July 1941, he had told Berlin: "According to reliable reports from countless German military and civilian observers, during the last few weeks, in town and country, the *Ustase* has

gone raving mad." One of Horstenau's reports stated: "We saw no sign of [guerrillas] but there were plenty of ownerless horses and cattle, not to mention innumerable geese. At Crkveni Bok, an unhappy place where, under the leadership of an *Ustase* lieutenant-colonel, some 500 country folk from 15 to 20 years had met their end, all murdered, the women raped and then tortured, the children killed. I saw in the River Sava a woman's corpse with the eyes gouged out and a stick shoved into the sexual parts. This woman was at most 20 years old when she fell into the hands of these monsters. Anywhere in a corner, the pigs are gorging themselves on an unburied human being. All the houses were looted. The 'lucky' inhabitants were consigned to one of the fearsome boxcar trains; many of these involuntary 'passengers' cut their veins on the journey."

Mussolini soon turned against his former protégés, and ordered his army to reoccupy Herzegovina, the birthplace of many of the *Ustase* leaders. In total, it is estimated that at least 30,000 Jews, 29,000 Roma and 600,000 Serbs — one-third of the pre-war population — were murdered in the four years of the Independent State of Croatia's existence.

In Serbia, a new pro-Nazi government was first established under the leadership of Milan Asimovic and later under former Minister of War General Milan Nedic, which governed until 1945. Nedic supported Hitler and met with him in 1943. This new government immediately established three concentration camps for Jews, gypsies and others. Nedic formed his own paramilitary storm-troopers known as the State Guard, which numbered 20,000. The guard was comprised of former members of the Chetniks, which had existed as an all-Serb paramilitary police force under Alexander and Paul to enforce loyalty from non-Serbian members of the armed forces. The Chetniks were essentially a Serb nationalist guerrilla force, named after the armed irregulars who had harassed the Turks in the nineteenth century. The most important group were those organized by Colonel Draza Mihailovic in the Ravna Gorge district of western Serbia.

Chetniks and partisans

When Yugoslavia disintegrated, one faction of Chetniks swore allegiance to the new Serbian Nazi Government. Another group remained under the pre-war leader Kosta Pecanac, who openly collaborated with the Germans. A third Chetnik faction followed the Serbian fascist Dimitrije Ljotic. Ljotic's units were primarily responsible for tracking down Jews, gypsies and partisans for execution or deportation to concentration camps (which often amounted to the same thing). By August 1942, the Serbian Government would proudly announce that Belgrade was the first city in the New Order to be Judenfrei or "free of Jews". Only 1115 of Belgrade's 12,000 Jews would survive the war, and 95 percent of the total Jewish population of Serbia was exterminated between 1941 and 1945.

Other Chetniks rallied behind Mihailovic, a 48-year-old army officer and monarchist who had been court-martialled by Nedic and was known to have close ties to Britain. Early in the war, Mihailovic offered some tepid resistance to the German forces while at the same time collaborating with the Italians.

Although Mihailovic conducted a propaganda campaign to convince the Allies that his Chetniks were inflicting great damage on the Axis, he in fact collaborated with both the Germans and Italians while fighting the *Ustase* and partisans. At its peak, Mihailovic's Chetniks claimed to have 300,000 troops (in reality, they never exceeded 30,000). At first, the Allies considered Mihailovic the most important figure in the Yugoslav resistance, but they eventually shifted their support to the partisans.

The partisans, founded by Josip Broz (Tito), a Croatian communist, represented the only real resistance to the Axis in Yugoslavia during World War II. They fought a tenacious campaign; and on 13 July 1943, a Democratic Republic of Croatia under the leadership of Andrija

Hebrang was declared in those areas occupied by partisan forces (by the end of 1943, the partisans numbered 300,000). By 1943, Allied support swung behind Tito; and by 1944, the partisans were the only recognized Allied-backed force fighting in Yugoslavia. But in 1941, the country was firmly under the heel of the Germans.

Soon after its formation, Pavelic's Croatia offered troops to fight on the Eastern Front. In a letter to Hitler, Pavelic stated that the Croatians were eager to join the battle of "all freedom-loving nations against communism". The call for volunteers yielded 9000 recruits which, by 16 July 1941, had been whittled down to 4000 men. They were formed into the 369th Reinforced Croatian Infantry Regiment, which consisted of a regimental staff, three infantry battalions and an artillery staff company. A training battalion was also formed, in the Austrian town of Stokerau, to process replacements when the regiment had been sent to the front.

In October 1941, the regiment was in combat east of the River Dnieper, where it received the surrender of thousands

Below: *The smallest element in the armed forces of the Independent State of Croatia (which was not independent at all) was the navy. As well as having a small navy of her own, Croatia supplied personnel for the German and Italian navies. This is the Croat Naval Legion Badge.*

of Red Army soldiers (who believed they would receive better treatment if they gave themselves up to fellow Slavs). The following year, in July 1942, the regiment was fighting near the River Don where it sustained heavy casualties. It was involved in the fighting in Stalingrad, which reduced its numbers still further. By 3 November 1942, for example, it was down to 191 men. In the face of privations and combat, the numbers dwindled further; and, to make matters worse, Colonel Pavicic, the regiment's commander, went insane. On 23 January 1943, 18 wounded Croatians were flown out of the Stalingrad Pocket, leaving behind a handful of their comrades to fight on under Lieutenant-Colonel Mesic. They were either killed or captured by the Red Army when the pocket was finally liquidated.

The Croat divisions

The positive response to German recruiting in Croatia led the Germans to raise a division, which began forming at Stokerau in August 1942. Built around a cadre from the 369th Regiment, the division soon achieved a high level of readiness under the leadership of German General-leutnant Fritz Neidholt, who had the assistance of German officers and NCOs (Neidholt was hanged in Belgrade in 1947 for war crimes in Yugoslavia). Soon it mustered 14,000 men in two regiments, the 369th and 370th, and was titled the 369th (Croat) Infantry Division, though its members nicknamed it the "Devil's" Division.

The Germans intended to send the division to the Eastern Front, but due to the growing partisan threat in Yugoslavia it was deployed to Croatia in January 1943. Its first operation, codenamed White, was in northern Bosnia and lasted from 20 January until the end of March. The operation failed to destroy the partisans in the area, who escaped at the Neretva River by fighting their way through Italian forces and wiping out a Serb Chetnik blocking force. In May, the division was engaged against the partisans again, this time near the town of Balinovac in the Montenegro-Bosnian border area. The partisans numbered four divisions and two brigades, who were trying to escape being surrounded by Axis forces. The 369th Division was the blocking force, and it inflicted heavy casualties on the partisans, though losing many men itself. And, once again, the partisans escaped.

In 1944, the division continued its anti-partisan sweeps, but by the end of the year Tito's forces had the upper hand in Croatia. In January 1945, for example, they pushed back the 369th Division from Mostar, and the Croat unit was forced to retreat to Austria. It surrendered to British forces on 11 May. The survivors were handed over to the partisans, who executed them.

The Germans raised a second Croat division, the 373rd (Croat) Infantry Division, to combat partisans in Croatia.

Nicknamed the "Tiger" Division by its members, it began forming in January 1943 at Dollersheim in Germany. Organized into the 383rd and 384th Croatian Infantry Regiments, it mustered 10,000 men and was heavily engaged throughout 1943 and 1944. It was badly mauled in December 1944 at Knin; and by early 1945, what was left of it was part of the German XV Mountain Corps. The survivors surrendered to partisans near Sisak in May 1945.

The third division raised by the Germans was the 392nd (Croat) Infantry Division, known as the Blue Division, again mustered at Dollersheim. It was formed in August 1943, and comprised the 364th and 365th Croatian Infantry Regiments. Assigned to the northern coastal area of Croatia, it was engaged against the partisans throughout its short career. Most of the survivors surrendered to the partisans north of Fiume in April 1945. All the Croat divisions had a majority of German officers and NCOs, with the rank and file being Croat.

Another Croat unit that deserves mention is the Fighter Squadron that was raised during the war, designated 15.(Kroatische)/JG 52. First formed in July 1941, over the next few months its personnel learnt to fly Bf 109 fighters. It was deployed to the Eastern Front, near Poltava, on 6 October 1941. By the end of January 1942, the squadron had shot down 23 Soviet aircraft. It continued to serve on the Eastern Front until July 1944, when it was withdrawn to Croatia to combat partisans. By this time, its tally totalled 283 enemy aircraft shot down for the loss of only two aircraft and five pilots.

SS recruitment in the Balkans

The Croat divisions and squadron were under army and air force control respectively, but it was inevitable that Himmler would try to recruit units from the Balkan region. However, his efforts would ultimately make a mockery of the ideal of the SS being a racially pure Germanic organization.

On 7 August 1940, Gottlob Berger, head of Waffen-SS recruiting, sent Reichsführer-SS Himmler a memorandum outlining his plans for the recruitment of ethnic Germans (Volksdeutsche) from the Balkans into the Waffen-SS. He estimated there were 700,000 Volksdeutsche living in Yugoslavia. Himmler approved the formation of a freiwilligen gebirgs division (volunteer mountain division) on 1 March 1942. The cadre around which the division was built was the SS-controlled Selbstschutz (Protection Force), made up of Volksdeutsche in Serbia; and the Einsatz Staffel (Action Squadron) from Croatia (in 1943, Himmler introduced compulsory military service for the Volksdeutsche in German-occupied Serbia; 21,500 ethnic Germans from Serbia would see service in Himmler's Waffen-SS).

What would be named the 7th SS Freiwilligen Gebirgs Division *Prinz Eugen* was formed between April and October 1942. Its command was entrusted to SS-Brigadeführer Artur Phleps who, on 20 April 1942, was promoted to SS-Gruppenführer. Phleps, who had been a soldier in the Austrian Imperial Army, was a Volksdeutsche himself from Transylvania and commanded a mountain corps in the Romanian Army until 1941. By 31 December 1942, the division numbered 393 officers, 2010 NCOs and 18,699 men (though the majority were volunteers, conscription was also resorted to). The officers and NCOs were almost entirely Reichsdeutsche (Germans from the Greater Reich), while the enlisted men were Volksdeutsche from Yugoslavia, Romania and Hungary. In general, the Reichsdeutsche had a low opinion of the fighting ability of the Yugoslav Volksdeutsche, though both Himmler and Berger were committed to exploiting the manpower of these ethnic Germans living outside the Reich.

In October 1942, the *Prinz Eugen* Division was ready and was transferred to the Uzice-Cacak region of western Serbia. In November, it was under the control of the German Twelfth Army, Army Group Southeast. The

Above: *Soldiers of the 369th (Croat) Infantry Division on the march in Bosnia in 1943. The photograph is dated 15 April, which indicates that they are returning from the abortive Operation White in northern Bosnia conducted between January and the end of March.*

"backbone" of the division was made up of Volksdeutsche from the Serbian Banat who had been officers and NCOs in the Yugoslav Army.

The primary mission of the division was to battle partisans, it was thus equipped with mainly obsolete and captured weapons, including French Renault tanks. Mountain divisions were designed to fight in difficult terrain, and thus had a high proportion of pack and horse transport. Support weapons were lighter than those in line divisions, and designed for easy breakdown into manageable loads. For example, the *Prinz Eugen's* 1st and 2nd Artillery Battalions were each equipped with two batteries of four 75mm mountain guns. In contrast, the *Wiking* Division's Artillery Regiment had battalions equipped with 150 heavy howitzers as well as with 105mm light howitzers.

In October 1942, the division took part in its first large-scale military operation, against Serbian forces under one of Mihailovic's commanders, Major Dragutin Keserovic, in the Kopaonik Mountains in the region of Kriva Reka. Phleps' orders to his subordinates indicated the type of war *Prinz Eugen* was going to fight: "The entire population of this area must be considered rebel sympathizers. Every man in Division *Prinz Eugen* will fight victoriously wherever the combat takes him. We now lay the groundwork for future operations. The division must fight to destroy our enemy, eliminate his headquarters and maintain the peace." However, according to Otto Kumm, who commanded the division between February 1944 and January 1945, this first military engagement against Mihailovic's Chetniks was a failure. Kumm noted in his history of the division: "The Chetniks had their spies in every town and were warned long beforehand."

Himmler visited the *Prinz Eugen* Division between 15 and 18 October, and according to Kumm "was pleased by the attitude and state of training". During the latter part of October, the *Prinz Eugen* attacked Mihailovic's guerrilla forces again, this time in Gorni Milanovac and Cacak. During the next two years, the division was almost continuously fighting partisans, though in January 1945 it also came up against Red Army units near Vukovar where it was badly mauled. *Prinz Eugen* ended the war in Slovenia where its officers surrendered to the partisans. As a result, most of the division's survivors were shot.

Fighting insurgents can be a frustrating business, and in Yugoslavia the SS often took out its frustrations on the local population. The *Prinz Eugen* committed a number of atrocities during its career. In May 1943, during Operation Black, the division invaded Montenegro from Herzegovina and occupied the Niksic district. The SS troops took punitive measures against the civilian population, burning entire villages, torturing and killing civilians in their homes. Pregnant women, infants with their mothers, the frail and the elderly were all butchered. In one village, 121 people, mostly women, were massacred, including 29 children between the ages of 6 months and 14 years, and 30 persons between the ages of 60 and 92. In March 1944, during a "purge action" from Sinj, 834 inhabitants were massacred and their bodies burned. More than 500 houses were also looted and set on fire.

Approval for the raising of a second Croatian SS division was given by Hitler on 17 June 1944. The new division was given the honorary title *Kama* (the word for a short Turkish sword) and assigned the divisional number 23. This new division was to be a mountain division titled the 23rd SS Waffen Gebirgs Division *Kama*. It was also decided that a mountain corps command would be created that would eventually be in charge of the *Handschar* and *Kama* Divisions. Recruitment for the *Kama*

Left: *A soldier of the 7th SS Freiwilligen Gebirgs Division Prinz Eugen, a unit formed in March 1942 from a core of Serbian and Croatian Volksdeutsche. It was raised principally to fight Tito's partisans, though in the process committed a number of atrocities against civilians.*

Below: *The cuffband of the Prinz Eugen Division. Equipped with obsolete and captured equipment, it was capable enough against lightly armed partisans. However, in 1944, it came up against the Red Army and was badly mauled. There were many desertions as a result.*

Above: The Grand Mufti of Jerusalem (wearing white turban) meets Azerbaijani members of the Waffen-SS. The Mufti arrived in Berlin via Persia and Italy in November 1941, but it was not until April 1943 that the Axis formally supported the Pan-Arab movement.

Division had already begun on 10 June 1944. Some German officers and NCOs were made available, as well as a number of Croatian officers and men from the *Handschar* Division. The entire Reconnaissance Battalion of the *Handschar* was also transferred to *Kama*. To this core of troops was added a batch of new recruits, mostly Croatian Moslems from Bosnia. At its peak in September 1944, *Kama* had 3793 men.

Hitler had planned to form the division in northern Croatia, but feared that Tito's partisans would seriously disrupt or even destroy the unit before it could finish training. He therefore ordered it to form in the Hungarian Bacska, which was populated mostly by ethnic Hungarians and Germans.

In September 1944, with the Red Army advance approaching the Balkans, the training bases of the *Kama* Division were suddenly dangerously close to the frontlines. The SS High Command attempted to get the division ready for combat, but soon realized that sending still raw recruits into combat would be folly. It was, therefore, decided to disband the unit and make as much use of the personnel as possible by transferring them as replacements to other divisions. The Moslems in the division were ordered to report to *Handschar*, but many

took the opportunity to desert. The others were generally incorporated into the forming 31st SS Freiwilligen Grenadier Division (a Dutch unit).

The Reichsführer-SS had several reasons for forming a Moslem SS division. For example, such a unit would be useful for taking advantage of the traditional Moslem enmity towards the Christian Serbs, who made up a large part of Tito's partisans. He was also attracted to the Islamic idea of the virtue of dying in a holy war (Jihad).

The Independent State of Croatia contained the province of Bosnia and Herzegovina. The province was an ethnic and religious mix, with Catholic Croats, Orthodox Serbs and Moslem Croats. It was the latter that the SS would target in its recruitment of a Croatian SS division. Himmler was fascinated by the Islamic faith, and regarded Moslems in general as fearless soldiers. He also subscribed to the theory that Croatians (and therefore the Croatian Moslems) were not Slavic people, but actually of Aryan descent. Of more interest to Hitler, the Germans were hoping to rally the world's 350 million Moslems to their side in a struggle against the British Empire. The creation of a Moslem, albeit European Moslem, division was considered a stepping stone to this greater end.

Himmler proposed the formation of a Bosnian Moslem division to Hitler in late 1942, but the Führer waited until 13 February 1943 before authorizing its formation. Prior to the creation of the division, however, approval also had to be granted by the Croatian Government, as its citizens were to be recruited – and on Croatian territory.

Himmler immediately began negotiations with the Croats. Their most serious objection to the concept was that they didn't want any boost given to Moslem

Below: The Grand Mufti during a visit to the base of the Handschar Division, a formation raised by the Germans from Croatian Moslems to make use of the traditional Moslem enmity against the Christian Serbs who made up the bulk of Tito's partisan forces.

separatism in Bosnia. The SS prevailed, and Pavelic eventually agreed to the division's creation on 5 March 1943. But the Croats tried to hinder the project, especially after the SS recruiters played up the glories achieved by the Bosnian units of Imperial Austria-Hungary, thus fanning the flames of Moslem separatism. The employment of the Grand Mufti of Jerusalem by the Waffen-SS to drum up more recruits further alienated the Croats.

These efforts were reasonably successful, though, as 8000 men had volunteered by 14 April, including a number of deserters from the Croatian military. This was well short of the target of 26,000, so a number of Volksdeutsche and Moslems from the Croat Army and *Ustase* were recruited. However, this was still inadequate, so Himmler reluctantly permitted Bosnian Catholics to enlist, but not to exceed 10 percent of the division's authorized strength (only 400 ultimately joined). Despite these additions, the division was firmly Moslem in practice: imams served at the battalion level, except for the all-German signal battalion; and mullahs were attached

Left: *An SS-Hauptsturmführer of the* Handschar *Division (left). Himmler remarked to Goebbels that "he had nothing against Islam because it educates men ... promises them heaven if they fight and are killed in action; a very practical and attractive religion for soldiers".*

manpower that had been defending the Moslem villages in Croatia from the depredations of the marauding royalist Chetniks, *Ustase* and communist partisans. The divisional strength reached the required 26,000 men by mid-1943, though not all men were volunteers (some being begged, bribed and outright kidnapped into service). Morale in the division dropped when reports were received of soldiers' villages being destroyed and their families killed.

The Handschar Division

The recruits were in training from July 1943 until February 1944 but problems soon emerged. Their German training officers, indoctrinated by years of Slav-baiting, did not share Himmler's enthusiasm at the prospect of Moslems becoming members of the Waffen-SS. They despaired at the sight of the men kneeling down on their prayer mats facing Mecca, praying to Allah, and made their feelings known in no uncertain terms. They called the recruits *Mujos* and behaved towards them in an overbearing and condescending manner. This led to friction between officers and men which culminated in a mutiny in the pioneer battalion, during which some German officers were shot out of hand. The mutiny was soon quelled, with 14 of the ringleaders being shot, and a large number of others being sent either to labour gangs working on the Siegfried Line or to concentration camps.

The division was ready by early 1944, being named the 13th SS Waffen Gebirgs Division *Handschar* (a "handschar" is a curved Turkish sword, traditionally the symbol of Bosnia). The division had two infantry regiments (Waffen Gebirgs Jäger Regiments 27 and 28), an artillery regiment (Waffen Gebirgs Artillerie Regiment 13), a reconnaissance company, a panzerjäger (anti-tank) company, a flak company, a pioneer battalion and other support units.

The division's first commander from 9 March 1943 until 1 August 1943 was SS-Standartenführer Herbert von Obwurzer. SS-Brigadeführer Karl-Gustav Sauberzweig took over until 1 June 1944, when SS-Brigadeführer Desiderius Hampel replaced him. Hampel commanded the remnants of the division until its surrender on 8 May 1945.

The uniform worn by the division was regular SS issue, with a divisional collar patch showing an arm holding a scimitar over a swastika. On the left arm was a Croatian arm shield. The oval mountain troop Edelweiss patch was worn on the right arm. Headgear was the Moslem fez in

to regiments. Books were produced encouraging their religion and were distributed throughout its ranks. It was even reported that Hitler sent each member of the division a pendant with a miniature Koran attached to it.

It was originally intended to form the division in Bosnia from a cadre supplied by the *Prinz Eugen* Division, but the training areas were too crowded with the 117th Jäger Division, which was also being formed. The SS was also tired of the Croatian Government's petty obstructions, and decided to train the division in Germany instead. The first trainloads of recruits were shipped to the Wildflecken training ground, not far from Schweinfurt, in late May. However, in early June, the SS decided to train the recruits in France instead. Thus, in July, the Bosnians were sent to various towns near the city of Le Puy. By this time, the Bosnians numbered only 15,000 and were desperately short of trained officers and NCOs (a number of the older men who had served in the Austro-Hungarian Army had been deemed unsuitable). To fill out the division, the SS demanded that all Moslems in Croat service be turned over and that a draft of military age men be carried out. This filled out numbers, but at the cost of stripping most of the field grey (normal service) or red ("walking out"), with the SS eagle and death's head emblazoned. Non-Moslem members could opt to wear the normal SS mountain cap.

Handschar began anti-partisan operations in the spring of 1944 from its base in Brcko, and took part in several large-scale anti-partisan sweeps. However, the 1st battalion of the 28th Regiment wasn't to stay long in Bosnia. It was composed of ethnic Albanian Moslems from Kosovo and Himmler ordered it to serve in the newly forming 21st SS

Waffen Gebirgs Division *Skanderbeg* being raised from Albanian Moslems. The battalion was reformed from new recruits and men from the rest of the division. This wasn't the last "donation" unit; on 28 May 1944, Hitler granted permission to form a second Bosnian division. *Handschar* had to provide a cadre for the new division – 23rd SS Waffen Gebirgs Division *Kama* – though ongoing operations prevented any men from being released until June. *Handschar* gave up 54 officers, 187 NCOs and 1137 men to *Kama*.

These losses, coupled with the previous leadership shortage, hampered its combat operations as few Bosnians were judged suitable for promotion. The addition of 500 young Croatian Volksdeutsche hardly compensated *Handschar* for its losses.

Below: *Four brothers serving in the Handschar Division. Note the distinctive collar insignia worn, which shows a "Handschar" scimitar in a hand with a swastika. Fez colours were either red (for parades) or field-grey.*

Above: *The Moslems of the* Handschar *Division never displayed a high commitment to the Nazi cause. They were good at killing unarmed civilians, but only engaged the partisans half-heartedly. Himmler was very disappointed, and disbanded the division in October 1944.*

As part of V SS Mountain Corps, *Handschar* was constantly engaged in anti-partisan warfare until September 1944 when it was withdrawn back to Brcko (just in time to receive the brunt of a fresh offensive by Tito's partisans). It was during this time that the desertion rate reached an all-time high: more than 2000 deserters were reported in the first three weeks of September, who also took their weapons with them. Many switched sides, especially after Tito offered an amnesty, but a number joined the *Ustase* or simply went home to defend their families. *Handschar* was now short of manpower, so Himmler ordered it reorganized on 24 September. Each of its Gebirgsjäger regiments had its third battalion disbanded, and most of its speciality units were removed and subordinated directly to IX SS Mountain Corps.

Widespread desertions continued until October. After 100 Bosnians of the divisional escort company deserted in mid-October, an enraged Himmler ordered all unreliable Bosnians to be disarmed and their weapons turned over to Germans. The Bosnians were pressed into service with labour units. The remnants became part of Battle Group Hanke and were deployed to Hungary, south of Budapest, Lake Balaton and Drava in March 1945. Thus ended Himmler's scheme of creating an all-conquering Moslem division.

As well as Yugoslavia, Himmler also looked to Albania to furnish recruits for his SS empire. During the Italian administration from 1941–43, Kosovo Serbs, Jews, gypsies and other non-Albanians were arrested, interned, deported or murdered. Serb houses were burned and their

Right: *Cossacks in Belgrade. Both the 1st and 2nd Cossack Divisions saw action against the partisans in Yugoslavia. Like many ethnic units in German service, once removed from their homelands the morale of the Cossacks fell and they were largely ineffective.*

Above: A village burns following its sacking by troops of the Skanderbeg Division, a unit raised by Himmler from Albanian Moslems to fight the communist partisans. Formed in April 1944, it went into action in August and proceeded to commit a number of atrocities.

inhabitants were driven out of Kosovo. Dozens of Serb Orthodox churches were also demolished and looted.

With the surrender of Italy in 1943, Germany occupied Albania and sought to strengthen Albanian nationalist groups and to recruit Albanians for German-raised units. On 16 September 1943, Dzafer Deva, a member of the *Balli Kombetar* (BK – National Union, an Albanian nationalist organization which sought to create an ethnically pure Greater Albania), organized the Second League of Prizren (the league was a nineteenth-century Albanian liberation movement) "in cooperation with the German occupation authorities", which intensified its efforts to ethnically cleanse Kosovo of Serbs and Jews and other non-Albanians. Attacks against Kosovo Serbs increased and intensified, and over 10,000 Kosovo Serb families were driven out of Kosovo.

The *Balli Kombetar* and the Second League of Prizren were instrumental in the creation of the 21st SS Waffen Gebirgs Division *Skanderbeg*, which was seen as advancing the cause of a Greater Albania by making Kosovo ethnically pure and cleansed of Serbs and Jews. Himmler was comfortable with the idea of an Albanian SS division as "anthropological studies" by the Italians during 1939–43 purported to show that the Ghegs of northern Albania and Kosovo-Metohija were Aryans who had preserved their racial purity for over 2000 years.

Bedri Pejani, the president of the Second League of Prizren, wrote to Himmler on 19 March 1944, asking him to organize Albanian military formations as part of the armed forces of the Third Reich: "Excellency, the central committee of the Second Albanian League of Prizren has authorized me to inform you that only your excellency is united with the Second Albanian League, that you should form this army, which will be able to safeguard the borders of Kosovo and liberate the surrounding regions."

On 17 April 1944, following instructions from Himmler, the *Skanderbeg* Division was formed. Himmler envisioned the formation of two Albanian SS divisions, but the war ended before the second could be raised. Approximately 300 Albanians from the *Handschar* Division were transferred to the new unit, making a total of 6491 ethnic Albanians, two-thirds of whom were from Kosovo-Metohija. To this Albanian core was added German troops – Reichsdeutsche from Austria – and Volksdeutsche officers, NCOs and enlisted men transferred from the *Prinz Eugen* Division then stationed in Bosnia and Herzegovina. The *Skanderbeg* Division was made up of Albanian Moslems of the Bektashi and Sunni sects of Islam and several hundred Albanian Roman Catholics. The total strength of the division was 9000 men of all ranks.

The first commander of the division was SS-Brigadeführer Josef Fitzhum, from April to June 1944. In June 1944, SS-Standartenführer August Schmidhuber, formerly an officer in the *Prinz Eugen* Division, was appointed divisional commander until August 1944. Thereafter, SS-Obersturmbannführer Alfred Graf assumed command of the remnants of the division until May 1945.

Militarily useless, the *Skanderbeg* Division essentially engaged in a policy of ethnic cleansing and genocide against the Serb Orthodox Christian and Jewish populations of Kosovo-Metohija and the Stara Srbija region. In Kosovo-Metohija, it massacred unarmed Serbs in a systematic plan of genocide. Its first operation in Kosovo-Metohija was the raid on Kosovo Jews in Pristina which took place on 14 May 1944. The SS troops raided apartments and homes where Kosovo Jews lived, looted their possessions, and rounded them up for deportation to concentration camps.

Following the defeat of Nazi Germany, both Yugoslavia and Albania became communist states. In November 1945, Tito proclaimed the Federal People's Republic of Yugoslavia; and in 1946, its southern neighbour became the People's Republic of Albania. Nationalist sentiments within both states were suppressed, and the wounds of a brutal war were seemingly healed. However, the hundreds of thousands of deaths that were caused by Nazi policy in the Balkans created a legacy of mistrust and thirst for revenge. These sentiments lay festering among the different ethnic groups in both countries, until they finally exploded into violence in the 1990s.

Below: *Recruits for the Skanderbeg Division. Only 6000 of the Albanians who presented themselves were judged suitable for military service, and most had deserted by September 1944. For the Waffen-SS, the second Moslem division had been a fiasco.*

Chapter 13

A SETTLING OF SCORES

Technically, all those foreign nationals who fought for Germany in World War II were traitors, and as such deserved a traitor's fate. Stalin was more than happy to shoot or work to death all those from the Soviet republics who had taken up arms against him, and also wreaked vengeance on their families for good measure. In the West, although there were thousands of trials after the war for collaborators, justice rather than revenge was the prime motive.

At the end of World War II, there were millions of men and women of non-German origin who had served Nazi Germany between 1939 and 1945 and whose fate had to be determined by the victorious Allies. This chapter will examine the contribution foreign nations made to the German war effort, and the fate that was meted out to them after May 1945.

The German Army, the agent for spreading Nazi ideology throughout Europe, made use of great numbers of foreign volunteer units. These included "sub-human"

Left: Austria, May 1945. Russian nationals who fought for the Third Reich are loaded on to cattle wagons for shipment back to the Soviets, and certain death.

Slavs, although Hitler had categorically forbidden the use of Russians by the German forces (an order that was largely ignored by divisional commanders). Their utilization not only occurred, it occurred on a vast and vital scale. It is a strange and ironic truth that without Russian aid Germany's war against Stalin could not have continued as long as it did. Desertion from the Red Army was massive in the early stages of the 1941 invasion. Many of the defectors offered their services to the Wehrmacht. Reluctant to turn away willing hands, the army took them on, albeit "off the record", as *Hiwis*. They may have been given uniforms and rations but old prejudices died hard — there was a kind of racist supremacy pleasure in seeing *Hiwis* digging ditches and latrines. But, then, especially during the winter of 1941–42, hundreds of *Hiwis* were

Left: *Jan Munk, a Dutch volunteer in the Wiking Division. After the war, he was tried in Holland for serving in the German armed forces. He got off relatively lightly, receiving a two-year prison sentence.*

sucked into the vortex of battle and became de facto combatants. Their courage and steadiness under fire, and their uncomplaining fortitude in the face of hardship and danger, won for them the respect of the German soldier at the front and did much to break down the psychological barrier between "sub-human" Slavs and "supermen" Aryans created by Nazi propaganda. Berlin would have never agreed, of course, and so the German Army never declared the *Hiwis*, and thus thousands of Russians never appeared on the recorded strengths of German divisions in the East. By the end of 1941, around 150,000 Russians were in the employ of the Wehrmacht. Less than a year later, this had risen to 500,000; of these, some 200,000 were in combat units. By the end of 1943, this figure had doubled. Large proportions of this manpower pool were later absorbed into the Waffen-SS.

Western and Eastern foreign nationals

The foreign volunteer programme was always central to the development of the Waffen-SS as the war developed, but was it worth it, both in terms of manpower and contribution to the German war effort? The SS was able to tap a useful source of high-grade manpower in the case of Western European volunteers, which the German armed forces would otherwise have found unavailable. The Western volunteers were usually highly motivated and their units well equipped, although there were a number of initial problems, not least that SS training grounds, officer and noncommissioned officer (NCO) schools were not set up to readily accommodate non-German recruits. As a result, the Western recruits fought well on the battlefield, the ultimate criterion for any military organization, and the *Nordland* and *Wiking* Divisions were among the best fielded by the Waffen-SS.

If there were problems integrating Western volunteers, then German policy with regard to the Eastern volunteers can only be seen as an almost unmitigated disaster. On the credit side, the German invasion of the Soviet Union did serve to galvanize foreign nationals, Western Europeans that is, by suggesting that it was a "European" undertaking intent on ridding the world of communism. This had less appeal to the Eastern volunteers, who may have wanted to

Left: *A hero in Germany, a traitor in Belgium. The soldier on the left is Remy Schrynen, a highly decorated member of the Flemish 27th SS Freiwilligen Grenadier Division Langemarck. He received a 10-year prison sentence.*

Above: *Former Dutch members of the Waffen-SS being held in a prison camp in Holland in 1945. The scale of collaboration in Holland mitigated against issuing severe sentences against individuals. Most offenders received light prison sentences.*

Below: *John Amery (left), the traitor who tried to raise a British legion for the Germans. His efforts came to nought, and after the war he stood trial in Britain accused of eight counts of treason. He pleaded guilty and was sentenced to death, being executed in December 1945.*

rid their homelands of the Bolsheviks but also wanted national self-determination. This was anathema to the Germans, of course, and so the Eastern volunteer units were never used to their full potential. They were employed for rear-area tasks, or even shipped off to the Atlantic Wall for garrison duties. And once away from their homelands, their morale plummeted. How much more effective they could have become had they been used to fight for the re-establishment of their homelands will never be known, but the ill-conceived German policy towards them hampered Nazi aims in the East. The ultimate example of this is the fiasco of Vlassov's army, which only became a reality when the war was already lost.

The whole Eastern programme could have been excused in 1941 or perhaps even as late as 1942 for its propaganda potential, but thereafter it siphoned off trained officers and NCOs desperately needed elsewhere when manpower and material shortages began to bite in 1943. In the same way, it frittered away essential stocks of war munitions on second-rate units.

Above: *Red Army soldiers prepare to execute Russians who had been serving in the Wehrmacht. Given the ideological nature of the war on the Eastern Front, justice was more often than not served by a noose or the barrel of a gun. Traitors could expect no mercy.*

What was the fate of those foreign nationals who had fought for Hitler? In Western Europe, the process of dealing with collaborators began as soon as the war ended. In Holland, special courts were established to enable the many thousands of collaborators, as well as those who had served in the German armed forces, to be tried, and the death penalty was reintroduced for the first time since its abolition in 1873. In all, 138 death sentences were pronounced, although only 36 were actually carried out. Anton Mussert was brought to trial at The Hague in November 1945 on a charge of high treason. On 12 December, he was unsurprisingly found guilty and sentenced to death. Eighteen Germans also received death sentences for crimes in Holland but only five, of whom one was Rauter, were executed.

The International Military Tribunal at Nuremberg dealt with Reich Commissioner Seyss-Inquart. The tribunal stated that he had been "a knowing and voluntary participant in war crimes and crimes against humanity which were committed in the occupation of the Netherlands". He was hanged on 16 October 1946.

Between 120,000 and 150,000 persons were arrested in Holland in the immediate post-liberation period but, by October 1945, only 72,321 men and 23,723 women remained in prison. Thirty-five special courts consisting of five judges each were set up to deal with major cases of collaboration, while smaller tribunals comprising one judge and two laymen dealt with less serious offences. Some 60,000 persons were deprived of their Dutch citizenship for entering foreign military service, and also had their property seized by the state. This was applied to all those who had served in the German Army, Navy, Air Force, the Waffen-SS, the *Landstorm Nederland*, German police or security formations, the guard companies of the Todt Organization and the German Labour Service (RAD). However, it did not include service with the Dutch Germanic SS or the German state railways. On the whole, the Dutch treated their collaborators with tolerance and humanity, though perhaps the very magnitude of the problem prevented harsh judgements.

Following its liberation, Belgium set up special courts consisting of two civilian and three military judges to try

Above: *A group of Russians from an unidentified German unit on the Eastern Front. This photograph is from Russian secret service files, and was used for identification purposes during the processing of German prisoners who fell into Soviet hands.*

Below: *This individual has been made an example of by the Russians, no doubt for collaborating with the enemy. A sign listing his crimes has been nailed to the gallows, which is being read by several Red Army soldiers. Note the T-34 tank in the background.*

Above: Members of Vlassov's POA, the army raised by the Germans from Russian nationals, in France. Thousands of Russians in German service were captured by the Western Allies during the fighting in France in 1944. They were subsequently sent back to the Soviet Union.

collaborators. Some 100,000 persons were arrested but only 87,000 were subsequently brought to trial; of these, around 10,000 were acquitted. Sentences of death were passed on 4170 persons (3193 were for military collaboration), of which only 230 were actually carried out. About 16,000 persons received long prison sentences. Léon Degrelle, the Rexist leader and famed Walloon commander, was sentenced to death *in absentia*, having escaped to Spain.

Those members of the Flemish Legion still serving in the Waffen-SS retreated from the River Oder and surrendered to the Americans near Schwerin on 2 May 1945. From there they were sent to the former German concentration camp at Neuengamme, which was being used by the British as a holding centre for SS prisoners. In the autumn, the Flemings were handed over to the Belgian Army, which transported them by cattle truck to the Belgian Army camp at Beverloo. This first contingent consisted of 1900 men and four Flemish Red Cross nurses. On arrival at Beverloo station, the prisoners were allegedly kicked and beaten as they made the 4.8km (three-mile) journey to the camp. Once inside the camp, the prisoners were subjected to the same brutality, indignities and lack of medical attention inflicted on inmates of German concentration camps.

In Denmark, the prosecution of collaborators was smaller in scale and intensity. The main reasons were that relatively few Danes had served in the German armed forces, and the occupation had been mostly lenient (at least until 29 August 1943 when the Germans had officially dissolved the Danish Government and instituted martial law), thus lessening the desire for revenge. In total, 15,724 Danes were arrested on charges of collaboration after the war. Subsequently, 1229 were acquitted, while the remainder were handed prison sentences ranging from one year to life (62 individuals received the latter sentence). The death penalty, abolished in 1895, was reintroduced under a special law of 1 June 1945 for extreme cases of collaboration or crimes against humanity. The courts meted out a total of 112 death sentences, but only 46 were carried out. K.B. Martinsen, commander of Freikorps *Danmark*, was executed on 25 June 1949. Prison sentences in excess of four years were passed on 3641 persons, 9737 persons were temporarily deprived of their civil rights and another 2936 had their civil rights removed permanently.

Denmark and Norway

The status of former members of the Freikorps became a delicate issue in post-war Denmark. At one stage during the war, the Danish war minister had consented to the enlistment of Danish military personnel into the Freikorps, but later changed his mind. After the war, volunteers were tried as collaborators, but claimed that they had been led to believe that the Freikorps had the backing of the Danish Government. The government replied that even if it had given its consent, the volunteers could not use this as a valid excuse since they should have realized that the government was acting under German pressure. The authorities then proceeded to cancel the volunteers' pension rights, and most volunteers were sentenced to one or two years' imprisonment (the Danish resistance blew up the Freikorps *Danmark* war memorial at Hovelte in May 1945).

In Norway, more than 90,000 persons were investigated by the police on suspicion of collaboration; of these, 18,000 were sent to prison and a further 28,000 fined (some also lost their civil rights). In the case of state employees, a fine also meant the loss of their jobs. About 3500 sentences of more than three years, and 600 of more than eight years, were meted out to collaborators. The death penalty, abolished in 1870, was reintroduced. Some 30 death sentences were passed although only 25 were carried out. For volunteers who had served in the German armed forces, sentences of imprisonment ranged from four to eight years dependent on rank and age.

Right: *Andrei Vlassov, the commander of the Russian Liberation Army. Captured by the Americans, he was handed over to the Soviets on 15 May 1945. On 1 August 1946, Radio Moscow announced that he and several of his associates had been hanged.*

Officers were held to be more culpable than other ranks. Arthur Quist, for example, the commander of the Freiwilligen Legion *Norwegen* between 1942 and 1943, was sentenced to 10 years' imprisonment. Female volunteers were not exempt from punishment, either.

Periodic amnesties lessened the severity of some initial punishments. A law of 9 July 1948, for example, allowed for the release of all those imprisoned for collaboration after the completion of half their original sentences. But there would be no leniency shown to the man whose name has since become a byword for collaboration: Vidkun Quisling. After voluntarily surrendering to the Norwegian Government, he was put on trial for treason. Found guilty, his seven-hour closing speech notwithstanding, he was sentenced to death and executed in October 1945.

In France, a country wracked with guilt over the Vichy regime, trials of collaborators lasted from September 1944 until the end of 1949. In court, 2071 persons were sentenced to death, which does not include those passed *in absentia* – another 4400. Of the 2071 capital sentences, only 768 were carried out (all death sentences passed on

women or minors were automatically commuted by General de Gaulle). In the armed forces, 3035 officers were dishonourably discharged and a further 2635 involuntarily retired. About 5000 civil servants, including 18 magistrates, were relieved of their posts. A further 6000 were punished in lesser ways. Former members of the *Légion des Volontaires Français* and French Waffen-SS were offered active service in Indo-China as an alternative to imprisonment. Many decided to take this offer, and were killed fighting the *Viet Minh*.

Britain stood alone in not being occupied by the Germans, except for the Channel Islands. The latter, with

Left: *General Keightley (left), the commander of the British V Corps, under whose jurisdiction the forced repatriation of Soviet and Yugoslav refugees (one of the most shameful episodes in the history of the British Army) took place in May 1945.*

Above: *Cossacks who had fought for Germany surrender their weapons to the British in Austria in May 1945. The British at first assured the Cossacks that they were being sent to Italy. However, when they found out they were being sent back to Russia, there was widespread panic.*

their short lines of communication to the continent and their high density of population, were ideal for denunciation, collaboration and fraternization. In general, denouncers had two motives, both of which were fuelled by pragmatism rather than ideology. A tiny minority of islanders had been recruited by the German police force as informers and received lump sums for keeping the German authorities up to date on public opinion and all movements in the civilian population. The second motive was more personal and was usually directed against particular individuals against whom people bore a grudge. In fact, British citizens under German occupation did not

behave dramatically differently to those under the Nazi jackboot on the continent.

At least three people from the islands ended up volunteering for the German forces: Eric Pleasants and John Leister both joined the British Freikorps; and Eddie Chapman became a double agent. But there were no large-scale trials for collaboration on the islands. On the other hand, cases were brought against Britons from the mainland who had fought for or collaborated with the Germans. The most notable was the trial of John Amery, who was charged with high treason. He pleaded guilty and was condemned to death, a sentence that brought many calls for clemency, particularly from the Duke of Bedford. They fell on deaf ears, though, and he was executed at Wandsworth Prison. William Joyce, "Lord Haw-Haw", was also charged with high treason, found guilty and likewise executed. Thomas Hellor Cooper, the most senior British national in the British Freikorps, was similarly charged with high treason, found guilty and condemned to death, though this was later commuted to life imprisonment.

Other members of the British Freikorps were charged with varying offences, those in the military being tried by courts martial and receiving varying terms of imprisonment of between two years to life. Civilians were tried

under the Defence of the Realm Act, and received prison sentences of between two and three years in length.

The Indians who fought for both Germany and Japan were tried at the Red Fort trials in Delhi, the symbol of past Mogul rule and the very location where Chandra Bose had boasted that his triumphant army would parade in a free India. For its part, the Congress Party, the main movement for Indian independence, saw in the trials a heaven-sent opportunity to attack the British. The first three officers selected to stand trial were Shah Nawaz Khan, commander of the Subhas Brigade and then of the 2nd Division of the Indian National Army (INA); P. K. Sahgal; and G. S. Dhillon. All three were charged with waging war against the King-Emperor. They were a cross-section of India's community: a Muslim, Sikh and Hindu. However, India was in no mood to hear words focused on the imperial past. Demonstrations on behalf of the INA occurred all over the country, and under pressure from public opinion a compromise was reached whereby the accused were found guilty but their sentences of transportation for life were suspended. They were cashiered, though, since the Commander-in-Chief in India, Field Marshal Sir Claude Auchinleck, emphasized that it was "in all circumstances a most serious crime for an officer or soldier to throw off his allegiance and wage war against the State". With this comment, the trials ended.

The consequences of Yalta

By the end of the war, there were huge numbers of Eastern peoples milling around in Central Europe awaiting their fate. They had fought for Germany, but would they be treated as prisoners of war (POWs) or traitors?

The ultimate fate of all those who served with the German war machine was first discussed at the Tehran Conference (28 November–1 December 1943). At that meeting, British Prime Minister Churchill was concerned that large numbers of British and Commonwealth troops were being held by the Germans in the Eastern territories, and he believed it was highly probable that they would be liberated by the advancing Soviet forces (with no second front in Western Europe, he thought the Red Army might even reach the Low Countries). These gains would leave the liberated POWs as pawns in the power struggle he predicted would occur after the final victory in Europe.

Stalin, too, wished to see the return of his own POWs held by the Germans, though for different reasons than

Left: *Men, women and children were forced on to the boxcars that would take them to face the vengeance of Stalin's Red Army or Tito's partisans. Many were shot within hearing of the British, while others endured a slow death in the Gulag or Yugoslav camps.*

also provided for Soviet control of the camps and "the [Soviet] right to appoint the internal administration and set up the [camps's] internal discipline and management in accordance with the military laws of their country".

The policy of repatriation had actually been voiced many months before. On 16 September 1944, US Political Officer Alexander Kirk sent a cable to US Secretary of State Cordell Hull which noted that an agreement had been reached between the Soviets and the British for repatriation of Soviet citizens held as prisoners of war "irrespective of whether the individuals desire to return

Churchill. He wanted the quick return of the "traitors" (he viewed any Russian who surrendered to the enemy as such). Ever suspicious, he also believed that if they were outside his control they could be used as a potential army of invasion equipped by the Allies to topple his regime. A possible civil war was the last thing he required after the destruction of his purges and the losses suffered in the war. Thus it was agreed that all nationalities would be returned to their native lands. Churchill was happy but, unwittingly, the Western Allies had acquiesced in what was to become the death warrant for millions of Soviet and Baltic citizens.

The status of POWs was formalized at the Yalta Conference (4–11 February 1945), the subsequent agreement stating: "All Soviet citizens liberated by forces operating under United States command will, without delay after their liberation, be separated from enemy prisoners of war and will be maintained separately from them in concentration camps until they have been handed over to the Soviet authorities." The agreement

Right: *The British entertained their Russian hosts as the prisoners were forced on to trains. Some refugees committed suicide rather than return to face certain death. Other horrific scenes included mothers throwing babies from trains into rivers.*

Above: To speed up the repatriation of the prisoners to the Soviets, an official memorandum to the officers of the British V Corps stated: "Individual cases will NOT be considered unless particularly pressed. In all cases of doubt, the individual will be treated as a Soviet citizen."

to Russia or not. Statements will not be taken from Soviet nationals in the future as to their willingness to return to their native country."

At the end of the war, the Soviets possessed large numbers of German POWs, who were placed in camps without differentiating the Waffen-SS from the other branches of the German forces. In the camps, the prisoners were expected to undertake any and all tasks allotted to them. They were employed in such hazardous pursuits as mine and bomb disposal without proper training. The principle was very simple: every able-bodied prisoner was to carry on living so long as he contributed to the rebuilding of the Soviet Union. He was kept alive to expunge his "crimes" by hard labour. By the tenth anniversary of the end of the war – 1955 – those who had survived had all been repatriated.

The Soviets also set up trials after the war, which investigated war crimes, crimes against humanity and "crimes against the Soviet system". Vast numbers of suspects were tried and subsequently executed. Those who had fallen into Allied hands were turned over to the Soviet authorities; their fate in most cases was horrific. Many were summarily executed within hours of leaving Allied hands. This was the case for thousands of Soviet prisoners handed over by the British in Austria. A sham parade was mustered that was overseen by General Keightley, commander of V Corps. Non-Soviet and non-Yugoslav citizens and Serbian royalists were supposedly exempt from the deportation order, but key military officials in the British chain of command surreptitiously included them also. As a result, many Russians waving French passports and British medals from World War I were all rounded up and delivered to Stalin. About 35,000 Yugoslavs were handed over to Titoists between 19 May and 4 June 1945, a substantial number being subsequently tortured, brutally treated and massacred.

The fate of the Cossacks

Up to 58,000 Cossacks, including XV SS Cossack Cavalry Corps, surrendered to British forces in southern Austria. They were repatriated by British soldiers using a substantial amount of violence and brutality in which several hundred were killed. As a German, von Pannwitz, their commander, was not obliged to exchange British for Russian captivity, but like a good officer he elected to share the fate of his men. He was hanged along with five senior Cossack leaders in Moscow in July 1947.

Stalin was determined that Vlassov would never live to head an anti-communist army under the patronage of the United States. In his case, he was not so much handed over by the Americans as snatched from them by a Russian armoured column. In July 1946, for "acting as agents of German intelligence and indulging in espionage and diversionary terrorist activity", Vlassov and 11 other leading figures in the POA-KONR movement were executed in Moscow.

The fate of those anti-Tito forces and their families who managed to escape from Yugoslavia at the end of the war is particularly tragic. The huge column, numbering perhaps as many as 500,000 soldiers and civilians, including Slovenes, Serbs and even Chetniks, finally came to rest in a small valley near the Austrian village of Bleiburg. One of the first groups to arrive at British headquarters was a contingent of 130 members of the Croatian Government headed by President Nikola Mandic. All were informed that they would be transferred to Italy as soon as possible by British military police. All were then loaded into a train and returned to the partisans for execution. It was the intent of the British to turn over all Croatians, as well as Serbs and Slovenes, to the communists from whom they had fled.

When the Croatian military leaders realized that they had led hundreds of thousands into a trap, many committed suicide on the spot. The British extradited thousands of Croatians. Some were shot at the border, while others joined the infamous "death marches" which took them deeper into the new people's republic for execution. Realizing the importance of the clergy to the Croatian people, most church leaders were arrested. Although Archbishop Stepinac was sentenced to death, he was saved by a massive outcry of world public opinion and died under house arrest in 1960. Two bishops, 300 priests, 29 seminarians and 4 lay brothers were less fortunate and were executed. The number of Moslem religious leaders executed has never been determined, although the figure is thought to be in excess of 600.

The Galicians

Not all Eastern people fell into the hands of Stalin and his henchmen. Before the war, Galicia had been part of Poland. Hitler had handed it over to Stalin at the conclusion of the Polish campaign under the terms of the Russo-German Non-Aggression Treaty. Hitler was aware of how the area had become an Austrian "Crown Land" in 1772, being confirmed with slight frontier adjustments in 1814, thus becoming the largest province in the Austro-Hungarian Empire. After the war's end, the Soviets reaped vengeance on the population for their support of the Germans (see Chapter 10).

Some Ukrainians escaped Soviet vengeance, such as the men of the 14th SS Waffen-Grenadier Division *Galicia* under Pavlo Shandruk. He was a former staff officer of the Polish Army and before that a soldier in the Ukrainian Republic of 1919–21. He was the overall Ukrainian leader and head of the Ukrainian National Committee, a body seemingly dedicated to achieving Ukrainian independence but actually a sham to bolster the Ukrainians' morale and keep them fighting alongside the Germans to the bitter end. Shandruk had planned on taking control of the division in March 1945 and renaming it the "First Ukrainian Division of the Ukrainian National Army". Himmler agreed to hand the division over to Shandruk, and between 25–30 April 1945 the men took a new oath of allegiance to the Ukrainian nation.

The division surrendered to the British near Radstadt on 8 May 1945. When Shandruk successfully convinced his captors that he and his men were Poles rather than Russians, they were spared the unenviable fate that surely would have followed compulsory repatriation to the Soviet Union (after struggling to convince the Germans

that they were Ukrainians rather than Galicians, the men of the 14th SS Division saved their lives by claiming to be Galicians after all). They negotiated with the British Army and retreated from the front across the mountains to a region agreed upon by the British. The Ukrainians were interned in the pleasant surroundings of Rimini, an Italian seaside resort on the Adriatic. The Soviets made many attempts to obtain the division, but with the Cold War intensifying this prospect was a non-starter. Finally, the Labour Government brought them all to Britain. One idea was that they would be a ready spearhead for any attack on the Soviet Union. To the relief of the men of the division, this idea came to nought; thereafter, many of them emigrated to the USA, Canada, South America and elsewhere.

These Ukrainians were lucky, but their country, like the Baltic states and the homelands of the other Eastern peoples, was under Soviet control. They and the other foreign nationals who had fought for Hitler had gambled, but they had lost.

Below: Two British soldiers watch the repatriation from Austria. Some British soldiers refused to take part in the exercise, saying they went to war to fight German soldiers not to club refugee women and children.

GLOSSARY OF GERMAN TERMS

abschnitt: sector or district. In the SS, a regional division of Germany and its headquarters; in the SD, a subordinate regional headquarters and its area.

abteilung: unit, battery, battalion or department.

Abwehr: Wehrmacht intelligence service.

Ahnenerbe Forschungs und Lehrgemeinschaft: Society for Research into and Teaching of Ancestral Heritage. Administered by the Pers. Stab RfSS, this office promoted research into family and national hereditary history, and the dissemination of racial theories.

Allgemeine-SS: the general body of the SS, composed of part-time, full-time and honorary members.

Allgemeines Heeresamt: General Army Directorate.

Amt A: main office, branch or directorate of a ministry, or an independent ministry.

amtsgruppe: a subordinate branch of a hauptamt.

armee: army.

aufklärung: military reconnaissance.

Auslands Organization: the NSDAP agency concerned with the care and supervision of Germans in foreign countries. Ranked as the 43rd gau of the NSDAP under Gauleiter and Foreign Office Staatssekretär Ernst-Wilhelm Bohle.

Auswärtiges Amt: Foreign Office. The Reich Ministry for Foreign Affairs.

bataillon: battalion.

Befehlshaber des Ersatzheeres: Commander-in-Chief Replacement Army.

Chef der Deutschen Polizei: Commander-in-Chief of the German Police (Heinrich Himmler).

Chef der Sicherheitspolizei und des SD: Chief of the Security Police and SD (Heydrich, then Kaltenbrunner).

Deutsche Arbeitsfront: German Labour Front, largest of the NSDAP's affiliated organizations comprising all the corporations, guilds and professional associations.

dienststelle: headquarters, administrative office, station or depot.

einsatz: action, operation or employment.

Einsatzgruppe: Special Action Squad or task force of the Sipo and SD formed for special missions (especially liquidations of Jews and communists) in occupied territories.

Einsatzkommando: detachment of the Sipo and SD; subordinate element of an Einsatzgruppe.

ersatz: training, depot or reinforcement.

feldgendarmerie abteilung: military police battalion.

freiwilligen: volunteer.

Führer: Leader. The title "Der Führer" was used only in reference to Adolf Hitler.

gau: main territorial division of the NSDAP. There were 42 gaue in the Reich and annexed territories, with the 43rd gau comprising the Auslands Organization.

gauleiter: highest ranking NSDAP official in a gau, with responsibility for all matters of politics, economics, labour mobilization and civil defence.

gebirgs division: mountain division of the Heer or Waffen-SS.

Geheimes Staatspolizei (Gestapo): Secret State Police. Amt IV of the Reichssicherheitshauptamt from 1939.

Generalgouvernement: the Government General – German-occupied Poland and its administration.

generalkommando: headquarters of an army corps.

Generalstab des Heeres: the German Army General Staff.

Germanische Leitstelle: Germanic Liaison Office of the SS-Hauptamt, responsible for the supervision of the Germanic SS.

Hilfspolizei: Auxiliary Police.

Hitler Jugend: Hitler Youth.

Höhere SS und Polizeiführer: Higher SS and Police Leader.

Kraft durch Freude: the Nazi "Strength through Joy" movement.

kreis: district.

kriegs: war.

Kriminalpolizei: Criminal Police; Amt V of the Reichssicherheitshauptamt from 1939.

Lebensborn e.V.: the "Fountain of Life" society, established by the SS in 1936. Attached to the Pers. Stab RfSS and affiliated with the SS-RUSHA. Main functions of the society were adoption of "racially suitable" children for childless SS families, encouragement and facilitation of procreation between "Aryan" men and women, and the promotion of SS racial policies.

nachrichten: signals.

Nationalsozialistische Deutsche Arbeiter Partei: National Socialist German Workers' Party (NSDAP).

Nationalsozialistische Flieger Korps: NS Flying Corps. Led by NSFK-Korpsführer/General der Flieger Christiansen until 1943, then by NSFK-Korpsführer/Generaloberst Alfred Keller until 1945.

Nationalsozialistische Kraftfahr Korps: NS Motor Corps. Led by NSKK-Korpsführer Adolf Huhnlein until

his death in 1942, then by NSKK-Korpsführer Erwin Krauss until 1945. Played an important role in military and paramilitary training.

Oberkommando der Marine: High Command of the Navy.

Oberkommando des Heeres: High Command of the Army.

Oberkommando der Wehrmacht: High Command of the Armed Forces (Hitler was supreme commander, while Wilhelm Keitel headed OKW).

Ordnungspolizei: Order Police. Regular uniformed police force of the Reich, consisting of the Schutzpolizei, Gendarmerie and Feuerschutzpolzie, as well as various technical and auxiliary services.

Organization Todt: semi-military government construction force, established in 1933 under Dr Fritz Todt.

osten: east.

Rasse und Siedlungshauptamt (RUSHA): SS Race & Settlement Main Office, responsible for racial purity of the SS and settlement of SS colonists in the occupied Eastern territories.

Reichsarbeitsdienst: Reich Labour Service, headed by the Reichsarbeitsführer/Reichsminister Konstantin Hierl.

Reichsführer-SS und Chef der Deutschen Polizei: Reich SS Leader and Chief of the German Police. Heinrich Himmler's title from June 1936.

Reichsgau: one of the 11 regions formed from territories annexed from Poland and Austria in 1938 and 1939.

Reichskommissar für die Festigung Deutschen Volkstums: Reich Commissioner for the Strengthening of Germanism. Title given to Heinrich Himmler in 1939, entrusting him with the repatriation of Volksdeutsche (ethnic Germans) and the settlement of German colonies in the East. A Stabshauptamt RKFDV was established under Ulrich Greifelt to put Himmler's plans for Germanic mastery into effect.

Reichskommissariat für die Ostland: German civil administration in the Baltic States (Latvia, Estonia, Lithuania) and White Russia (Belorussia), 1941–45. The

Reich Commissar Ostland, with his headquarters in Riga, was Gauleiter Heinrich Lohse.

Reichsleiter: the highest rank in the NSDAP hierarchy.

Reichsministerium für die Besetzten Ostgebiete: Reich Ministry for the Occupied Eastern Territories, under Reichsleiter Alfred Rosenberg.

Reichssicherheitshauptamt: Reich Security Main Office.

Reichstag: German Parliament.

Reichswehr: the armed forces of Germany from 1919 until the enactment of the Defence Law of 21 May 1935; on that date its title was changed to Wehrmacht.

Schutzmannschaften: auxiliary police units composed of foreign elements and Volksdeutsche; the first Schuma unit was set up in the Ukraine in August 1941.

Schutzpolizei: Protection Police. The regular uniformed municipal and country police forces, comprising most of the membership of the Ordnungspolizei.

Schutz Staffel (SS): Protection Squad. Established in 1925 from the *Stosstrupp Adolf Hitler*, the SS became, under Heinrich Himmler, the most powerful organization in the Third Reich.

Selbstschutz: a German nationalist self-protection organization formed in Silesia in 1920. Also a self-protection militia recruited from the Volksdeutsche in Poland by the SS.

Sicherheitsdienst des RfSS: the SS Security Service established by Reinhard Heydrich in 1931 as the intelligence organization of the Nazi Party.

Sicherheitspolizei: Security Police, composed of the Gestapo and Kripo.

Sigrunen: the runic double "S" insignia of the Schutz Staffel.

sonderkommando: special detachment.

SS und Polizeiführer: SS and Police Commander in the Eastern occupied territories, subordinate to the HSSPF.

stab: staff.

Sturmabteilung (SA): Storm Troops, also called Brownshirts. The original defence formations of the NSDAP, founded in 1921. Purged in June 1934 (the Night of the Long Knives) when it became too radical and unwieldy, prompting Hitler to wipe out most of its leadership, including Ernst Röhm. The purge of the SA was carried out by Himmler's SS, initially a sub-unit of the SA. In its wake the SS gained considerable power.

Totenkopfverbände: Death's Head units, employed in the concentration camps as guards. Formed the nucleus of the *Totenkopf* Division when this unit was formed in October 1939.

trupp: squad or detail. An SA (and in its early years, SS) unit equivalent to a platoon.

unterführer: noncommissioned officer.

verband: a formation or unit.

Volksbund fur das Deutschtum im Ausland: The League for Germans Abroad. Pre-Nazi organization concerned with activities of the Volksdeutsche (ethnic Germans). Taken over by the NSDAP in 1930 and eventually absorbed by the Volksdeutsche Mittelstelle under SS-Obergruppenführer Werner Lorenz.

Volksdeutsche: ethnic Germans.

Volksgruppe: an ethnic group

Waffen-SS: Armed SS.

wehrkreis: military district.

Wehrmacht: the armed forces, consisting of the German Army (Heer), Navy (Kriegsmarine) and Air Force (Luftwaffe).

Wehrwirtschaft: military or war economy.

FURTHER READING

Atkin, Nicholas. *Pétain.* Harlow: Pearson Education, 1997.

Bartov, Omer. *Hitler's Army: Soldiers, Nazis and War in the Third Reich.* Oxford: Oxford University Press, 1992.

Bennett, Rab. *Under the Shadow of the Swastika: The Moral Dilemmas of Resistance and Collaboration in Hitler's Europe.* New York: New York University Press, 1999.

Bloch, Marc. *Strange Defeat.* New York: Norton Library, 1968.

Bond, Brian. *Britain, France, and Belgium, 1939–40.* New York: Brassey's, 1990.

Boog, Horst et al. (eds.). *Germany and the Second World War, Vol. IV: The Attack on the Soviet Union.* Oxford: Clarendon, 1998.

Brett-Smith, Richard. *Hitler's Generals.* London: Osprey, 1976.

Burleigh, Michael. *The Third Reich: A New History.* London: Pan, 2001.

Burleigh, Michael, and Wippermann, Wolfgang. *The Racial State: Germany 1933–1945.* Cambridge: Cambridge University Press, 1991.

Butler, Rupert, *Hitler's Jackals.* Barnsley: Pen & Sword Books, 1998.

Carell, Paul. *Hitler Moves East, 1941–1943.* Boston: Little, Brown & Co., 1964.

Carell, Paul. *Scorched Earth.* New York: Ballantine, 1971.

Cooper, Matthew. *The German Army, 1933–1945: Its Political and Military Failure.* New York: Random House, 1978.

Cooper, Matthew, and Lucas, James. *Hitler's Elite.* London: Grafton, 1990.

Creveld, Martin van. *Hitler's Strategy 1940–1941: The Balkan Clue.* Cambridge: Cambridge University Press, 1973.

Cross, Robin. *Citadel: The Battle of Kursk.* London: Michael O'Mara, 1993.

Davies, W.J.K. *German Army Handbook 1939–1945.* London: Military Book Society, 1973.

Downing, David. *The Devil's Virtuosos.* London: New English Library, 1976.

The Editors of Command Magazine. *Hitler's Army: The Evolution and Structure of German Forces.* Pennsylvania: Combined Publishing, 2000.

Erickson, John. *The Road to Stalingrad.* New York: Harper & Row, 1976.

Glantz, David M., and House, Jonathan. *When Titans Clashed: How the Red Army Stopped Hitler.* Lawrence, KS: University of Kansas Press, 1995.

Glantz, David M., and House, Jonathan. *The Battle of Kursk.* London: Ian Allan Publishing, 1999.

Haupt, Werner. *Assault on Moscow 1941.* Atglen, PA: Schiffer, 1996.

Haupt, Werner. *Army Group Center.* Atglen, PA: Schiffer, 1998.

Hitler, Adolf. *Hitler's Table Talk,* London: Weidenfeld & Nicolson, 1953.

Knappe, Siegfried. *Soldat: Reflections of a German Soldier, 1936–1949.* New York: Dell Publishing Co., 1993.

Lehman, Rudolf. *The Leibstandarte.* Manitoba: JJ Fedorowicz, 1990.

Littlejohn, David. *Patriotic Traitors: A History of Collaboration in German-occupied Europe.* Heinemann: London, 1972.

Littlejohn, David, *Foreign Legions of the Third Reich Vol. 1, Norway, Denmark and France.* San Jose, CA: Bender Publishing, 1987.

Littlejohn, David. *Foreign Legions of the Third Reich Vol. 2, Belgium, Great Britain, Holland, Italy and Spain.* San Jose, CA: Bender Publishing, 1987.

Littlejohn, David. *Foreign Legions of the Third Reich Vol. 3, Albania, Czechoslovakia, Greece, Hungary and Yugoslavia.* San Jose, CA: Bender Publishing, 1994.

Littlejohn, David. *Foreign Legions of the Third Reich Vol. 4, Poland, the Ukraine, Bulgaria, Romania, Free India, Estonia, Latvia, Lithuania, Finland and Russia.* San Jose, CA: Bender Publishing, 1987.

Lucas, James. *German Army Handbook 1939–1945.* Stroud: Sutton Publishing Limited, 1998.

Lucas, James. *War on the Eastern Front: The German Soldier in Russia 1941–45.* London: Greenhill Books, 1979.

Manstein, Erich von. *Lost Victories.* Chicago: H. Regency Co., 1958.

Mitchell, Samuel. *Hitler's Legions.* London: Leo Cooper, 1985.

Müller, Rolf-Dieter, and Ueberschär, Gerd R. *Hitler's War in the East 1941–45: A Critical Assessment.* Oxford: Berghahn, 1997.

Nafziger, George F. *The German Order of Battle: Panzers and Artillery in World War II.* London: Greenhill Books, 1999.

Nafziger, George F. *The German Order of Battle: Waffen-SS and Other Units in World War II.* Pennsylvania: Combined Publishing, 2001.

O'Neill, Robert J. *The German Army and the Nazi Party 1933–39.* London: Cassell, 1966.

Perret, Bryan. *Panzerkampfwagen III.* Oxford: Osprey Publishing, 2001.

Schreiber, Gerhard et al. (eds.). *Germany and the Second World War, Vol. 3: The Mediterranean, Southeast Europe and North Africa 1939–41.* Oxford: Clarendon, 1995.

Seaton, Albert. *The Russo–German War, 1941–45.* New York: Praeger, 1970.

Seaton, Albert. *The German Army, 1933–1945.* London: Weidenfeld & Nicolson, 1982.

Stein, George. *Waffen–SS: Hitler's Elite Guard at War, 1939–1945.* Ithaca, NY: Cornell University Press, 1984.

Stroop, Juergen. *The Stroop Report.* London: Secker & Warburg, 1979.

Sydnor, Charles. *Soldiers of Destruction: The SS Death's Head Division, 1933–1945.* Princeton, NJ: Princeton University Press, 1977.

INDEX

PICTURE CREDITS

Christopher Ailsby Historical Archives: 8, 10, 11 (both), 15 (bottom), 18, 21 (top), 22 (both), 23, 24, 26, 27, 28 (both), 29, 30, 32, 33, 34, 35, 36, 37 (both), 38 (both), 39 (both), 40, 42, 44 (both), 45 (both), 46, 47, 48 (both), 49, 50 (both), 53, 54, 56 (bottom), 58, 59, 60, 62, 63, 64 (both), 65 (all three), 66, 67, 68 (both), 69 (both), 70, 71, 72 (both), 73, 74, 75, 76, 78, 79, 80, 81 (both), 83, 86, 87 (top), 89, 94, 95 (both), 96, 98, 99, 100 (both), 101 (both), 102 (both), 103, 104, 106, 107 (both), 108 (both), 109, 110, 111, 112, 113, 114 (both), 115, 118, 119 (both), 120 (both), 124 (bottom), 125, 126, 127, 128 (top), 131 (both), 132, 133, 134, 135, 136, 137 (both), 140, 144, 145, 146 (both), 147, 150, 155 (both), 156, 157, 161, 162, 164, 165, 166, 169, 170, 172 (both), 173 (bottom), 174, 175 (both), 176, 177, 178, 180, 181 (both), 182, 183.
History in the Making: 138, 142, 143 (both), 149.
Robert Hunt Library: 12, 14, 15 (top), 16, 17, 19, 20 (bottom), 21, 43, 51, 52, 56 (top), 57, 82, 84, 85, 87 (bottom), 90, 91, 93, 116, 121, 122, 123, 124 (top), 128 (bottom), 129, 130, 141, 152, 153, 154, 159, 160, 163, 167, 168, 173 (top).